Reading: Issues and Directions

edited by

CHARLES GAINS

and

DAVID WRAY

Published by NASEN Enterprises Ltd.

Published in 1995

ISBN 0906730 73 2

Published by NASEN Enterprises Ltd.
NASEN Enterprises is a company limited by guarantee, registered in England and Wales. Company No. 2637438.

Further copies of this book and details of NASEN's many other publications may be obtained from the Publications Department at its registered office: 2 Lichfield Road, Stafford ST17 4JX. (Tel: 01785 46872; Fax: 01785 41187)

Cover design by Graphic Images.
Typeset in Palatino and printed in the United Kingdom by Impress Printers (Stoke-on-Trent) Limited.

Contents

Contributors

Charles Gains is Editor of *Support for Learning*, a journal of the National Association for Special Educational Needs. He has experience in primary and secondary schools, in a support service and as a tutor to in-service courses in higher education. He has written widely in the field of special educational needs and the teaching of reading and is co-author (with Mike Hinson) of *The NASEN A-Z: Graded List of Reading Books* (NASEN, 1994).

David Wray is Senior Lecturer in Primary Education at the University of Exeter. He has researched and published widely in the field of literacy development and is currently editor of the United Kingdom Reading Association journal *Reading*. His recent publications include *Literacy and Language in the Primary Years* (with Jane Medwell), published by Routledge, and *Literacy and Awareness*, published by Hodder and Stoughton. He is currently director of the Exeter Extending Literacy (EXEL) Project.

Martin Coles is Lecturer in Primary Education at the University of Nottingham.

Michael Connor is an educational psychologist with Surrey County Council.

Henrietta Dombey is Professor of Literacy in Primary Education at the University of Brighton.

Usha Goswami is a University Lecturer in Experimental Psychology at Cambridge University and a Fellow of St John's College.

Cyril Hellier is a Senior Educational Psychologist with Tayside Regional Council.

Maureen Lewis is Research Officer on the Exeter Extending Literacy Project at the University of Exeter.

Michael Lockwood is Lecturer in Education at the University of Reading.

Jane Medwell is PGCE Courses Leader at the College of St Mark and St John, Plymouth.

Henry Pearson is Lecturer in Education at Chester College.

Val Potter is an educational psychologist employed in a Dorset School.

Louise Poulson is Lecturer in Education at the University of Exeter.

Jean Prance is Adviser for Reading Recovery with Surrey County Council.

Angela Redfern is Lecturer in Education at the University of Reading.

Patricia Rospigliosi is learning support teacher for a cluster of schools in West Devon.

Chris Sawyer is an educational psychologist working in Dorset.

Katy Simmons was a Lecturer in Education at the Oxford Brookes University and is now Co-ordinator for IPSEA.

Trish Taylor is a senior education officer working in Dorset.

Keith Topping is Director of the Centre for Paired Learning at the University of Dundee.

Martin Turner is Head of Psychology at the Dyslexia Institute, Staines.

Anna Wright is Head of Educational Psychology Service, Surrey County Council.

Acknowledgements

The editors and publishers gratefully acknowledge the help of Basil Blackwell Publishers.

Introduction

DAVID WRAY

Living in interesting times

The ancient Chinese saying, 'May you live in interesting times', sounds as if it might be used as a blessing but, in fact, is used as a curse, condemning its recipient to a life of turmoil and uncertainty. By this token, educators with an interest in the teaching of reading certainly appear to have been condemned to 'interesting times' over the past few years. The teaching of reading has hit the headlines of national newspapers and been discussed by television and radio newscasters. It has been the subject of television documentaries, ministerial broadcasts and parliamentary select committees. It has even featured as a topic on 'Question Time' on more than one occasion and been commented upon by members of the Royal family. Although as professionals we have often cringed at the polarised way the topic has usually been treated in the media, we have also recognised that in a period of public disquiet it well behoves us to ensure that we are familiar enough with issues underlying the debates to contribute to them from a position of professional strength. The chief purpose of the present volume, therefore, is to bring together papers written, for the most part, in the last four years which explore the issues surrounding these debates. The papers are also intended to take the debate forward and to explore ideas and directions which are currently emerging from professional discussion.

All the papers included here have been previously published or are about to be published in either *Support for Learning* or *Reading,* which are the journals of The National Association for Special Educational Needs (NASEN) and United Kingdom Reading Association (UKRA) respectively. The book's publication represents, therefore, a very productive collaboration between the two associations as well as, we hope, a 'state of the art' summary of issues in the teaching of reading.

A fresh look at reading

The teaching of reading has always generated its share of controversy among theoreticians, researchers and teachers. Far from having resolved the 'Great Debate' about reading teaching (Chall, 1967), current controversies have refined and redefined this debate (Wray, 1989). The reactions of the national press to the furore over reading standards suggest that this topic remains of pressing interest to the public at large, and a source of some confusion to educational practitioners. The current debate about the teaching of reading in Britain centres on the relative efficacy of approaches which focus, on the one hand, on learning to read as an 'apprenticeship' (Waterland, 1985) using 'real' books (Wade, 1990) with a concentration upon children making meaning from text, and, on the other, on the teaching of reading through structured materials or schemes with an emphasis on the development of decoding skills. The former of these approaches, usually known as the real books approach, seems to have received the backing of those in a position to influence teachers' actions, such as local authority advisers, and many schools are being advised to adopt teaching methods based on this approach. The extent of its take-up seems, however, to be less in fact than a reading of the popular press would lead one to believe (DES, 1990). As yet there have been no significant research studies into the effectiveness of the real books approach in comparison with alternative methods and little is known about the extent to which schools have actually changed their teaching methods, nor the homogeneity of any such changes.

Although the real books approach to the teaching of reading has not been thoroughly evaluated by research studies, the philosophy underlying it does have a long-standing, if controversial, theoretical base. Research evidence about the nature of the reading process for both adults and children is itself disputed. Some studies of adult readers have suggested that they tend to read for meaning rather than attend too much to surface representations (Kolers, 1973), and some very influential models of reading (e.g. Goodman, 1970) have developed from this line of evidence, conceptualising the process as one of prediction and 'guessing'. On balance, however, research evidence tends to support the view that adults recognise the majority of the words they read on sight rather than predicting them from context (Oakhill & Garnham, 1988). A number of studies of young readers have suggested that when they read they appear to try to make sense of their reading (e.g. Weber, 1970) relying heavily on context, although it is possible that this might be explained simply by a relatively underdeveloped sight vocabulary. Many recent studies of 'emergent readers' have, however, suggested that young children immersed in a literate environment absorb lessons about the nature and the functions of print inevitably founded upon its role as a conveyor of meaning (e.g. Harste, Woodward and Burke, 1984).

Fresh insights into the nature of reading have also come from literary theory which suggests a theory of reading involving a complex process in which meaning is a negotiation between reader and writer (Iser, 1978). Literary reading has been conceptualised by Rosenblatt (1985) as a 'transaction' between reader and text, a term taken up by Goodman (1987) to conceptualise the reading act itself. It has been suggested (Smith, 1988; Meek, 1988) that, for young readers, part of the message taken from such transactions with the books they read is an increased understanding of the nature of reading itself and of how books work. Books themselves, and their authors, thus become active teachers of reading. Reading is conceived as much more than a process of decoding symbols to adduce meaning, but rather as a complex process of interaction between the world of meanings represented by an author and that within the reader's head.

This concept does not imply that the teacher is redundant in the process of a child learning to read. Instead the role is redefined from that of direct instructor to facilitator of interactions between child and book. Young children coming to books for the first time will not be able to derive any meaning from them since they lack the requisite abilities to unlock the author's representation. The teacher acts as intermediary between child and book. This mediation is itself based upon well-elaborated theories of learning. Renewed interest in the socially based learning theories of Vygotsky (Wertsch, 1985) has led to developments in 'apprenticeship' approaches in which the learner is inducted into more complex activities then he/she is individually capable of by being guided and assisted by a more skilful cooperator. This cooperator provides the 'scaffolding' (Bruner, 1985), to enable the learner to succeed at the task.

The real books approach to the teaching of reading does have a theoretical basis both in terms of the conceptualisation of the reading process towards which it is working and in the teaching strategies it adopts. These theoretical principles do not, however, command acceptance from all quarters. A recent thorough review of research into beginning reading (Adams, 1990) makes a strong case for the teaching of phonics, although the very terms of this review are themselves not universally accepted (Goodman, 1991). Such fiercely argued disputes are characteristic of the beginning reading field, as demonstrated by exchanges in academic journals (e.g. McKenna et al (1990); Edelsky (1990)).

Drawing conclusions from the vast range of research into reading and its teaching itself invites controversy but the following points might command wide acceptance among teachers and researchers alike:

- Reading is an extremely complex process. This means that 'simple' approaches to teaching children to read will probably have little chance of success. The approach of 'put children in a room full of wonderful books and they will learn to read' is just as simplistic as that of 'teach children to recognise and pronounce letters and they will thereby learn to read', and neither is likely to be successful.

- Teaching reading needs to build upon what children do well (look for meaning, attend first and foremost to functional aspects of print, learn through stories) before introducing aspects which they find more difficult (apply a range of cues simultaneously, respond to text without relying upon its physical context to give them its meaning).

- Children need to be taught the technicalities of reading, but these must be set into a context of meaning. As Marilyn Jager Adams puts it in her comprehensive review of research into beginning reading:

  'In both fluent reading and its acquisition, the reader's knowledge must be aroused interactively and in parallel. Neither understanding nor learning can proceed hierarchically from the bottom up. Phonological awareness, letter recognition facility, familiarity with spelling patterns, spelling-sound relationships, and individual words must be developed in concert with real reading and real writing and with deliberate reflection on the forms, functions, and meanings of texts.'

The present volume

The present collection of papers take us forward from these conclusions about reading and explore various aspects of the reading process and the ways we might think about its teaching in the mid-1990s. We hope that readers will find this an interesting and stimulating collection, with plenty of implications for the development of practice.

References

Adams, M (1990) *Beginning to Read*, MIT Press.

Bruner, J (1985) 'Vygotsky: a historical and conceptual perspective' in Wertsch, J (ed) *Culture, Communication and Cognition: Vygotskyan Perspectives*, Cambridge University Press.

Chall, J (1967) *Learning to Read: The Great Debate*, McGraw-Hill.

DES (1990) *The Teaching and Learning of Reading in Primary Schools*, HMSO.

Edelsky, C (1990) 'Whose agenda is this anyway?' in *Educational Researcher*, Vol. 19 (8), pp. 7-11.

Goodman, K (1970) 'Reading: a psycholinguistic guessing game' in Singer, H and Ruddell, R (eds) *Theoretical Models and Processes of Reading*, International Reading Association.

Goodman, K et al (1987) *Language and Thinking in School*, Richard Owen.

Goodman, Y (1991) 'Beginning to read: a critique' in *The Reading Teacher*, Vol. 44 (6), pp. 375-8.

Harste, J, Woodward, V and Burke, C (1984) *Language Stories and Literacy Lessons*, Heinemann.

Iser, W (1978) *The Implied Reader*, Johns Hopkins University Press.

Kolers, P (1973) 'Three stages of reading' in Smith, F (ed) *Psycholinguistics and Reading*, Holt, Rinehart and Winston.

McKenna, M et al (1990) 'Whole language: a research agenda for the nineties' in *Educational Researcher*, Vol. 19 (8), pp. 3-6.

Meek, M (1988) *How Texts Teach What Readers Learn*, Signal.

Oakhill, J and Garnham, A (1988) *Becoming a Skilled Reader*, Basil Blackwell.

Rosenblatt, L (1985) 'The transactional theory of the literary work: implications for research' in Cooper, C (ed) *Researching Response to Literature and the Teaching of Literature*, Ablex.

Smith, F (1988) *Joining the Literacy Club*, Heinemann.

Wade, B (1990) *Reading for Real*, Open University Press.

Waterland, L (1985) *Read with Me*, Signal Press.

Weber, R (1970) 'First graders' use of grammatical context in reading' in Levin, H and Williams, J (eds) *Basic Studies on Reading*, Basic Books.

Wertsch, J (1985) *Culture, Communication and Cognition: Vygotskyan Perspectives*, Cambridge University Press.

Wray, D (1989) 'Reading: the new debate' in *Reading* 23 (1).

SECTION 1

Setting the Scene - The Reading Debate

1 - Finding out

MARTIN TURNER

An explanation of the numbers involved in the June 1990 revelations of falling reading standards has often been requested. I have written (Turner, 1991) a factual narrative account for educational psychologist colleagues of the extraordinary events of last summer [1990], and will not go over this ground again. Readers of *Support for Learning* may know that ten local education authority (LEA) school psychological services had been in informal contact for a period of six months, and that representatives of nine of these LEAs met together on 22 June and decided to communicate their finding that the data of eight LEAs showed (to varying degrees) a significant downward trend.

The massive public response, however, got off to a bad start: the average decline over the eight authorities of 3.23 points of standard score over 5 years was reported variously as 'a 3.5 per cent fall', or occasionally 'a 2 per cent drop'. Other variants are still current today. The numbers of children allegedly involved varied also, swinging between dangerously large, but quite inconsistent, six figure numbers. Because of the scale of public concern, coupled with an alarming dearth of hard information in the public domain, I published a short account (Turner, 1990), giving a statistical summary together with research background, educational context and an infamous 'hypothesis' (see below).

The then Secretary of State, John MacGregor, quickly commissioned, in July 1990, two government investigations into the claims, and these reported on 10 January 1991. As one, the survey by the National Foundation for Educational Research (NFER) into LEAs' historical test data (Department of Education and Science 1991a), found that fully 73 per cent of LEAs willing to submit data for analysis showed evidence of a decline since 1985, exactly as we had said, information on the original eight may now be thought to be a matter of diminishing interest.

However, the original eight included some of the largest county areas in the country and the NFER report nowhere gives actual numbers of children affected. Moreover, by comparing private information with the lists of responding LEAs in Appendix 1 of the NFER report, it is possible to arrive at a minimum total of thirty-one LEAs showing some evidence of a decline over the period. (The psychologists involved in the original meeting, including myself, have on no occasion, despite considerable pressure, identified the authorities concerned. Since, as a witness to the Parliamentary Select Committee for Education, Science and Arts enquiring into reading standards on 27 February 1991, I was not asked, under the pains and privileges of parliamentary authority, to name them, it is unlikely now that the list will ever become public.)

Clearly the scale - geographical and numerical - of the decline has surpassed the most pessimistic expectations. The second government report, that of Her Majesty's Inspectorate (HMI) (Department of Education and Science 1991b), made no bones about the importance of teaching methodology in achieving good reading results in schools (more on this below). On the face of it, strong support has been forthcoming from quarters from which whitewash has not, in the past, been unknown. The machinery of cover-up has creaked and groaned but the main point has been conceded. Prominent academics have very visibly altered their positions. Nevertheless, two outstanding issues concern me: there has been no recognition, as far as I can see, of the extraordinary size and significance of the phenomenon; and, with all the publicity, little or no real curiosity has been evinced about what is really going on. Is it, for instance, as some evidence suggests, an international phenomenon? No research proposals are forthcoming.

The original evidence

But first let us consider the original evidence once more. The eight authorities used all manner of reading tests. The decline appears, as a unitary phenomenon, on all of them. At least two LEAs quite properly conducted further research on their declining scores, first by changing tests, and then by giving further tests to the poorer readers. The results of changes of test are instructive: scores continued to decline, but from x to y, instead of from a to b. (Tests correlate strongly, but not perfectly, with each other.) Nor is the type of test used a critical factor. Word recognition, sentence completion, Cloze, passage reading - all give the same message. One authority even reverted to its original test (Young's group reading test) and found the decline appeared to accelerate. The investigation into characteristics of poor readers found that their general cognitive (usually verbal) abilities were little different from those of a random sample of the population. Attainment in number skills, though these often involve threshold levels of competence with written language, appeared to be unaffected. Thomas and Hagedorn (1990) have published figures based on IQ/RQ differences which are strongly suggestive of a similar situation; Thomas (1990) has also stated that 'the fourfold increase in the number of pupils with the significant underfunctioning in reading was ... most apparent in the more affluent area, not as one normally expects, in a socially deprived area'.

One line of defence, little heard now, is that there are all sorts of ineffable powers which enable readers to siphon meaning straight from the page but which do not show up on tests. This becomes a little like the proposition that readers do not have to look at the text or do not have to turn the pages. Of course there are higher order reading skills (which can be tested) but these do not develop in the absence of lower order, decoding skills. It is important to make serious, substantiated, informed criticisms of psychometric tests; but, in this technically highly developed, sophisticated field, few people in education seem able to make knowledgeable comments.

I have even heard it argued, seriously, that all tests show downward trends. Not so. Three, at least, of the larger counties recorded stable mean (average) scores throughout the 1970s. Only from about 1980 did the means begin to dip. The main reason for the frequency of the 1985 date for the beginning of test scores' decline is that most authorities did not survey infant reading systematically before this date; where they did, in three cases, an earlier decline is apparent.

And what of the numbers involved? If one takes, first, the actual numbers of children whose scores contributed to means during a period of decline, one arrives at a figure of 457,500. (These include good and bad readers alike, across a wide geographical range, over a period varying from 10 to 4 years.) The size of the primary populations in the areas concerned (the populations of 5- to 11-year-olds at any one time) is approximately 373,200. Reckoned as a proportion of the nation's 7-year-olds, the total size of the annual cohorts obtaining test results in these authorities, 57,000, is about 9.2 per cent of all 7-year-olds in the maintained system. I should emphasize that these figures are conservative and do not make assumptions, for instance, about other areas in an authority for which test data were available for only one.

The magnitude of the decline is best understood by averaging differences between two mean scores (from the onset of decline until the end or most recent year) over the period in question. Again this must be done fairly as it is quite easy to exaggerate a decline by selective choice of high and low points. Test scores are reported in terms of standard scores or quotients (mean 100; standard deviation 15) which permit direct comparison of children of different ages. A point of standard score has been expressed as: 'in very rough terms about two months of development for the average child' (Department of Education and Science 1991a). In the eight authorities the decline averaged from between 0.40 to 0.94 points of standard score per annum. Over the 5 years which we reported as the most pronounced period of decline, this amounts to the loss of about 28 weeks of development (3.23 points of standards score). Such a 'loss of attainment' is considerable: about 7 months in 5 years.

To put this in perspective, consider the recent Evaluation and Monitoring Unit report on maths (Foxman, Ruddock and McCallum, 1990). Over a 4-year period (1984-8) it was found that 'the decline in 11 year olds' understanding of decimals and fractions could be up to three-quarters of a year of average progress'. This relative decline is clearly of the same order of magnitude. 'Perhaps', the authors speculate, 'the efforts made to come to terms with broader approaches has meant a lowering of emphasis in more traditional areas.' (One is reminded of the frantic outcry against 'narrow, mechanistic' methods in the teaching of reading.) However: 'Age 11 pupils in Northern Ireland were very much more successful than those from other countries.' Schools there 'timetabled more mathematics and gave pupils more mathematics homework'. Northern Ireland 11-year-olds are, by this reckoning, fully 3.7 years ahead of their mainland counterparts! Not surprisingly, by age 15 (though not at 11), 'pupils ... displayed more favourable attitudes to mathematics than their counterparts in England and Wales'.

Longer term results?

Could it be the case, as is often argued, that new reading teaching methods do not work as quickly as traditional ones - but nevertheless work better, in terms of interest, motivation and range of skills, in the medium and longer terms? Unfortunately, one (unpublished) analysis of reading test scores for children on the Neale test at 7 and later for the same children on the Hunter-Grundin at 11 finds a correlation coefficient of 0.725 between the two sets of scores. The relationship between reading status at 7 and at 11 is nearly as strong as if the children had been given different tests a week apart. This study is broadly in line with the generality of research findings: reading achievement at 7 is strongly predictive both of later reading success and attitudes (self-concept, attitude to school) throughout the school years.

But what is there by way of explanation of such a marked national slowdown in the rate at which our infant age children are acquiring literacy skills? Here we run into trouble. To whatever extent one now accepts this, there has been an undeniable de-emphasis throughout the 1980s on the actual skills of learning to read. A 'progressive' movement has attempted to influence teacher behaviour away from phonic instruction and towards learning through 'real books' (commercially available titles). At the same time thirty-one of the LEAs which test reading systematically have registered a downward movement in reading attainment after level or rising standards in the 1970s. Research would suggest that the two phenomena are not unconnected.

HMI in its report (Department of Education and Science 1991b) gives the teaching and organization of reading prominence in thirteen paragraphs (28-40). Although, in my view, the earnest avoidance of extremes (reliance upon a single method) by reference to a 'mixture of methods' obscures the importance of the *sequence of methods,* this report does tackle the professional issues head on, a welcome change from HMI's recent empty pronouncements on the subject. 'There was a clear link between higher standards and systematic phonic teaching' (para. 31). 'Of the 20% of schools where reading was less than satisfactory, two-thirds were in areas suffering various degrees of disadvantage. However, the wider picture was mixed: schools serving disadvantaged areas also featured significantly among those whose standards of teaching and learning were high. Plainly the policies and practices of these schools were powerful in mitigating the effects of disadvantage' (para. 60). And: 'In just over half the schools where standards were satisfactory or better there was strong parental interest and close co-operation between the home and the school' (para. 62). One implication of this is that the other half of the schools were succeeding in the absence of such support!

HMI also very sensibly expresses a preference for successful initial teaching of reading over the 'remedial' variety: 'The teaching of phonics was often more prominent when children showed signs of reading failure. The approach was commonly used for "remedial" groups and by peripatetic teachers of reading. Sometimes a concentration on phonics was seen as the last resort "when all else had failed" ... A balanced approach which included more systematic phonic work from an early stage might well have benefited these children' (para. 32).

Nevertheless, my hypothesis that the 'whole language' movement (or whichever of the myriad of names you prefer) is responsible for the decline remains controversial. At high political and academic levels there is consternation; at classroom level there is instant understanding of what I am talking about! Indeed one tragic insight is the extent to which what individuals think and say privately differs from what they feel free, against the prevailing orthodoxy, to say in public. There is the ever-present and oppressive sense of threat. How has the education service achieved this isolation of almost Cuban proportions?

The components of the hypothesis

The hypothesis is best approached, not as a simplistic single cause explanation, advanced with vain confidence, but as a serious, provisional account based on the weight of research findings in what must be the best researched area in education. Let us therefore take it in a number of component parts.

1. The traditional first resort of researchers, reaffirmed by HMI in the passages cited above, is to consider teaching *method* as the most important of factors influencing reading. Not the *only* factor, note, but the most important. That the decline has nothing to do with teaching method must be regarded as provocatively implausible. The burden of proof must be on those who support an alternative explanation to produce their evidence.

2. The phenomenon of decline is both widespread and prolonged. Such a unitary phenomenon is unlikely to arise from a multiplicity of causes. In this, the expert view lies close to a lay or commonsense one.

3. Other universal explanations (varying rates of TV watching, social breakdown, environmental pollution) are either unsupported by evidence or easy to refute.

4. The rise of the new orthodoxy parallels exactly the decline in reading achievement. Here one takes virtually any factor shown by research to promote reading achievement, contrives its exact opposite, and arrives at current Good Primary Practice. A small clique, it appears, having established an extraordinary dominance in the reading world, propagates a narrow, impoverished ('psycholinguistic') view of reading.

5. There is the evidence from observations at different levels of the schools system. I have myself researched the curriculum effect after reduced attainment among average or bright children, after 3 years of 'the storybook method', was brought to my notice by concerned teachers. A comparison between two 'emergent reading' schools and one traditional school showed underachievement (IR/RQ differences) roughly

double in the 'emergent' schools. This curriculum effect may be observed at classroom, school, LEA, national and international levels.

6. As I have argued in *Sponsored Reading Failure* (Turner, 1990), concurrent test evidence shows that children failing at reading are not less bright and may sometimes be unaffected in number attainment. This strongly implicates the curriculum.

The hypothesis remains just that. Has no one a better one to propose? Is there to be no experiment, no research endeavour, to investigate the scale and cause of this tragic national educational setback?

I take some comfort, it is true, from the large extent to which educationists now privately accept the truth of my assertions. But then I am left wondering at the lack of curiosity one way or the other.

Does nobody care to find out?

References

Department of Education and Science (1991a) *An enquiry into LEA: Evidence on standards of reading of seven year old children.* A report by the National Foundation for Educational Research. HMSO: London.

Department of Education and Science (1991b) *The teaching and learning of reading in primary schools.* Report of Her Majesty's Inspectorate. HMSO: London.

Foxman, D, Ruddock, G and McCallum, I (1990) *Assessment Matters No. 3: APU Mathematics Monitoring, 1984-88 (Phase 2).* Schools Examination and Assessment Council (Evaluation and Monitoring Unit). HMSO: London.

Thomas, D (1990) Letter to *The Teacher*, Dec., 16.

Thomas, D and Hagedorn, J (1990) Reading between the lines. *Times Educational Supplement*, 6 April.

Turner, M (1990) *Sponsored Reading Failure.* IEA Education Unit: Warlingham Park School, Warlingham, Surrey.

Turner, M (1991) Squaring the diamond. In Lindsay, G (ed.) *Research and Social Policy*, Special issue, *Educational and Child Psychology.* British Psychological Society: Leicester.

(First published in *Support for Learning*, Vol. 6, No. 3, 1991.)

2 - A chapter of errors: A response to Martin Turner

DAVID WRAY

The statements and writings of Martin Turner over this past year [1991] have stirred up so much emotion that it is quite difficult to stand back and examine what he has to say and evaluate the claims he makes without getting emotionally involved oneself. In what follows I shall try to be as dispassionate as possible, but, in case I fail from time to time to maintain this stance, let me come completely clean and begin by stating clearly at the outset the mixed feelings I have about the Turner position and, most particularly, his 'infamous hypothesis'. As a specialist whose passion for matters educational, and especially literate, borders on the obsessive, I have welcomed the increased attention given over the past year to the teaching of reading. I have certainly felt very deeply the decline in interest in this area since the heady days immediately following the Bullock Report (Department of Education and Science (DES) 1975). It is good to see it back high on the agenda. But, and it is a big 'but', I have many times over the past months felt extremely angry at Mr Turner for sparking off such a wave of teacher- (and teacher educator-) bashing in the media. When dedicated, gifted teachers are labelled as 'trendy', 'incompetent', 'assassins of the alphabet' and have the ills of society blamed upon them ('Trendy reading lessons blamed for crime wave', *The Daily Express*, 1 October 1990), I am afraid I find it hard to remain academically detached. Demoralised personnel in an underfunded and overextended service (of which more later) need nurture and support, not gratuitous attacks.

Evidence

Having made my personal position clear, I want to try to examine as calmly as possible some of the claims Turner has made, and I shall do this by reference to the actual evidence before us. I shall begin by looking at the evidence underlying the alleged decline in reading standards. This is, of course, ground which has already been thoroughly covered (Harrison, 1991 and elsewhere) and I shall summarise it fairly briefly here. Has there been a decline?

The initial source of evidence on this was that 'leaked' by Turner himself in the summer of 1990. It is a cause of some concern that this has still not been made fully public and, despite Turner's (1991) claim that, in the light of subsequent evidence, it 'may now be thought to be a matter of diminishing interest', the secretive and 'shady' way in which this evidence was presented is still a very serious weakness in the case which Turner tried to make. However, some local education authority reading test results since made public do tend to give some support to the idea of declining standards. Bald (1990) quotes the results of Derbyshire's reading screening test for the years 1981 to 1989 inclusive and these show a two point drop in mean quotients between 1985 and 1989. Results from Buckinghamshire (Lake, 1991) echo this drop (although with the rider of a totally different explanation for it, as will be discussed later). Other sources of evidence are less clear cut.

The report of Her Majesty's Inspectorate (HMI) on reading standards (DES, 1990) found that standards of reading were satisfactory or better in 80 per cent of primary schools (and high in about 30 per cent). While reading in 20 per cent of schools was in need of attention, this proportion had changed little since the 1978 national Primary Survey (DES, 1978). HMI concluded therefore that there was no evidence that there had been a fall in standards of reading in primary schools. They also found that there was 'no evidence of teachers and schools rushing into a single method of teaching reading' (p. 2), and that 'phonic skills were taught almost universally and usually to beneficial effect' (p. 2). They go on to state that the highest standards were found in schools with a clearly defined reading policy which involved children experiencing a wide range of texts and of approaches.

Although the survey of the National Foundation for Educational Research (Cato and Whetton, 1991) does show declining scores on reading tests in nineteen out of the twenty-six authorities which produced usable information, it admits that this evidence is suspect because of its origin in a mixture of tests, none of which assesses 'how competent readers read in real life; that is silently through (usually) lengthy passages seeking the meaning of the piece as a whole'. This survey also found no evidence of the conspiracy which Turner suggests among advisers, teacher educators and language post-holders to promote dogma which ordinary class teachers do not, in their heart of hearts, believe in. On the contrary, by suggesting that children should read a much wider range of texts than a graded reading scheme, these 'conspirators' would seem to be advocating exactly the kind of practices which the HMI report links to higher standards!

Finally, the report of the House of Commons Education, Science and Arts Committee (1991), set up in response to public concern over reading standards, states that the evidence available does not prove beyond reasonable doubt that standards of reading have fallen in recent years. The report further states that, if there has been a decline, it is most unlikely that a swing towards 'real books' methods has been the cause.

Validity of evidence

The evidence, therefore, is inconclusive. It becomes even more so when one begins to question its status. Turner is very scathing about attempts to do this, and in particular to question the validity of the source of the evidence - standardised reading tests. Yet, as he himself admits (Turner, 1991), 'it is important to make serious, substantiated, informed criticisms of psychometric tests', which several commentators have tried to do (Hynds, 1990, Harrison, 1991). A very useful way to look at this is to consider, as Dombey (forthcoming) has done, the features of children's reading which standardised tests cannot tell us, yet which are extremely important for teachers to know about. Standardised tests do not, according to Dombey, tell us *how* children recognise words (simply whether they do), how well children identify words in compelling texts, how children see themselves as readers, the range and depth of children's experiences as readers, and so on. It should be noted specially that this is *not the same* as claiming that 'there are all sorts of ineffable powers which enable readers to siphon meaning straight from the page but which do not show up on tests', to quote Turner. His very metaphor of 'siphoning meaning' suggests that he has a very limited conception of what reading involves, and it is a much richer and complicated act than he seems to allow, and certainly than the psychometric tests currently in use measure.

If one adds to these doubts worries about testing reliability, such as the fact that some authorities seem to have changed their testing instruments during the period under investigation, one is left with some very serious caveats to the evidence as it now stands. However, let us, for the sake of argument, allow that there may have been a decline, and go on to examine Turner's hypothesis about the causes of it.

Causes of the 'decline'

This hypothesis comes in two parts, namely that: (1) there has been a fundamental change in methods of teaching reading over the last five to seven years, and (2) this change in teaching methods has led to a decline in teaching standards. I shall focus on each part separately.

The first part is actually very easily dismissed. Evidence from the HMI report (DES, 1990) suggests that very few schools actually espouse a 'real books' approach. Over 95 per cent of classes used graded reading schemes. A survey reported in *Child Education* (Janaury 1991) reveals that only 6 per cent of the respondents were operating a real books policy and 89 per cent were using a structured programme of phonics teaching. From research which will be described more fully later (Lake, 1991), only two schools out of forty-nine, in an area which did seem to be witnessing slightly declining reading standards, were using what could be called a real books approach. These findings completely contradict Turner's claims. Indeed, it is possible to turn this argument on its head. Perhaps it is the fact that the vast majority of schools still teach reading using structured materials which has itself led to the apparent decline in standards. Reading in the real world has changed and a simple ability to recognise words does not go as far as perhaps once it did.

The second part of the hypothesis obviously becomes meaningless if the first part is rejected. However, there are still several interesting points to be made in this area.

The first is a simple statistical point which one would have expected a trained psychologist to recognise. This is the impossibility of attributing cause and effect to correlational evidence. The fact that two phenomena coincide would not, in itself, be proof that there was a link between them.

The second is that there are clearly several plausible alternative explanations available which might account for declining standards, most of which in fact will ring a lot more bells with teachers than the essentially conspiracy theory which Turner advances. These include the underfunding of schools, teachers being bombarded with demands upon their time which have eaten into the time available for teaching and developing reading, the difficult years of teacher industrial action in the mid-80s, the emphasis in development initiatives and in-service opportunities over the last few years on other areas of the primary curriculum such as science and technology (Martin, 1990). These factors have undoubtedly had an influence upon teachers. There are, however, two further areas which have probably had even greater influence.

Demoralisation

One is the progressive demoralisation of teachers which we have witnessed over the last five years or so and which Barton (1991) documents so well. The evidence for this in terms of sheer teacher turnover, with some areas of the country witnessing 25 per cent and more turnover in a year (Smithers, 1990), is powerful enough. Even more disheartening is the constant message which comes from those teachers who remain in post that the profession is undervalued, over-scrutinised and, particularly, underpaid. As a teacher educator, it has become a routine activity to attempt to counteract the very negative messages about teaching which students almost universally receive during periods of school experience. Lack of stability, the continuous drain of experienced staff, and downright cynicism on the part of those who remain does not, with the best will in the world, make for quality teaching. How have schools reached this position? One thing is certain. It has not been caused by the 'ever-present and oppressive sense of threat' which Turner in his article disgracefully attributes to the influence of the 'whole language movement'. It has not, Mr Turner, been advocates of whole language who, over the last ten years, have engaged in a systematic attack on teachers, 'modern' teaching methods, teacher education and indeed any attempt to establish an intellectual basis for educational practice. On the contrary, whole language advocates have been consistently distinguished by their emphasis on teacher- (and child-) empowerment. The attacks have come from the very people chosen by Turner to publish his booklet *Sponsored Reading Failure*, right-wing 'think' tanks who have had and continue to have an extraordinary influence on educational policy.

Social background

A second area which has come back into the headlines is social background. A study recently published (Lake, 1991) goes a long way to answering several of the methodological concerns about the evidence so far available on reading standards. It presents the results of the same reading test, carried out at the same time of year on 1500 children of the same age every year since 1979 (although full results are given only for the period 1985-90, the crucial period of decline according to Turner). Assessments are given of the interactions of these results with factors such as school catchment area, school reading policy, changes in this policy, and children's general knowledge scores. The crucial factor seemed to be catchment area, which related much more strongly to declining reading scores than any other. Among children classed as 'late starters' according to the reading test results, general knowledge seemed to have declined. The author argues that it is likely that deterioration in children's background experiences over the period may well have been at the root of the declining reading scores. No relationship was found between school teaching practices and reading achievement. Where schools had changed their policies for the teaching of reading, there did seem to be a link with declining performance, but the data suggest that the changes were a *result* of schools' concerns over performance rather than a cause of it.

This research study is undoubtedly one of the most important to have emerged from the current 'reading debate' and seems to contradict the Turner hypothesis of changes in teaching methods being responsible for declining standards. Lest it should be thought that this is just another example of passing the blame on to parents, it should be pointed out that the past decade, as well as seeing constant attacks on the teaching profession, has also witnessed an increase in poverty, unemployment, homelessness and a decrease in welfare provision of many kinds, all of which have increased the pressure on many families to such a degree it would be surprising if there had not been a deterioration in children's breadth of experience.

There are thus many question marks over Turner's position, both his claim about declining reading standards and his attribution of it to changes in teaching methods. But what about these teaching methods? I want now to move to a more fundamental examination of the theoretical position underlying Turner's article and much of his other writing; namely that the teaching of reading should ideally begin with a thorough treatment of phoneme-grapheme correspondences. Of course, Turner is not alone in taking this position, and debate about the merits of a phonics-first approach to beginning reading has been raging for some considerable time. (Books such as that written by Hubert Jagger (1929) contain fierce denunciations of the phonic approach and, in their turn, refer to writing on the same topic dating back to 1887.) Turner, and other phonics apologists, continually make the claim that 'the weight of research findings' supports their position. It is useful to examine some of this research evidence, and some alternative evidence which is rarely, if ever, cited by phonics advocates.

Psychological research

There are several traditions of research which have attempted to shed light on how people learn to read and become literate, and one of the most important of these has been grounded in psychology. A great deal of work has been done, often using measures of eye movement, on the mechanisms whereby skilled readers recognise words. This tradition was seriously challenged in the 1970s by psycholinguistic research, particularly that of Paul Kolers (1973), which suggested an enhanced role for context in reading. Subsequent work (Zola, 1984, Ehrlich and Rayner, 1981) has suggested that, while context does play an important part in word recognition, and hence reading, it is, for adults, only one cueing system among many. Adults seem to be able to process several sources of information at once (knowledge about language structures, knowledge about the world, semantic and syntactic context, graphic and phonic cues, discourse knowledge and so on) to make very rapid decisions about words on the page, and also which words to attend to and which to virtually ignore. This extremely complex process takes place almost without conscious thought and is best described as an interaction between reader and text (Rumelhart, 1985).

For beginning readers, however, because they lack the automatic control of these cue systems, the process seems to have different emphases. Ehrlich (1981) found that beginning readers were much more dependent upon context to read words than were older readers, a finding which goes some way to explaining the evidence from Weber (1970) and Clay (1969), to name but two, that young readers are more likely to substitute synonyms and similar grammatical words in oral reading, and are facilitated in their reading by being given meaningful (that is, context-embedded) text to read (Goodman, 1965). An approach to teaching which built upon what children do well would emphasise context and meaning.

Another line of psychological research has been that concerned with developments in children's awareness of sounds, superbly summarised in Goswami and Bryant (1990). It has certainly been well demonstrated that the more able young readers tend to be those who have greater phonological awareness, but there is no support here for the idea, advanced by some phonics theorists, that beginning with direct teaching about phoneme-grapheme relationships will thus accelerate reading progress. Goswami and Bryant in fact argue that it is through learning to read that children become aware of phonemes rather than vice versa. An awareness of phonemes is a product of learning to read rather than a precursor, and, indeed, children's nascent awareness is more likely to show itself in their writing than in their reading for quite some time.

Another important area of research, coming from a completely different tradition, has examined the impact upon children's literacy development of experiences external to the school. It is quite clear that becoming literate is a cultural phenomenon and takes on different meanings in different cultures (Heath, 1983). Children are alert to these differences from a very early age (Teale, 1986). It has also been established by a myriad of studies that young children are engaged in making sense of the literate environment which surrounds them from the moment they are born (Ferreiro and Teberosky 1983, Harste, Woodward and Burke 1984, Sulzby 1986). The vast majority of children arrive at school with an emergent understanding of how print functions as a carrier of meaning in the world around them. This understanding, as with all linguistic developments, is founded upon the interactions which take place between adult and child, and child and child, and one of the most important settings for these interactions is the sharing of stories (Snow and Ninio, 1986). The emphasis, therefore, in good infant classrooms upon story as a way into reading is thoroughly justified.

A narrow, impoverished view

It should be fairly clear that approaches to the teaching of reading based upon this breadth of research demonstrate anything but 'a narrow, impoverished view of reading', in Turner's words. Indeed, in the face of this, it would be a phonics-first approach which would be in greater danger of being narrow and impoverished. This point is made very strongly by Adams (1990) in perhaps the widest ranging review yet of research into phonics approaches to teaching reading. Because this report itself has been used by phonics advocates to support their position, it is worth quoting from its concluding chapter.

> Finally, none of these programs embodies the misguided hypothesis that reading skills are best developed from the bottom up. In the reading situation, as in any effective communication situation, the message or text provides but one of the critical sources of information. The rest must come from the reader's own prior knowledge. Further, in the reading situation as in any other learning situation, the learnability of a pattern depends critically on the prior knowledge and higher-order relationships that it evokes. In both fluent reading and its acquisition, the reader's knowledge must be aroused interactively and in parallel. Neither understanding nor learning can proceed hierarchically from the bottom up. Phonological awareness, letter recognition facility, familiarity with spelling patterns, spelling-sound relationships, and individual words must be developed in concert with real reading and real writing and with deliberate reflection on the forms, functions, and meanings of texts. (p. 422)

If we examine carefully the teaching programmes suggested by writers often classed as advocates of whole language, it is usually apparent that the concern in this final sentence is very much at the heart of these programmes. That suggested by Holdaway (1979), for example, is full of activities which concentrate attention upon letters and sounds, but which, crucially, begin from real experiences with real texts. Those described by Butler and Turbill (1984) likewise make constant reference to words, letters and sounds, but again set these into a meaningful context. Whole language programmes are clearly not built upon a 'narrow, impoverished view of reading'. They are, in fact, far more in tune with the findings of a whole range of research than are the methods seemingly proposed by Turner.

I shall conclude by giving a simple answer to the question at the very end of Turner's article. Of course, people want to find out more about reading, reading standards and teaching methods. We have ourselves at Exeter several research projects under way and planned and I do not doubt that the same is true elsewhere in the country. What I hope, however, is that research and investigation into these matters does take into account the complexity of what is being investigated. The teaching of reading is far too important and far too complex for simplistic analyses such as that of Martin Turner to be any use whatsoever in its development.

References

Adams, M J (1990) *Beginning to Read.* MIT Press: Cambridge, Mass.

Bald, J (1990) Problems with reading? *Language and Literacy News,* No. 3.

Barton, L (1991) Teachers under siege: A case of unmet needs. *Support for Learning,* 6, 3-8.

Butler, A and Turbill, J (1984) *Towards a Reading-Writing Classroom.* PETA: Rozelle, NSW.

Cato, V and Whetton, C (1991) *An Enquiry into LEA Evidence on Standards of Reading of Seven Year Old Children.* HMSO: London.

Child Education (1991) Reading survey confirms structured teaching approach. *Child Education,* 68 (January).

Clay, M (1969) Reading errors and self-correction behaviour. *British Journal of Educational Psychology,* 39, Part 1.

Department of Education and Science (1975) *A Language for Life* (The Bullock Report). HMSO: London.

Department of Education and Science (1978) *Primary Education in England.* HMSO: London.

Department of Education and Science (1990) *The Teaching and Learning of Reading in Primary Schools.* HMSO: London.

Dombey, H (forthcoming) Reading standards: What teachers need to know. In Wray, D (ed.) *Standards in Reading.* University of Exeter: Exeter.

Ehrlich, S (1981) Children's word recognition in prose contexts. *Visible Language,* 15.

Ehrlich, S and Rayner, K (1981) Contextual effects on word perception and eye movements during reading. *Journal of Verbal Learning and Verbal Behaviour,* 20.

Ferreiro, E and Teberosky, A (1983) *Literacy before Schooling.* Heinemann: London.

Goodman, K (1965) A linguistic study of cues and miscues in reading. *Elementary English,* 42, No. 6.

Goswami, U and Bryant, P (1990) *Phonological Skills and Learning to Read.* Lawrence Erlbaum: Hove.

Harrison, C (1991) The state of reading: A personal view. *Language and Literacy News,* No. 4.

Harste, J, Woodward, V and Burke, C (1984) *Language Stories and Literacy Lessons.* Heinemann: Portsmouth, New Hampshire.

Heath, S B (1983) *Ways with Words.* Cambridge University Press: Cambridge.

Holdaway, D (1979) *The Foundations of Literacy.* Ashton Scholastic: Sydney.

House of Commons (1991) *Standards of Reading in Primary Schools.* HMSO: London.

Hynds, J (1990) Are the educational psychologists right? *Language and Literacy News,* No. 4.

Jagger, H (1929) *The Sentence Method of Teaching Reading.* Grant Educational: London.

Kolers, P (1973) Three stages of reading. In Smith, F. (ed.) *Psycholinguistics and Reading.* Holt, Rinehart and Winston: New York.

Lake, M (1991) Surveying all the factors. *Language and Learning,* No. 6.

Martin, T (1990) Struggling readers. *Language and Literacy News,* No. 4.

Rumelhart, D (1985) Toward an interactive model of reading. In Singer, H and Ruddell, R (eds) *Theoretical Models and Processes of Reading.* International Reading Association: Newark, Delaware.

Smithers, A (1990) *Teacher Loss.* Interim report, School of Education, University of Manchester.

Snow, C and Ninio, A (1986) The contracts of literacy: What children learn from learning to read. In Teale, W and Sulzby, E (eds) *Emergent Literacy: Writing and reading.* Ablex: Norwood, New Jersey.

Sulzby, E (1986) Writing and reading: Signs of oral and written language organisation in the young child. In Teale, W and Sulzby, E (eds) *Emergent Literacy: Writing and reading.* Ablex: Norwood, New Jersey.

Teale, W (1986) Home background and young children's literacy development. In Teale, W and Sulzby, E (eds) *Emergent Literacy: Writing and reading.* Ablex: Norwood, New Jersey.

Turner, M (1991) Finding out. *Support for Learning,* 6, 99-102.

Weber, R M (1970) First graders' use of grammatical context in reading. In Levin, H and Williams, J (eds) *Basic Studies on Reading.* Basic Books: New York.

Zola, D (1984) Redundancy and word perception during reading. *Perception and Psychophysics,* 36.

(First published in *Support for Learning,* Vol. 6, No. 4, 1991.)

SECTION 2

Providing a Reading Environment

3 - Reading: What children need to learn and how teachers can help them

HENRIETTA DOMBEY

What we want and where we are

We all want the children we teach to be able to get the words off the page, but that is not all. We want more, not just for the brightest, nor just for those nearing the end of Year 2. We want all our primary children to become *readers*. Although fluent word recognition is of course essential, becoming a reader means much more than this. It is a complex matter that cannot easily be summed up in a few simple precepts, much less made to happen by following simple rules. Yet those of us involved in one capacity or another in the teaching of reading in publicly funded infant schools are castigated, almost daily, often by those with no experience of infant teaching, for failing to recognise the central simplicity of the enterprise. We are living through a public 'debate' about the teaching and learning of reading in which the early stages of learning to read are presented as a straightforward collection of 'skills' whose teaching and learning are quite unproblematic, necessitating only a proper discipline on the part of the teacher.

It could have been worse. Thankfully, Dearing has recognised that teachers and children should have a two year breathing space [as of 1993] before any decisions are made about changing the content of the National Curriculum - including English. Baroness Blatch's pragmatically positive response to this has saved us from the threatened confines of a narrowly conceived set of 'initial reading skills' (National Curriculum Council, 1993). So we have gained an unexpected breathing space, but we have not changed the terms of debate.

We cannot afford to plan our children's learning without taking a larger and more informed view of the issues involved. Yet attempts to bring a more measured approach to the treatment of reading in the public media have been largely unsuccessful: even the education editors of 'quality' newspapers see discussion informed by sound evidence and considered argument as less interesting than quack remedies. So we must do the job for ourselves in our own journals - and then go out and talk to others about it. In this article I intend to make a start by exploring what children need to learn, and the part teachers can play in the making of readers.

To do this I am going to leave aside the ten level framework of the National Curriculum, both as we have it now on the Statute Book, and as we might have it in the future. I do so because the ten level framework imposes an incremental view of development in reading, dealing in discrete items of observable behaviour, and so inevitably lacks depth and dynamism. The tactics and items of knowledge set out in the present attainment targets are not irrelevant to learning to read, but they are far from being a sufficient account of the process. No list of 'statements of attainment' can show us a living reader, much less the process that has brought her to this state. To do this we need to enlarge our attention to include more elusive qualities such as the attitudes children have towards reading, their experiences of reading texts of various sorts, and the strategies they habitually use to make sense of these texts. Such attitudes, experiences and strategies weave together with the tactics and knowledge set out in the National Curriculum to make children readers. They are not collections of discrete behaviours learnt one at a time in a set, predetermined order, but qualities and habits of mind which develop and deepen over time.

Children possessing these qualities are set fair to become committed and capable adult readers. But skilled reading should no longer be the preserve of an élite. We need to help more of our pupils towards this goal. When they are adults, all children now in infant school will need to read texts that are more varied, more demanding and more pervasively significant in their lives than those that make up the reading matter of most of their parents now. The less skilled and flexible their reading, the more impoverished and less autonomous their lives will be.

What children need to learn

These qualities can be thought of as lessons - the lessons children must learn if they are to put reading to work for them and enrich their lives through it. Some of these lessons are learned relatively quickly, but others develop over a long time. Some are of central importance and others more peripheral. However they do not fall into a neat linear pattern and cannot be set out in a neat order of importance or of teaching. I certainly do not claim that the list is definitive or exhaustive: you may well want to add other lessons. And of course many children have begun to learn many of these lessons long before they enter the reception class.

Attitudes

Children need to learn:

- *Pleasure and satisfaction: to see books and other texts as a powerful source of enjoyment, information and understanding.* Children who do not learn this lesson early have little reason to invest the energy and attention in learning to read that it demands. This point cannot be overstressed.

- *Confidence: a firm belief that they will learn to read.* Children need to see learning to read as something normal and themselves as capable of achieving it. Teachers must have faith in their pupils' capacities.

- *Concentration and persistence.* Particularly in the early stages, learning to read requires considerably more of these qualities than most other activities that young children engage in. They are, of course, closely linked with self-confidence and the experience of pleasure.

- *Toleration of uncertainty.* Even in the early stages a reader must be prepared to put up with not knowing exactly what is going on, what a word means or why a character is acting in a particular way, and be prepared to find the answer by reading on. Again this attitude cannot be clearly separated from others: you are more likely to tolerate uncertainty if you are confident and convinced of the ultimate reward.

- *Tentativeness: a readiness to correct error and revise ideas about the text and its content.* This is essential to the development of fluent and accurate reading for meaning, and to construction of the complex sense demanded by stories, poems and information texts. Expectations are crucial to reading, but so too is a willingness to admit that texts can carry surprises.

Strategies

Children need to learn:

- *To make sense of a text, to focus on making it mean.* Unless children learn to approach a text in the spirit of making it mean something, they cannot be said to be reading. Reading is essentially about making meaning from texts: word identification is a means to that end.

- *To draw on their experience of the world and of other texts to aid them in the process of meaning-making.* To understand most texts we draw on a wide range of physical and cultural knowledge. We also draw on knowledge of the patterns and structures of texts as various as fairy tales and recipes. This enables us to make sense of the particular section of text being read, to fit it into the larger whole and develop appropriate expectations about what is to come. Children need to learn to do this.

- *To make use of the information provided by the pictures to aid them in the process of meaning-making and in word identification.* Young children do, of course, find pictures easier to read than words. We should neither dismiss this meaning-making activity, nor assume that all children are highly skilled in it. They may need more help than we realise in making sense of pictures, and in following a story through a sequence of pictures.

- *To make use of the information provided by the letters (and punctuation marks) on the page.* If children are not doing this they are not reading. Most word identification involves attention to the marks on the page.

- *To make use of their knowledge about the world in general and about the subject matter of the text being read in particular.* Attention to the letters on the pages is not enough on its own for accurate word identification. Children also need to draw on appropriate semantic knowledge of what might 'make sense' in terms of the developing meaning of a text.

- *To make use of their knowledge of written language.* If they are to identify words efficiently children also need to draw on syntactic and lexical knowledge. Through 'tuning in' to the language of a text they need to make use of their knowledge of the kind of words and sentence structures to be expected.

- *To orchestrate these strategies for word identification and put them to the service of meaning-making.* Children need to learn to put all these strategies together in one harmonious super-strategy, thereby achieving a fluent, accurate and thoughtful reading of text. No one source of information - phonics, spelling patterns, syntactic, semantic or textual cues - can provide the reader with the means for fluent and accurate word identification, or with a valid conception of the meaning of the text.

Knowledge and tactics

These larger strategies imply further areas of knowledge and tactics. Children need to learn:

- *The language of books.* The language of written text is very different from the language of the spoken word. There is a great difference between the organized and patterned language of texts written for young children and the fluid fragmentary quality of the conversation they experience.

- *The conventions of the English writing system: left to right, top to bottom etc.* Many children in our schools encounter writing systems at home that operate according to different rules. Others come to school unaware of such conventions.

- *That the text is the same on each re-reading and that the marks on the page tell you what to say.* Again this is not self-evident. Many children begin by thinking that it is the pictures that tell the reader what to say.

- *That language is composed of separable words.* Like other non-literate people, young children apprehend language as a continuous stream, not as a succession of entities called words.

- *To conceive of words as sequences of separable sounds, or phonemes.* Many children find this lesson very hard indeed, since they are habituated to thinking of words in terms of their meaning. Thus playing 'I spy' with four and five year olds can be a slow and erratic business, as they appear at first incapable of detaching the phoneme a particular word begins with. Until they can manage to do so, phonics teaching will be useless.

- *To relate these phonemes to the letters or groups of letters that represent them.* Unfortunately these phonic rules are both complex and unreliable. And children vary markedly in the ease with which they learn to use this information. But learning to use these rules is essential to fluent reading.

- *To recognise irregular but common words immediately.* Very many of the words most commonly used in written English do not obey straightforward phonic rules. Exceptions abound, particularly in very common words such as 'one' or 'you', so these must be learned as 'sight words'.

- *To recognise the common spelling patterns of English, together with common prefixes, suffixes and root words.* Much of our English spelling is not simply phonetic. The spelling of words such as 'magician' or 'heard' carries information about their meaning and grammatical status.

Experiences

Attitudes, strategies, tactics and items of knowledge are of course gained through experiences of many sorts. Some experiences seem to be particularly powerful and to have their own intrinsic value. They are lessons in their own right, crucial to the development of children as readers.

Children need substantial experience of:

- *Hearing written language read aloud.* Children need to be immersed in the language of the written word, thoroughly experienced in making sense of it and in savouring its cadences, through hearing stories, poems and information that arrests, involves and satisfies them. Extraordinarily complex learning can take place as children listen to a story that holds their attention and excites their interest in language. At one and the same time children can learn about the kinds of meanings that you can make through stories, the new words and sentence structures of which these meanings are made, the intonation patterns that give them life and make them more comprehensible, and also many of the larger strategies and even many of the tactics involved in intelligent reading.

- *Using many types of texts for many purposes.* Children need experience of reading stories, poetry, information books and texts on the computer screen, and of reading these in different ways for different purposes. The new forms of literacy that are developing so swiftly mean that flexibility and an awareness of difference are more important than ever.

- *Re-reading favourite texts and authors.* If children are to become avid readers, they need early on to know certain texts very well indeed. It may be a book on African Wildlife which appeals at first through the power of its pictures, and which initially the child needs help in making sense of. Or it may be a book of rhymes or a storybook, with texts that are memorable because of their patterned language as well as the meanings they convey. Knowing stretches of texts so well that they almost possess them by heart gives a feeling of mastery as well as a solid familiarity with linguistic forms and a growing understanding that texts can endure and yield more on a second or even a third reading.

Classroom practice

If children are to learn to read well, to learn lessons of the sort itemised above and to learn many of them, we must be deliberate about how we provide for them, support them, prompt them and teach them. We cannot let this learning be a *laissez faire* enterprise, a by-product of random encounters with books and adults. Teachers have many roles to play.

Teacher as provider

From nursery on, the infant classroom needs to be rich in informative, alluring and legible print. It is not just a matter of a lively book corner, important though that is: children need poems on the wall to reread and savour, labels on drawers to tell them what is inside, and notices that add to the displays they accompany. To help them think of words as sequences of sounds, and to learn to relate these to the letters that represent them, children also need alphabet friezes, at a height where they can see and touch them, and plastic letters to manipulate. To give the written word a sense of closeness and personal importance, they need books and other texts composed by themselves and their classmates. These materials need to be organised so that they are accessible to the children, and should be supplemented by a well stocked and well organised school library, including plenty of picture books, fiction and poetry, as well as information books.

So what about reading schemes? Surely these can give, as they claim, a clear framework for progress? Although most scheme books these days are less bland and artificial than they used to be, most still offer very limited fare. The stories lack the drive and force of 'real' books. The pictures seldom add to these thin texts. The focus of teacher and learner is narrowed down to word identification, with the emphasis on the visual information provided by the letters on the page. With these thin texts the children can make only limited use of context or picture cues, and little progress in the business of learning how to make coherent and satisfying sense of the words on the page. The complex orchestration of different kinds of information, the essential skill of reading, is not fully fostered or stimulated.

If you or your school choose to use a scheme for the structure and forward impetus it seems to provide, you should be aware of its limitations and recognise the central importance of lessons that only more substantial texts can teach. No scheme book can teach a child that the words on the page can be savoured, or can yield richer meanings on a second reading. As they are marshalled through a scheme, children cannot develop their own tastes or pursue their own interests. Reading-scheme books cannot teach children the purposes or pleasures of reading, and can teach only a limited version of the process. So those who are taught on a reading scheme need many additional lessons and many other texts.

And even if you provide a wealth of other texts, there is a very real danger that the reading scheme, with its structured appearance and institutional status, will come to represent 'real reading' in the eyes of children, parents and teachers, and the other books will be seen as no more than optional extras - extra-curricular entertainment.

Teacher as model

The purposes, pleasures and processes of reading need continual demonstration. Otherwise, for many children reading can be an activity as pointless as it is baffingly invisible. With every note about the eye inspection teachers have an opportunity to show something of what reading can do for us and how we go about it. Talking one's way through the process of finding a passage that tells you how parrots make their nests demystifies the process of seeking information from large library books, and makes it that much more accessible.

Story-time, through which children can gain the familiarity with written language that is so crucial to them, gives a daily opportunity for modelling reading in action. By her excited commentary, the nursery teacher can show how turning the pages will help everyone find out whether Rosie will get safely back. With the aid of large format 'big books', the reception teacher can show something of how to identify unfamiliar words. With these and other more conventionally sized books she can help children make illuminating connections with other books and other experiences, demonstrate excited involvement and share her own tentative predictions of what might happen. By sharing her interpretation, the Year 2 teacher can help children understand complex plots and hold various possibilities in their heads, and model some of the extraordinarily subtle and complex meaning-making that modern picture books permit.

Teacher as co-reader

As well as allowing the modelling of much of the reading process in ways that are visible to the watching children, big books let one invite the whole class or a smaller group into a reading partnership. In rhythmic and familiar stories and rhymes, children can 'read' parts of the text long before they can read through a book unaided or recognise words out of context. But the teacher's support in this early reading is vital, if the experience is to give the children pleasure in the text and a sense of achievement. It is a matter of knowing when to read on, clearly articulating each word without losing its part in the whole pattern, and when to pause, encouraging the children to take over. With each re-reading of the text, the children should be able to take over more for themselves.

Until they have developed a degree of independence, young readers also need co-reading on a one-to-one basis, where it can be more sensitively tuned to individual children's needs, interests and strengths. Reading and re-reading a book with tactful and stimulating support gives children a far more substantial and pleasurable introduction to the process of reading than attempting to memorise words in isolation. After they can tackle a text largely on their own, children continue to need regular sessions with their teacher where they receive this one-to-one support. This should help them use the various cueing systems more efficiently and harmoniously - to orchestrate the act of reading, and thus gain in fluency and independence.

Teacher as guide

Children need to be allowed some choice in the texts they read if they are to develop their tastes and their commitment to reading. But they cannot always know whether they will find a particular book unrewarding or pleasurable, challenging or too daunting. Some of these discoveries they have to make for themselves, and they will be the more experienced as a result of making them. But the teacher's role as guide is important too. Children left to make all their own choices may stick with a small range of familiar texts, and remain undeveloped both in terms of the range of books they read and their level of difficulty. Or they may continually choose books whose pictures hold their interest, but whose text they make no attempt to read. This does not mean that their progress should always be onward and upward: re-reading familiar texts can give children greater confidence and a deeper sense of the meanings a text can yield, as well as allowing the legitimate pleasures of revisiting old haunts and old friends. And sometimes it can be very necessary to follow the reading of a demanding text with one that is much easier. Seven-year-old Linda followed her reading of Serraillier's *The Silver Sword* with Holmelund Minarik's *A Kiss for Little Bear.* But young readers need an overall pattern of increasing challenge, in terms both of words to be recognised and worlds to be constructed. This progress needs to be discernible to parent, teacher and child.

Teacher as reading companion

Children need to talk about the texts they read, interpreting and commenting on the events, facts and characters, and relating them to those they know from their own first and second hand experience. They need to express and share their enjoyment, pleasurable fears, puzzlement and pondering, the sources of so many of the more important meanings they will make from books. This companionship should be generous, allowing and encouraging children to make their own meanings, but extending and challenging these they are narrow or at odds with the text.

Teacher as phonics tutor

All the roles itemized up to now imply that children can learn much implicitly; from seeing what reading can do and how people go about it, being allowed to join in with the recitation of familiar text, and moving through books of increasing challenge, whose meanings they discuss companionably. But unless they can also get a purchase on the complex system of sound-symbol relations that governs English spelling, children will not become the confident effortless readers we wish them to be.

Through nursery rhymes, nursery and reception teachers can help their children savour the sounds of words and begin to mentally detach these from each other. Tongue twisters can refine this process. Alphabet friezes are invaluable, especially where the children are invited to make their own additions. So are those old favourites 'I Spy' and 'The Caretaker's Cat'. Magnetic letters and ongoing lists of rhyming words also have a place in helping children to perceive the sounds in words and relate these to letters. Of course the emphasis in the early stages is on the simplest and most straightforward sound-symbol relationships, such as the initial sounds of 'car', 'cat' and 'caretaker' and what Goswami and Bryant (1990) call the 'rimes' of 'hat', 'cat' and 'sat'. Much of this early activity will take place outside the reading of meaningful text, but connections should be made, particularly in the reading of familiar rhymes. All children should be given clear opportunities to infer regularities from seeing words grouped by the similarity of their spelling pattern and sound.

Some children catch on to the phonic principle very readily. Others learn this crucial tool much more slowly and need careful monitoring and extensive support. But this should accompany the other reading lessons they are learning, not replace them. For phonics learning to be of value it must be orchestrated with many other lessons.

Teacher as organiser

The desultory encounter between distractible child and randomly chosen book is one of the many enemies of progress in reading. Children need a sense of pattern and purpose in their experience of reading in and out of school. They need to experience reading time as focused and productive, as time when they learn a number of different lessons that combine to help them make meaning from written texts. Organisation can make or break the teaching of reading. Sensitive, subtle interactions between a teacher, a child and a text are of little use if the rest of the class is in disorder. As HMI observe, classrooms where reading is good are orderly places, where children have appropriate tasks, often self-chosen, from which their attention is not expected to wander (HMI, 1991).

Sometimes the children work in twos or larger groups, reading the same text together and helping each other. Teachers may place more able readers with the less competent, or may group children of similar competence together. Sometimes classes are paired so that, for example, Year 4 children read with children in Year 1. Where such groupings work best, teachers have carefully chosen particular arrangements for particular reasons, kept the groups relatively stable, and provided other regular opportunities for individual and whole class reading.

Time spent with big books (commercial or homemade) is similarly focused and productive. Individual reading gives rise to conversation about books, making reading a less lonely enterprise than it is for many children, but is not extinguished by this talk. Parents and other helpers in the classroom work in close co-operation with the teacher. Home-school co-operation (of which more below) is similarly part of a large overall plan in which parents, teachers and children work together, each with a clear idea of where they are going, how and why.

Taped stories, games involving rhyming and other word play fit into a general pattern, as do regular visits to the school library, perhaps even the public library. Reading weaves in and out of many activities, in maths, science, technology and other curriculum areas, is supported and focused on when it is encountered, but also has its own daily protected space. This should be a time when other concerns, such as the exchange of early morning news, do not compete, and when the children are fresh for the imaginative and intellectual effort reading requires of them. Many teachers find that the first half hour of the afternoon is best for this quiet reading, ERIC as it is sometimes called - Everyone Reading In Class.

Organisation should not just be an individual classroom matter. As well as an agreed policy on the teaching of reading, infant teachers need to share ideas on practical matters, and plan these harmoniously. Expectations set up in children and parents in the reception class need to be met and extended throughout the infant years. Daily story and daily quiet reading, regular continuing work on developing phonemic awareness and the orchestration of the phonic, syntactic, semantic and pictorial cueing systems need to thread right through this vital time in children's development as readers.

Teacher as partner with parents

Twenty-five years ago, when Margaret Clark carried out her study of children who could read on school entry, she found that most parents were embarrassed to admit to their child's proficiency, regarding it as something as shameful as bed-wetting (Clark, 1976). Reading was the school's province: parents who aimed to help at home were seen as interfering with their children's progress along the smooth path laid down at school. Things are very different in most schools now as teachers recognise how crucial parents can be in helping their children take their reading forward. But exactly how productive this partnership is depends on how it is formed, fed and organised. Parents need to be wooed and actively recruited to the business of helping their children learn to read, not to have their participation taken for granted. Explanatory times for individuals after school and home visits for those who lack the time or confidence to talk about reading on school premises need to be organised very early on in the reception year.

Parents need the school's policy, expectations and ways of teaching explained to them. Their part needs to be made clear and attractive. Book bags and home-school reading diaries with daily entries are vital to the well-being of home-school reading links. And all this needs to be well integrated with the reading carried on in the classroom. Home reading will not play its full part if the books that go home in the bags are chosen rapidly at the end of the day when the children's minds are elsewhere, or if the teacher's entry in the diary never engages the concerns of the parent or reveals any of the important lessons she is hoping the child might tackle and achieve.

Teacher as assessor and recorder

Record-keeping and assessment are vital if teachers are to help their children along a broad front of literacy-learning. At the simplest level, teacher, parent and child need a record of books read by the child and how well she tackled them, with perhaps a note of what she made of them. But more is needed if children's experience is to develop coherently. Since the attitudes, experience and strategies that contribute vitally to children's growth as readers are qualities that develop slowly over time, in ways peculiar to individual children, ticking statements of attainment when children appear to have achieved them is not enough. Descriptive and interpretive records are essential to allow the teacher to reflect on where each child has got to, what has helped this learning and where she might go next.

Parents and children have much to contribute to such assessment and should be invited to do so at least once each year. As well as providing the teacher with invaluable extra information, the act of reflection on the reading process can help both parents and children think more deliberately about what they are doing and where they are going.

To be a maximal value, teacher assessment needs to be written down in a way that gives it dignity and permanence, and puts the emphasis on future action. The Primary Language Record, produced by teachers working with the staff of the Centre for Language in Primary Education provides the most comprehensible and manageable format for this (Barrs et al, 1988).

Where children appear not to be making satisfactory progress, more intensive assessment is needed if extra help is to be tailored to their specific needs. The PLR shows various ways of approaching this, notably through miscue analysis, the procedure devised by Ken and Yetta Goodman that reveals the tactics the reader is using to identify words (Goodman et al., 1987). But talking to the children about what they think about reading may be equally revealing. It should not be assumed that all readers fall behind simply because of inadequate proficiency in using phonics. Clear record-keeping and thoughtful descriptive assessment make full and purposeful collaboration between teacher, parent and child a real possibility. Without them it is at best a hit or miss affair.

So what does this add up to?

To become literate in a language with an alphabetic writing system, all children need to learn phonics - that is they need to grasp the relation between speech sounds and letters. But if they are to recognise words efficiently they need far more than this, and to become *readers* they need more still. Children need the width and depth of experience that can come only from experience of reading a range of high quality texts, in which they can find satisfying stories and poems, and information that will extend their understanding of how the world works.

But books on their own teach few children to read. We need to do far more than throw our pupils into a swimming pool of lovely books in which they are invited to wallow. If children are not given human support and armbands, and taught a stroke or two, they may be submerged. Children need to make progress and to be seen by all concerned to be doing so. To achieve this, we need a clear sense of what children have to learn, what progress looks like and what different texts and different experiences have to offer.

Despite repeated media assertions, the evidence suggests that the teaching of reading in our infant schools is not in a state of serious decline. We certainly need money for materials, time to plan and assess, and classes small enough to allow children individual attention. We probably also need a wider recognition that in the infant school reading is central, not just one of more than a dozen attainment targets. But what we do with the material, time and children available to us can vary enormously in its scope and effectiveness. Despite all the upheavals of the National Curriculum, now seems a useful and necessary time to reassess our teaching in the light of developing knowledge and changing demands.

References

Barrs, M et al (1988) *The Primary Language Record.* Centre for Language in Primary Education: London.

Bussis, A et al (1985) *Inquiry into Meaning: An investigation of learning to read.* Lawrence Erlbaum Associates: Hillsdale, NJ.

Clark, M (1976) *Young Fluent Readers: What can they teach us?* Heinemann: London.

Goodman, Y (1987) *Reading Miscue Inventory: Alternative procedures.* Richard Owen: New York.

Goswami, U and Bryant, P (1990) *Phonological Skills and Learning to Read,* Lawrence Erlbaum Associates: Hove.

HMI (1991) *The Teaching and Learning of Reading in Primary Schools.* DES: London.

National Curriculum Council (1993) *English for Ages 5-16.* Department for Education and the Welsh Office: London.

4 - The role of analogies in reading development

USHA GOSWAMI

How do young children set about making connections between written words and the sounds of spoken words when they begin learning to read, and why do some children find this connection such a difficult one to make? Recent research in developmental psychology has begun to provide some intriguing answers to this question. It is becoming clear that a very important factor in an individual child's reading and spelling development is that child's *phonological awareness:* the child's ability to segment spoken words into their constituent sounds. Although phonological awareness tasks are purely oral, children's ability to succeed on these tasks is an important predictor of how well they will learn to read and to spell. In particular, children with special difficulties in phonological tasks will almost certainly have contingent difficulties in reading.

Levels of phonological awareness and the development of phonological skills

One important research finding has been that there is more than one level of phonological awareness (figure 4.1). The traditional view was that spoken words could be segmented into either *syllables* or *phonemes.*

Syllabic	*'wigwam'*	=	*'wig' + 'wam'*
Phonemic	*'wig'*	=	*/w/+/i/+/g/*
Onset-Rime	*'trip'*	=	*/tr/+/ip/*
	'wig'	=	*/w/+/ig/*

Figure 4.1 - Levels of phonological awareness

Syllabic segmentation was relatively simple. A word like 'wigwam' could be segmented into two syllables, 'wig' and 'wam'. A word like 'butterfly' contained three syllables, corresponding approximately to 'but-ter-fly'. There was some linguistic debate about whether the syllabic boundary came at 'but-ter' or 'butt-er', but there was no doubt that two syllables were involved.

Phonemic segmentation was more difficult. A phoneme is the smallest unit of sound that changes the meaning of a spoken word. Thus, 'pig' and 'dig' differ by a single phoneme, and so do 'pig' and 'pit'. All of these words contain three phonemes, corresponding approximately to the sounds of the alphabetic letters making up the words. For example, the phonemes in 'pig' correspond to the sounds of the alphabet letters 'p', 'i' and 'g'. However, the relationship between phonemes and alphabetic letters is not a straightforward one. Words like 'soap' and 'rain' also have three phonemes, even though they have four letters, and so do words like 'shop' and 'chat'. Words like 'light' and 'cough' have three phonemes too, even though they have five letters. This is because letter clusters like 'igh', 'ou', 'oa', 'ai', 'sh' and 'ch' can all correspond to a single phoneme.

As these examples might lead you to expect, young children have great difficulties with *phonemic* awareness tasks. Five- and six-year-old children can segment words like 'wigwam' and 'butterfly' into their constituent syllables with ease, but the same is not true of segmenting words like 'soap' and 'pig' into their constituent phonemes (see, for example, Liberman, Shankweiler, Fischer and Carter, 1974). In fact, until the children begin being taught to read, they can hardly perform phonemic segmentation tasks at all. The same is true of tasks requiring them to delete phonemes. Twenty years ago, Bruce showed that 5- and 6-year-olds had great difficulty in deleting the 'j' sound in 'jam' to leave 'am', or the 'k' sound in 'pink' to leave 'pin' (Bruce, 1964). Again, it was only when the children were being taught to read that they began to succeed in these phonemic tasks.

More recently, linguists have identified another level of phonological awareness (see Treiman, 1988). This level is intermediate between the syllable and the phoneme, and divides spoken words into the two units of the *onset,* corresponding to any initial consonants, and the *rime,* corresponding to the vowel and any final consonants. The onset of a word like 'pig' corresponds to the 'p', and the onset of a word like 'chat' corresponds to the 'ch'. Both these onsets are single phonemes, but onsets can also correspond to groups of phonemes, as in 'speak' ('sp'), 'twist' ('tw'), 'spring' ('spr'), and 'straw' ('str'). The rime of a word like 'pig' corresponds to the letter cluster 'ig', whereas the rime of 'chat' corresponds to the letter cluster 'at'. The rime of 'light' is 'ight', and the rime of 'cough' is 'ough'. Rimes may correspond to just the vowels in written words, as in 'tree' ('ee'), 'zoo' ('oo') and 'go' ('o'). However, whereas all words have rimes, not all words have onsets. Words like 'eat', 'oak', 'end' and 'out' are examples of words that consist only of rimes.

Interestingly, research has shown that onsets and rimes are psychologically distinguishable units for children long before they begin learning to read. The phonological awareness tasks that measure onset-rime awareness are tasks that involve rhyming and alliteration, such as the 'odd man out' task developed by Lynette Bradley and Peter Bryant. They asked children to select the 'odd word out' of sets of words like 'rod', 'rot', 'rock' and 'box', or 'pan', 'fan', 'tin' and 'man'. They found that even 4-year-olds could succeed in this task, and that preschoolers' ability to categorise words on the basis of onsets and rimes was a strong predictor of their reading and spelling ability 4 years later (Bradley and Bryant, 1978, 1983). Recent studies comparing onset-rime awareness with phonemic awareness within the same task have confirmed that whereas onset-rime awareness is present prior to learning to read, phonemic awareness develops largely as a consequence of reading. For example, children who are asked to make 'same-different' judgements do much better when pairs of words share onsets ('plea', 'plank') or rimes ('spit', 'wit') than when they share single phonemes ('plea', 'pray'; 'rat', 'wit'; Treiman and Zukowski, 1991).

Relating phonological skills to reading: the role of analogies

Why should rhyming be related to reading? The answer seems to be that an awareness of rhyme alerts children to the possibility of using *analogies* between spelling patterns in words when they begin learning to read. Take the example of the word 'light', which is generally considered to be an irregular word. Although this word is indeed irregular in terms of its individual letter-sound correspondences, it is highly *consistent* in terms of the spelling pattern of its rime, 'ight'. In fact, there are ninety other words in written English that use the 'ight' unit ('bright', 'sight', 'night', 'flight', ...) including multisyllabic words ('brightness', 'nightie'), and there are no exceptions. This means that a child who begins to read by segmenting English words into onset-rime units is at a great advantage. That child is much more likely to meet spelling-sound consistency when reading: in our example, all the new words that the child comes across with the spelling unit 'ight' in the rime will share the same rhyming pronunciation. So a child who learns how to pronounce the letter string 'light', and then uses that word as a basis for analogies to similar words like 'night' and 'bright', will be at a distinct advantage.

My own research has shown that many young children use such analogies spontaneously in reading. In a series of experimental studies, I have found that children are much more likely to make analogies between spelling units that reflect onsets and rimes (such as the consonant cluster 'tr' in 'trim' and 'trap', or the letter cluster 'eak' in 'beak' and 'peak') than between matched spelling units that cross the onset-rime boundary (such as the letter cluster 'bea' in 'beak' and 'bean', or the consonant cluster 'sk' in 'desk' and 'mask'; Goswami 1986, 1988, 1991, in press). Children who learn to read 'beak' go on to read 'peak' and 'weak' by making analogies based on rimes. Children who learn to read 'trim' go on to read 'trot' and 'trap' by making analogies based on onsets (figure 4.2).

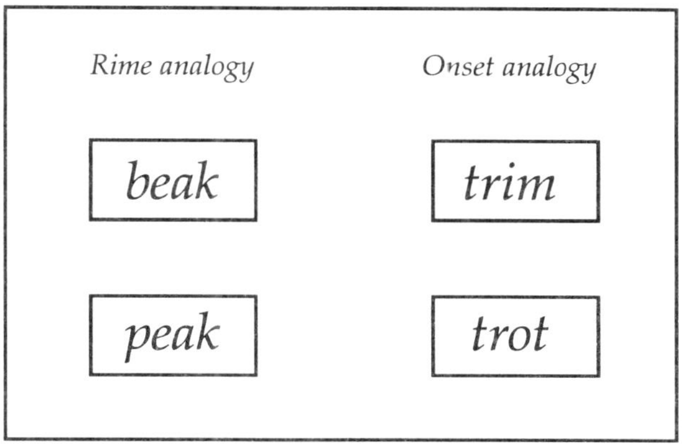

Figure 4.2 - The clue word task.

Although my original studies used a 'clue word' task, in which the children were taught a basis for analogy as a clue word (such as 'beak'), and were then given single words like 'peak' and 'bean' to try and read, the same effects are found when the analogous words are embedded in passages of prose (Goswami, 1988, 1990a). This analogy effect is not simply an artefact of rhyming, as children do not often make analogies between words like 'head' and 'said', words that share rhymes but that have different spelling patterns for the rime unit (Goswami, 1990a). Analogies in reading thus seem to show some analysis and comparison of the spelling sequence in words.

Furthermore, there seems to be a direct link between a child's phonological awareness at the onset-rime level and their use of analogies in reading. Children who have better rhyming skills make more analogies (Goswami, 1990b, Goswami and Mead, 1992). The developmental sequence suggested by these findings can be modelled in the following way (Goswami and Bryant, 1990). A child who has good onset-rime skills prior to being taught to read has the ability to categorise words on the basis of shared sounds. That child might have formed rhyming categories of words like 'light', 'fight' and 'night', or 'beak', 'weak' and 'speak'. When that child begins learning to read, she will find that these rhyming categories often map onto spelling categories. Words that share the same spelling patterns, such as 'light' and 'fight', also share rhyming sounds. It is a small step to move from recognising this relationship to *using* it by making analogies. A child who has good phonological categories will be able to predict the sounds of unfamiliar words on the basis of their shared spelling patterns. If a child can read the word 'light', and then meets the new word 'night', that child can decode 'night' by making an analogy from 'light' (figure 4.3).

Early experiences with rhyme

⇩

Awareness of onset and rime units

⇩

Use of analogies in reading

Figure 4.3 - Causal connections in reading.
(Source: Goswami and Bryant, 1990)

The implications for teaching

These research findings have a number of important implications for teaching. Let us summarise the main findings discussed above. The first is that there is a clear pattern of phonological development. Awareness of onsets and rimes emerges before an awareness of phonemes. The second is that there is a connection between onset-rime awareness and reading. Children with good rhyming skills become better readers. The third is that beginning readers can use analogies between the spelling patterns representing the onsets and rimes in words, using the spelling pattern of a familiar word, such as 'light', to decode an unfamiliar one, such as 'night'. Taken together, these findings suggest that teaching children about the connections between spelling units and onsets and rimes might be a very good way to begin teaching them about spelling-sound correspondences in reading.

However, there are some important additional points that should be made. The first is that a good grounding in phonological skills might be *crucial* if a child is to benefit from being taught to use analogies. A child with good rhyming skills has the necessary phonological basis (sound categories) to begin using analogies (spelling categories). A child with poor rhyming skills does not. The second is that some letter-sound knowledge is required to use analogies successfully. Although knowledge of a word like 'light' will give the child the basis for an analogy to 'night', some additional information is needed, which is the pronunciation of the onset 'n'. Thus teaching reading by analogy will also mean teaching a child individual letter-sound correspondences, but only when these letter-sound correspondences are onsets, such as 'ch' or 'l'. Reading by analogy is not the same thing as using a traditional phonics programme. These programmes may rely *exclusively* on sounding out unfamiliar words letter by letter, and may focus on letter-phoneme correspondences *within* the rime. By encouraging children to use analogies, teachers can introduce children to spelling-sound correspondence at the phonological level that is most *accessible* to the beginning reader, the level of onsets and rimes, and can leave the teaching of individual phonemes within the rime until some reading facility has been acquired.

Using analogy in the classroom

The training studies that have looked at the effects of teaching reading by analogy in the classroom have shown encouraging results. The majority have shown significant gains in reading for the analogy groups compared to the control groups (see, for example, Peterson and Haines, 1992, White and Cunningham, 1990). However, the studies that have worked best have given the children *phonological* training in rhyming and alliteration to accompany the *analogy* training of grouping words by shared spelling patterns. The best way to do this seems to be by focusing on word families.

In a landmark study that concentrated on phonological rather than analogy training, Bradley and Bryant (1983) gave a group of thirty children training in rhyming and alliteration for a period of 2 years, beginning when the children were 5 and 6 years old. They then measured the effects of this training on later reading and spelling development. They found a clear effect of rhyme training on later reading, but this effect was especially marked for fifteen of the children who had received supplementary instruction with plastic letters. These children had learned to spell out the words in the rhyming categories with plastic letters, interchanging onsets and rimes (PEN→HEN→MEN). In effect, they were receiving instruction in analogy.

More recently, two Canadian researchers gave twenty-four 5- to 6-year-olds explicit training in analogy. Peterson and Haines (1992) taught the children to read a clue word, such as 'ball', and then gave them practice in segmenting the clue word at the vowel ('b-all'). The children were given a family of analogous words ('hall, fall, call ...'), and were encouraged to segment these by onset and rime too, and to compare the spelling patterns of the shared rime units (such as 'all'). The links between the shared sound (rhyme) and the shared spelling units was stressed, and the children were taught to use their clue word to read the new words by analogy. After a month of training, which involved learning ten word families overall, the children showed significant gains in single word reading compared to a control group of children from the same classes who were not trained to use analogies.

A larger-scale study of reading by analogy was carried out by White and Cunningham (1990), who gave analogy training to around 300 6- to 7-year-old children in a whole school district in Hawaii. This was achieved by training some of the classroom teachers in this school district to teach reading by analogy. A programme for teaching dyslexic children developed by Irene Gaskins and her colleagues was adapted for this purpose (the 'Benchmark' programme, Gaskins, Downer and Gaskins, 1986). The crucial features of this programme are the systematic teaching of a large number of 'clue' words (about 200), lots of training in rhyming skills, and a focus on word families. During the course of the school year, the children in the analogy classrooms learned the 200 clue words, which were displayed on a 'word wall'. They also practised assigning new words to the correct families, either on the basis of their spelling pattern or their sound. For example, if the class was learning about the 'mat' and 'nine' families, a new word like 'spine' would be introduced, and discussion of which family it belonged in and how to spell it would take place. At the end of the school year, the children in 'analogy' classrooms were significantly ahead in reading and spelling compared to children in 'non-analogy' classrooms, who had simply received normal classroom teaching. Interestingly, these gains were not just in decoding. White and Cunningham (1990) reported a significant improvement in reading *comprehension* as well.

The drawback of these two analogy training studies is that they both used 'unseen' control groups, groups of children who did not receive extra training in something else to counter the possible 'Hawthorne' effects of being in the experimental group. Thus their positive findings require further confirmation. However, it is interesting to note that the children in White and Cunningham's study were attending schools in a catchment area that served a low socio-economic group, schools that had a large number of children who were experiencing difficulties in learning to read. White and Cunningham believe that reading by analogy is especially appropriate for children who are slow in beginning to read, and Gaskins and her colleagues share this belief. If they are correct, it may be because children who have poor phonological skills find it *easier* to learn to read by analogy, as analogies exploit a phonological level that the children find more accessible, the level of onsets and rimes. Although children with reading difficulties usually have phonological difficulties as well, and the importance of phonological training as well as analogy training cannot be stressed enough, these children should find that beginning to read with onsets and rimes is easier than beginning to read with phonemes.

Summary

A good phonological foundation is required if a child is to benefit from using analogies in reading. Many children come to school with such a foundation already present, as they have good rhyming and alliteration skills at school entry. These children can be introduced to reading via analogies and word families straight away, and will soon move on to working with individual phonemes, especially as they begin learning to *spell*. Children with reading difficulties usually have very poor phonological skills. For these children, extra phonological work with rhyme and alliteration will be necessary in order for them to develop the phonological skills necessary to use analogies. However, just like normally progressing children, they will be helped by beginning to learn about print at the most accessible phonological level, the level of onsets and rimes. For older children with reading difficulties as well as for young beginning readers, using analogies can provide a useful means of learning how spelling patterns and sound correspond.

References

Bradley, L and Bryant, P E (1978) Difficulties in auditory organisation as a possible cause of reading backwardness. *Nature*, 271, 746-7.

Bradley, L and Bryant, P E (1983) Categorising sounds and learning to read: A causal connection. *Nature*, 310, 419-21.

Bruce, D J (1964) The analysis of word sounds. *British Journal of Educational Psychology*, 34, 158-70.

Gaskins, I W, Downer, M A and Gaskins, R W (1986) *Introduction to the Benchmark School Word Identification/Vocabulary Development Program*. Benchmark Press: Media, Pa.

Goswami, U (1986) Children's use of analogy in learning to read: A developmental study. *Journal of Experimental Child Psychology*, 42, 73-83.

Goswami, U (1988) Orthographic analogies and reading development. *Quarterly Journal of Experimental Psychology*, 40A, 239-68.

Goswami, U (1990a) A special link between rhyming skills and the use of orthographic analogies by beginning readers. *Journal of Child Psychology and Psychiatry*, 31, 301-11.

Goswami, U (1990b) Phonological priming and orthographic analogies in reading. *Journal of Experimental Child Psychology*, 49, 323-40.

Goswami, U (1991) Learning about spelling sequences: The role of onsets and rimes in analogies in reading. *Child Development*, 62, 110-23.

Goswami, U (in press) Towards an interactive analogy model of reading development: Decoding vowel graphemes in beginning reading. *Journal of Experimental Child Psychology.*

Goswami, U and Bryant, P E (1990) *Phonological Skills and Learning to Read.* Lawrence Erlbaum: Hillsdale, N J.

Goswami, U and Mead, F (1992) Onset and rime awareness and analogies in reading. *Reading Research Quarterly*, 27 (2), 152-62.

Liberman, I Y, Shankweiler, D, Fischer, F W and Carter, B (1974) Explicit syllable and phoneme segmentation in the young child. *Journal of Experimental Child Psychology*, 18, 201-12.

Peterson, M E and Haines, L P (1992) Orthographic analogy training with kindergarten children: Effects on analogy use, phonemic segmentation, and letter-sound knowledge. *Journal of Reading Behaviour*, 24, 109-27.

Treiman, R and Zukowski, A (1991) Levels of phonological awareness. In S. Brady and D. Shankweiler (eds), *Phonological Processes in Literacy.* Lawrence Erlbaum: Hillsdale, N J.

White, T G and Cunningham, P M (1990) Teaching disadvantaged students to decode by analogy. Paper presented at the annual meeting of the American Educational Research Association, Boston, Mass., April.

(First published in *Support for Learning*, Vol. 9, No. 1, 1994.)

5 - Stories and learning to read

HENRY PEARSON

It has become fashionable to knock reading schemes, and many are easy targets for ridicule. Though the incidence of stilted text is becoming less common and is being replaced by more appetising, engaging prose and poetry in many schemes, some children are still being subjected to unnecessarily excessive phonic and vocabulary control. 'Reading books are getting better' concede Oakhill and Garnham (1988), 'but even so, graded reading schemes stop just where real reading - reading for pleasure and information - starts' (p. 3). In such scheme books literacy is treated as merely mechanical - an approach which fails to offer young children the enrichment that could be afforded to them through reading. Moreover, children may witness a conflict of philosophy: the books read to them *by* the teacher are quite different from the ones that they are required to read *to* the teacher.

Exponents of the so called apprenticeship approach, on the other hand, argue that it is possible, nay desirable, for emerging readers to learn the technique of reading without the need for structure and prescription and through exposure only to freely chosen real books. At first glance this is persuasive: no more the need for turgid and contrived text. However, it is only to be expected that such ideals are challenged by parents and teachers, and sometimes with just cause. The impression often given is misleading; emerse children in good books and they will learn to read; there is no need to teach, just facilitate. This may not be a complete account of how apprenticeship in reading works, but it is the sort of reputation it has acquired. For example, the glossary attached to an article in *The Independent* concerned with different schools of thought over the best way to teach children to read (Bagnall, 1989) defines the apprenticeship approach as 'child picks up the trick of reading by sitting by parent'! It is small wonder that, in the face of such misrepresentation, the 'progressives' get such a bad name and that there is an increased call for a return to the basics. Perhaps Stainthorp (1989) is justified in questioning such *laissez faire* approaches which devalue the role of the teacher and leave the learning of literacy to chance.

> In the past few decades the desire to present children with *real* books so that learning to read could be fun and lead to understanding and enjoyment of the texts, has led many people to appear to be suggesting that, as long as children are given enough experience with books, they will automatically learn to read. (p.69)

Stainthorp goes on to argue for a 'more rational phase in our approach where we take account of what children actually do when they learn to read' (p.70).

There can be no doubt that it is preferable for children to learn to read through exposure to good story books, but there are important issues that need first to be addressed if we are to prevent commitment to this method from being no more than an act of blind faith. For example, if we accept Jill Bennett's (1985) assertion that 'it is the books themselves, or rather their artists and authors, who are the real teachers' (p.3) - what is the role of the classroom teacher? If children are no longer to be guided through a series of programmed, numbered books, how are their individual needs to be accommodated? In the absence of cumulative text control, where is the structure? To argue that real books are better because they appeal to children and provide incentive for reading is important, but it is not sufficient in itself. Reading is creative, imaginative and recreational, but it is also a technical ability. Is it possible then, for stories to both entertain and teach technique? I believe it is. Furthermore, I suggest that apprenticeship approaches, in their best form, using good story books and with judicious intervention by teachers, can be rigorous and need not assume, as Mudd (1989) warns, that 'a reading environment alone will enable all children to understand the reading process' (p.84).

Since a hallmark of apprenticeship approaches is the importance attributed to stories, then it should be within their substance and structure that some essential ingredients for reading tuition are to be found. Indeed, the National Curriculum appears to endorse this notion: amongst the attainment targets in English for key stage one, the word story appears 25 times! Here, children are to be encouraged to *tell, retell, read, use, discuss, select, describe, explore, compose, create* and *write* stories.

Exposure to story seems to be an important predisposing factor in learning to read. Clark (1976 and 1984) found that experiencing stories read aloud was a prerequisite for those who became young fluent readers, and Wells (1986) suggests that telling and reading stories to pre-school children is an invaluable pre-literacy activity. In such circumstances, children learn about story genre and narrative structure in preparation for experiencing this form of language in print. Moreover, opportunities for exposure to story are manifold; this is one way in which the medium of television is promoting the literacy cause. Even the creators of advertisements have realised the potential of narrative form to engage the viewer. At the time of writing this article, one commercial for blended coffee is now in its fourth instalment! Since young children are likely to have experienced story, an since narrative is, as Hardy (1977) describes a 'primary act of mind, transferred to art from life' (p.12), then it follows that the substance of children's reading texts might be composed of something other than the contrived and esoteric language with which pre-school children are not familiar. Indeed, Simmons (1987) working with 10-12 year olds established some close relationships between children's story-telling and their ability to read. This was with particular reference to the children's understanding of story structure and 'grammar', syntactic complexity, the use of special linguistic devices, their acknowledgement of audience and their awareness of features of written, as opposed to spoken, versions of language in stories. 'All the more reason' she suggests, 'to expose children with reading difficulties to narrative form ... through a variety of narrative based experiences' (p.50).

Not all books offer the quality of narrative based experience that is helpful to children and their reading, nor is the distinction clearly defined between scheme and the misleading term 'real' books. Some books which appear to be real offer less enrichment than individual titles featured in some reading schemes. Two examples will serve to illustrate this point and may also highlight a possible distinction between good story on the one hand, and mere narrative on the other.

The first example is *Mrs Wishy-Washy* from Nelson's scheme 'Story Chest':

'Oh, lovely mud,' said the cow,
and she jumped in it.
'Oh, lovely mud,' said the pig,
and he rolled in it.
'Oh, lovely mud,' said the duck,
and she paddled in it.
Along came Mrs Wishy-washy.
'Just look at you!' she screamed.
'In the tub you go.'
In went the cow, wishy-washy, wishy-washy.
In went the pig, wishy-washy, wishy-washy.
In went the duck, wishy-washy, wishy-washy.
'That's better,' said Mrs Wishy-washy,
and she went into the house.
Away went the cow.
Away went the pig.
Away went the duck.
'Oh, lovely mud,' they said.

The second example is Rod Campbell's *My Presents* (Blackie):

It's my birthday.
I'm having a party.
All my friends have brought presents ...
shall we open them?

Susan gave me a ...
He's big and fluffy.
I like cuddling him.

Robert gave me some ...
They are all different colours.
I like building with them.

Sally gave me a ...
It's round and bouncy.
I like catching it.

John gave me a ...
It has a little brush.
I like making pictures with it.

Wendy gave me a ...
It makes me laugh.
I like putting him on my hand.

William gave me a ...
It has lots of pieces.
I like putting it together.

Jane gave me a ...
It makes a loud noise.
I like blowing it.

The last present is from Mummy and Daddy.
They gave me a ...
She's warm and fluffy.
I like her best of all.

Obviously it is difficult to appreciate the full impact of either book without seeing the layout, presentation, colour and illustrations. Campbell's book, for example, features pictures of presents hidden behind flaps suggesting the wrappers. However, the absence of the pictures here does allow us to focus on the differences between the texts. Ironically, the intricacy of Campbell's illustrations serves only to act as distraction from an otherwise dull and uneventful text. This is in contrast to the rich and humourous story of *Mrs Wishy-Washy*. Also significant is the prevalence of repetition in both texts - a much sought after ingredient by many teachers. But in *Mrs Wishy-Washy* this repetition is used to good advantage: it has a poetic resonance which makes it a delightful story to read aloud. In Campbell's book the repetitiveness is tedious.

The animal triumvirate in its defiance, and Mrs Wishy-Washy with her kindly 'Oh, look at you' help to create appealing characters in the reader's imagination. This opportunity is not provided for in *My Presents:* names are cited but characters remain 'off-stage' and afford little with which the reader can identify. Moreover, Rod Campbell's narrative is simply a string of similar events (the opening of presents) arranged chronologically, and the ordering is random. Save the last present, these could have been opened in any order. The effect is one of mere narrative.

In *Mrs Wishy-Washy* the story, though simple, is carefully shaped and structured - a problem identified, the situation acknowledged and resolved. The events develop and, with a predictable but delightful twist, the circumstances revert with the possibility of the cycle repeating itself. If we are looking for structure in children's reading tuition, it is in stories like this and within the children themselves that it might be found. Apprenticed readers are able to bring to such text their own knowledge and experience of story - its structure and conventions (Fox, 1983, 1989). This, combined with their abilities in using natural language, enables children to interact with the text - to bring their own script to bear in recognising its features. 'The structure' argues Fisher (1988) 'lies within the child's active involvement with learning and the task of the teacher is to facilitate this' (p.59). In its turn, the best text is user-friendly. It asks to be re-read. It neither tests nor constrains but rather invites the would-be reader first to recite, and eventually to read, the words.

I have spent some time observing young children with books in an attempt to find out something of what they do when learning to read. I cannot endorse the view that children will learn to read if left to their own devices, but I am increasingly impressed by the extent to which they can involve themselves with text when allowed time and opportunity to browse through books by themselves. This is particularly the case when a book has been read to them so that it has become familiar. One of the most delightful phenomena is to witness a child, curled up in comfort, saying the words of a familiar book with enthusiasm and expression - what Holdaway (1979) calls 'reading-like behaviour'. This ability to recite, rather than to technically and accurately decode the text, has an important function *en route* to reading. Rather than insisting from the outset on accuracy and precision, there should be a period during which children are allowed to approximate in, even play at, their reading. If precision is required, with no allowance to be made for error, then it follows that foolproof and restricted text will need to be used. Children are unlikely to make mistakes with a text which reads *Look, look, look in here!* However, if some approximations are encouraged to begin with, then opportunities are offered for the use of more enriching, less restricting, stories in text.

Whilst watching these children in a reception class, I became more aware of the importance of story in their reading development. I noticed that they were able to remember the stories of books that had been read to them, some recalled even most of the actual words. Stories are literally memorable, lists of words and mere narrative are not so. Which of the texts, *Mrs Wishy-Washy* or *My Presents* do you recall most readily now? Having remembered the story, children were then in a position to recite and eventually to read the text.

I was intrigued to watch the children's behaviour while enjoying these stories. Often a finger was inserted under the next page, poised to turn it over but waiting patiently for the current page to be completed before continuing. It occurred to me that it was the story that was propelling these readers through the pages of the book. The books that they chose were often the most predictable - if they could predict what was going to happen next, they could read what was going to happen next at the level of words, phrases, events and meanings. Having enjoyed certain books by themselves, the children would often ask an available adult to read the text with them. It was during these times, when the spade work was being done for them, that much of the learning was being undertaken. When following the text, a child being read to is left free to go about the business of recognising and eventually learning the words. None of this is cheating; when they re-read, memorise, predict or enlist someone's help in deciphering the text, they are simply finding their own ways of making the text accessible - as it were, facilitating their own learning.

This gives some indication of how the teacher's intervention might operate in a storybook approach. The author provides the material for the lesson through engaging, propelling, predictable and structured story text. The teacher acts as a go-between by communicating the author's words to the apprentised reader, by demonstrating how reading is done and by using the opportunities provided by the book to alert the apprentice to some textual features. For example, the teacher may read the story aloud and encourage the child to predict the text and to join in with the reading. Specific features can be highlighted and drawn out from their context for closer scrutiny. This might include alerting the reader to significant words and phrases in the text, or to initial letter sounds.

Ideally, and when possible, this needs to be undertaken on an individual basis, though the valuable work of reading stories to and with children might be undertaken by surrogate parents and other adults, or even by a tape recorder. Big books provide the opportunity for a one-to-one situation to be simulated with a group of children. When children are invited to join in with the reading of a big book they are each able to respond at their own level: some may prefer to watch and listen, others may manage to read out parts of the text, some the whole text. Sharing big books becomes particularly useful when miniatures are available for children to practise with by themselves. Hence, the cycle continues.

Amongst the ideas that are presented here, a structure is emerging; there is order in the way that reading can be introduced to children. As regards appropriate reading materials, the structure is within each story text rather than between a series of graded books. Thus, each read of each book offers a unique learning experience, but readers take with them, from one book to their next, an accumulation of knowledge. Good authors, through their stories, are adept not only at entertaining but also at making learning to read easy for the child. Such authors help the apprenticed reader to recognise the text, and this invariably means using not too many words so that the task is less daunting for the child. There is also an order which comes from within each child. I have suggested, for example, that there is a sequence of learning from playing at reading, to reciting text, to recognising words in the text, to reading the text. Eventually readers do learn the words; I would argue only that recognition of words in context precedes the learning of words.

Such approaches then are not haphazard, they are rigorous, but they do have the children's interests at heart.

References

Bagnall, N (1989) 'Dan and Nan hit the fan' in *The Independent* 8.6.89.

Bennett, J (1985) *Learning to Read with Picture Books.* The Thimble Press (3rd edition): Stroud.

Clark, M (1976) *Young Fluent Readers.* Heinemann: London.

Clark, M (1984) 'Literacy at home and at school: insights from a study of young fluent readers' in Goelman, H, Oberg, A and Smith, F (Eds) *Awakening to Literacy.* Heinemann: London.

Fisher, R (1988) 'The storybook approach to reading: where is the structure?' in *Education 3-13,* Vol. 16.1, 57-60.

Fox, C (1983) 'Talking like a book: young children's oral monologues' in Meek, M (Ed) *Opening Moves.* Heinemann: London.

Fox, C (1989) 'Children thinking through story' in *English in Education,* Vol. 23.2, 25-36.

Hardy, B (1977) 'Narrative as a primary act of mind' in Meek, M et al. (Eds) *The Cool Web.* The Bodley Head: London.

Holdaway, D (1979) *The Foundations of Literacy.* Ashton Scholastic: London.

Mudd, N (1989) 'What Katie did' in *Reading,* Vol. 23.2, 80-84.

Oakhill, J and Garnham, A (1988) *Becoming a Skilled Reader.* Blackwell: Oxford.

Simmons, K (1987) 'Children's story telling: what it can tell us about reading difficulties' in *Reading,* Vol. 21.1, 43-52.

Stainthorp, R (1989) 'A balanced approach to the teaching of literacy' in *Reading,* Vol. 23.2, 69-79.

Wells, G (1987) *The Meaning Makers.* Hodder and Stoughton: London.

6 - The 'real books' approach: Is apprenticeship a weak analogy?

MARTIN COLES

The approach to teaching reading currently invigorating many schools has two main strands. The first is the rejection of reading schemes in favour of 'real books', which phrase I take to mean books written by authors and illustrators with the prime purpose of interesting children and without confining requirements such as the need to use a limited vocabulary of key words or repeated particular phonetic patterns.

This desire to move away from offering children a graded series of books, as their initial reading material in schools, is not new; nor is the connected criticism of the quality of the text in such schemes. In 1908 for instance Huey was saying this of reading primers:

> No trouble has been taken to write what the child would naturally say about the subject in hand, nor indeed to say anything connectedly or continuously, as even an adult would naturally talk about the subject.

In the 1960s the Schools' Council Breakthrough to Literacy project attempted to encourage teachers to see that a child's own oral language experience could be used as a basis for the teaching of reading and writing. In the 1970s some schools moved away from using a single reading scheme in favour of the colour-coding system. And in 1975 the government report, *A Language for Life* ('The Bullock Report') welcomed the initiative of schools which provided 'real books' and other reading materials for young children:

> we would welcome the further development of the kind of scheme to which it is difficult to apply such simplistic labels as 'phonic', 'look and say', 'linguistic' etc. We welcome the enterprise of those schools which have successfully planned the teaching of reading without the use of a graded series ... every infant class needs a wide range of books and other printed materials.

It has to be said however that Bullock's recommendations were not taken up by the majority of Primary Schools at the time, as HMI noted:

> The use of graded reading schemes was universal in 7 year old classes and in nine out of ten of these classes children's reading practice was extended through use of supplementary readers associated with these schemes. A very similar picture emerged in the 9 year old classes. By the age of eleven some children in three-quarters of the classes were making use of reading schemes.

More recently Waterland (1985) published *Read With Me*. This short book, written by a practising teacher who was so obviously aware of the potential problems of moving away from a reading scheme, found a wide and receptive audience and in the four years since then there has been a sudden explosion in the number of schools who have adopted a 'real books' approach.

The subtitle of Waterland's books is 'An Apprenticeship Approach to Reading'. This phrase points to the second strand in the recent innovations, one which has no history similar to that outlined above but is of a more recent provenance, except perhaps it could be argued that an apprenticeship approach characterises much of what enthusiastic parents have always done.

Those schools which decide to move away from teaching via reading schemes can not simply change the texts they offer children. The theoretical basis for such a change demands that schools review the approach they take to the whole of the reading curriculum - the reading instruction offered by the teacher, classroom organisation of reading, assessment and record-keeping, the involvement of parents etc. I want here to consider just one aspect of this major review of the methods a school uses for developing children's reading, a review that is a necessary part of the move towards a 'real books' approach - the notion of the beginning reader as an apprentice. Is it a fruitful analogy and if so what does it imply for classroom practice?

Waterland explains her understanding of the concept as it relates to beginning readers thus:

> I came to adopt instead, a view of the learner not as passive and dependent like the cuckoo chick but rather as an active and already partly competent sharer in the task of learning to read. Here the model is apprenticeship to a craftsman. Consider the way apprenticeship works; the learner first undertakes the simplest parts of the job, then

gradually the more complex ones, increasing the share he can cope with and all the time working alongside, under the control of and with the help of, the craftsman. The apprentice does not sit passively with his mouth open; he works actively with the tools of his trade in his hand.

On the face of it this last sentence indicates a weakness in the analogy. Traditional apprenticeship occurs in the field of manual tasks. Reading on the other hand, is a cognitive activity. Drawing parallels between tasks which are different in such an important respect might well lead to inappropriate descriptions of beginning reading. There are other problems too with With Waterland's brief analysis. She asks us to consider the way apprenticeship works: 'the learner first undertakes the simplest parts of the job then gradually the more complex ones.' Now this is certainly how some classrooms work. Tasks and problems can be chosen to suit the stage of learning that a child is at. Teachers can, for instance, slowly increase the complexity of reading tasks and materials provided for children. But traditional apprenticeship is set in the workplace and the problems and tasks that are given to learners arise from the demands of the workplace. Tasks are therefore clearly and obviously purposeful; but letting the job demands select the tasks for students to practise is still one of the great inefficiencies of traditional apprenticeship.

So in traditional apprenticeship the tasks are selected either by job demands, or by the 'master', who takes the job demands into account. Yet Waterland advocates allowing the child, not the teacher, to specify the task in reading apprenticeship. Children choose their own books. In this way at least, the child is in charge and controls the actions of the adult, a reversal of the traditional master-apprentice relationship.

Furthermore, apprenticeship very often works on the basis of building a series of subskills to the point where they can be integrated in the efficient performance of the target task. As Waterland herself points out though 'reading is not a series of small skills fluently used; it is a process of getting meaning and must be so from the start.'

But criticisms of this kind imply that apprenticeship is being used as an exact model for teaching and learning reading when it is perhaps more sensible to consider apprenticeship as a suggestive rather than an exact analogy.

If we look at apprenticeship in this way, as suggestive, what are the structural features of traditional apprenticeship and what lessons might it have for teaching and learning reading? There are, I think, two crucial features of traditional apprenticeship which can usefully be applied to learning to read. The first is to do with methods of observation, coaching and practice, and the second with social context. (My description of traditional apprenticeship depends on that of Lave, J explained in Collins, A et al 1988.)

Observation, coaching and practice

Apprenticeship highlights methods for carrying out a task. Apprentices learn their methods through observation, coaching and practice. The apprentice repeatedly observes the master carrying out a task, modelling the process. An apprentice then attempts to execute the same process with help and guidance from the master i.e. coaching. A key aspect of this coaching is aid in the form of reminders and other help that the apprentice requires to complete the task. Once the apprentice has a grasp of the skill, the master reduces participation, providing only limited hints and feedback to the learner who continues to practise until the skill approximates to that of the master.

If we follow this model it becomes obvious that an apprenticeship approach is not a matter of laissez-faire. It is not simply a matter of 'catching' reading as if cognitive skills could be caught in the same way as one catches a cold. An apprenticeship approach following this paradigm does not mean just providing children with good books and assuming that it is enough, as some claim, simply to apprentice children to the authors and illustrators. Rather it is a case of 'read with me'. The pattern is one where, broadly, the child moves from listening to the adult read (observation), through reading with the adult (coaching), to reading independently (practice).

Several points are worth emphasising here. Traditional apprenticeship works in domains where the skills are usually external and readily available in both learner and teacher for observation. Applying apprenticeship methods to largely cognitive skills requires the externalisation of processes which are usually carried out internally in order that the learner can observe the expert strategies that the teacher is using. Of course this means reading aloud but also implies incidental conversation about the text and a commentary on the reading aloud in a one-to-one situation. So, for instance, at either of the first two stages - observation and coaching - the teacher might mention their change of voice as the speech marks provide a signal; they might wish to point out a miscue or two that a child corrected while reading, asking the child how they knew to make the correction; they might also point out significant uncorrected miscues when they occur - 'that can't be house can it? House doesn't make sense. Horse makes sense don't you think?'; they may, at a certain point, ask for a summary of the passage since summarising forms the basis for comprehension monitoring; they might too ask questions of the text which require the reader to predict in order to encourage an overall reading strategy of hypothesis formulation and testing. The teacher might sometimes model these activities for the learner by summarising herself or, in a conversational way, making a prediction about the way the story is going in an attempt to reflect the fact that skilled reading involves developing expectations and evaluating them as evidence accumulates from the text. She might too, offer some interpretative comments on the text as a demonstration that meaning is not somehow all in the text, to be extracted entirely through some sort of decoding, but relies on a reader's response.

Of course, all this has to be done with some sensitivity remembering that the eventual goal is for the teacher to fade from the scene. The learner must be helped to move from coaching to practice, and overwhelming interruption is unlikely to help motivate a reader or to allow pleasure to be gained from the book. Judging the what, when and how of intervention, and matching this to the learner's experience calls for sensitive, informed judgement. In practice a sensible compromise has to be reached between the need for coaching and the goal of nil intervention, but alternation between expert and novice efforts in a shared problem-solving context makes it possible to sensitise learners to the details of expert performance if they are highlighted by sensitive and skillful verbal description.

Social context

A second key observation about traditional apprenticeship concerns the embedding social context in which learning takes place. Apprenticeship derives many of its characteristics from its embedding in a subculture in which most members are visible participants in the target skills. Apprentices have continual access to models of expertise-in-use. It is not uncommon for apprentices to have access to several masters and thus to a variety of models of expertise. Moreover apprentices have the opportunity to observe other learners who have varying degrees of skill. Among other things this encourages them to view learning as an incrementally staged process while providing them with benchmarks against which they can measure their own progress.

Margaret Donaldson's now famous book *Children's Minds,* is just one of the many inquiries which are helping us to understand the importance of social context in all learning. Donaldson explains how thought and language depend upon the interpersonal contexts within which they develop. The apprenticeship approach to teaching reading recognises the significance of this aspect of learning by carrying with it a package of practical measures which help to create the embedding social context of apprenticeship in general. For instance, many schools adopting this approach ensure that the child has access to more than one reading teacher by ensuring that parents play a crucial role in the reading 'life' of the child, some schools have sessions of USSR (Uninterrupted Sustained Silent Reading) or ERIC (Everyone Reading In Class) where readers are made very obviously aware that they are part of a community of readers; other schools adopt peer-tutoring and paired-reading practices where children can play the role of both teacher and learner and thus begin to understand the nature of progress in reading by meeting and reading with other learners of varying degrees of skill.

There is a further relevant aspect of the social context in which traditional apprenticeship takes place. It has to do with the economic bias in traditional apprenticeship. Apprentices are encouraged at an early stage to learn skills that are useful and therefore meaningful within the social context of the workplace. Apprentices have opportunity to realise the value, in concrete economic terms, of these skills: well executed skills result in saleable products. Apprenticeship reading, as well as finding a way to create in the school a culture of expert practice for children to participate in and aspire to, must devise incentives for progress parallel to the economic incentives of traditional apprenticeship if it is to follow that model.

So how can apprentice readers realise the value of their developing skills? Well, primarily perhaps through the pleasure principle. The joy of reading good books can itself be the reward for increasing independence in reading. Moreover reading fiction can, even for very young children, be an experience which, as Hall (1987) noted, helps to extend an understanding of life and what it means to be human, and offers rewards in those terms. But it is also the case that reading is linked to work and instrumental effort. If this is to be recognised the classroom must provide a literacy environment and genuine literacy activities where children can 'cash-in' their skills and begin to see the purpose of acquiring them for instrumental reasons also.

Summary

If, when considering reading, we treat apprenticeship as a suggestive, rather than exact, analogy, there are useful insights to be drawn from traditional apprenticeship. Two features particularly hold messages for how we help children learn to read.

First, the movement in traditional apprenticeship from observation, through coaching, to practice can act as a model for reading instruction. It highlights, for instance, that a 'real books' approach is not laissez-faire, that coaching is required and that, in a cognitive area, part of this coaching involves making explicit to the learner processes which are usually internalised in skilled performance. The implications for teachers are radical. A number of traditional practices, such as hearing children read as kind of ritual, almost a magical laying on of hands, require major revision.

Second, a close look at traditional apprenticeship provides evidence for the importance of the social context in which learning takes place. Again teachers of beginning readers can use the model of traditional apprenticeship to reflect on their own school/classroom practices, to see whether they help create a culture of expert practice for instance, and offer the opportunity for learners to realise the value of their increasing skills. Practices such as peer-tutor schemes and the increasing involvement of parents in reading teaching illustrate that many schools are already working out the implications of this understanding.

If teachers are more aware of those areas of relative weakness and strength in the apprenticeship analogy they will have a more principled basis for using the approach in their teaching and a more stout defence against those who might argue that if the analogy is weak, a 'real books' approach is to be avoided.

References

Collins, A, Brown, J and Newman, S (1988) 'Cognitive Apprenticeship: Technical Report' (Abridged) in *Thinking,* Vol. 8, No. 1, pp. 2-10.

Department of Education and Science (1975) *A Language for Life.* HMSO: London, para, 7.25.

Department of Education and Science (1978) *Primary Education in England.* HMSO: London, para. 5.26/27.

Donaldson, M (1978) *Children's Minds.* Fontana: Glasgow.

Hall, N (1987) *The Emergence of Literacy.* Hodder and Stoughton: London.

Huey, E B (1908) *The Psychology and Pedagogy of Reading.* Macmillan: New York.

Waterland, L (1985) *Read With Me; An Apprenticeship Approach to Reading.* Thimble Press: Stroud.

7 - Comprehension monitoring, metacognition and other mysterious processes

DAVID WRAY

Reading some particularly densely written background material before writing this article, I noticed that it was becoming increasingly difficult for me to concentrate. My mind kept drifting to other, lighter, topics and several times I came to with a jerk to realise that I had understood nothing of the several paragraphs I though I had 'read'. In the language I shall use in this article, this was a metacognitive experience, and my comprehension monitoring had alternately lapsed and kicked into action. These terms are probably unfamiliar to many people, yet the processes to which they refer have been increasingly demonstrated to be of special importance in intellectual development and in the operation of many intellectual activities, in particular that of reading. This article will explore the areas of metacognition and reading, focusing in particular upon comprehension monitoring, before briefly reviewing the practical ways in which teachers might respond to these insights. (Much greater detail about the issues referred to here will be found in Wray, 1994).

Metacognition and comprehension monitoring

Vygotsky (1962) suggested that there are two stages in the development of knowledge: firstly, its automatic, unconscious acquisition (we learn things or how to do things, but do not know that we know these things); and secondly, a gradual increase in active conscious control over that knowledge (we begin to know what we know and that there is more that we do not know). This distinction is essentially the difference between the cognitive and metacognitive aspects of knowledge and thought. The term 'metacognition' is used to refer to the deliberate conscious control of one's own cognitive actions (Brown, 1980) - that is, cognition about cognition: thinking about thinking.

There is a hierarchical relationship between the terms 'metacognition' and 'comprehension monitoring' (Baker and Brown, 1984). Metacognition can be seen as the wider concept, applying to knowledge about cognition in general. Comprehension monitoring is seen as applying mainly to the comprehension of connected discourse, which may, of course, involve either reading or listening. In thinking about this topic the following kinds of questions tend to get asked (Wagoner, 1983):

- What do readers know about their own comprehension - that is, what they comprehend and how they comprehend?
- Are they aware of when they comprehend adequately and when they do not?
- How do readers decide when their comprehension is adequate?
- What kinds of strategies do readers use when they realise they are not comprehending what they read in order to compensate for this?

Some fairly clear answers to these questions have emerged from research, and they are answers with important implications for teachers of reading.

Comprehension monitoring in reading

An analysis of the operation of comprehension monitoring during the reading process must begin with a description of what this process involves. Good reading has been described as follows:

> A good reader proceeds smoothly and quickly as long as his understanding of the material is complete. But as soon as he senses that he has missed an idea, that the track has been lost, he brings smooth progress to a blinding halt. Advancing more slowly, he seeks clarification in the subsequent material, examining it for the light it can throw on the earlier trouble spot. If still dissatisfied with his grasp, he returns to the point where the difficulty began and rereads the section more carefully. He probes and analyses phrases and sentences for their exact meaning; he tries to visualise abstruse descriptions; and through a series of approximations, deductions, and corrections he translates scientific and technical terms into concrete examples. (Whimbey, 1975, p. 91)

While it is, of course, true that all readers do not follow precisely this sequence of actions, most theories of reading have suggested similarly strategic models for the comprehension process. According to Brown (1980), some of the metacognitive activities involved in reading are:

- clarifying one's purposes for reading - that is, understanding the explicit and implicit demands of a particular reading task;

- identifying the important aspects of a text;
- focusing attention on these principal aspects rather than on relatively trivial aspects;
- monitoring on-going activities to determine whether comprehension is taking place;
- engaging in self-questioning to check whether the aims are being achieved;
- taking corrective action if and when failures in comprehension are detected.

Reading for meaning therefore inevitably involves the metacognitive activity of comprehension monitoring, which entails keeping track of the success with which one's comprehension is proceeding, ensuring that the process continues smoothly and taking remedial action if necessary. It thus involves the use of what have been called 'debugging' skills (Brown, 1980).

Although mature readers typically engage in comprehension monitoring as they read for meaning, it is usually not a conscious experience. Brown (1980) distinguishes between an automatic and debugging state. Skilled readers, she argues, tend to proceed on automatic pilot until a 'triggering event' alerts them to a failure or problem in their comprehension. When alerted in this way they must slow down and devote extra effort in mental processing to the area which is causing the problem. They employ debugging devices and strategies, all of which demand extra time and mental effort. Anderson (1980) suggests that efficient readers need not devote constant attention to evaluating their own understanding and he suggests the existence of an 'automated monitoring mechanism' which 'renders the clicks of comprehension and clunks of comprehension failure'.

The events which trigger such action may vary widely. One common triggering event is the realisation that an expectation held about a text has not been confirmed by actual experience of the text. For example, in reading a sentence such as *The old man the boats,* the fourth and fifth words will probably cause a revision of the reader's sense of understanding and therefore take longer to process. Another triggering event is the meeting of unfamiliar ideas at too rapid a frequency for the reader to maintain a tolerance for the subsequent lack of understanding. The usual reader reaction to this is to slow down the rate of processing, devoting time and effort to the task of sorting out the failure in comprehension. The reader enters a deliberate, 'aware' state quite distinct from the automatic pilot state, and the smooth flow of reading abruptly changes (Baker and Brown, 1984).

Realising that one has failed to understand is only part of comprehension monitoring; one must also know what to do when such failures occur. This involves the making of a number of strategic decisions. The first of these is simply to decide whether or not remedial action is required. This seems to depend largely upon the reader's purposes for reading (Alessi, Anderson and Goetz, 1979). For example, if a reader's purpose is to locate a specific piece of information, a lack of understanding of the surrounding text will not usually trigger any remedial action. On the other hand, if the purpose is to understand a detailed argument, then practically any uncertainty will spark off extra mental activity.

In the event of a decision to take action, there are a number of options available. The reader may simply store the confusion in memory as an unanswered question (Anderson, 1980) in the hope that the author will subsequently provide sufficient clarification to enable its resolution; or the reader may decide to take action immediately, which may involve rereading, jumping ahead in the text, consulting a dictionary or knowledgeable person, or a number of other strategies (Baker and Brown, 1984).

The occurrence of this range of strategies has been studied by Winser (1988), who asked readers of various ages to think aloud as they tried to understand difficult texts. The strategies they used when they encountered comprehension difficulties included the following:

- *reading on:* reading more of the text to see if more information could be gained;
- *sounding out:* examining letters and sounds carefully (this strategy was used most often by younger readers);
- *making an inference:* guessing a meaning on the basis of textual clues and previous knowledge;
- *rereading:* reading the difficult section again;
- *suspending judgement:* waiting to see if the text provided more clues.

Research on comprehension monitoring in action

Two important studies of the comprehension monitoring of undergraduate students have given us insights into how this operates in mature, skilful readers. Baker (1979) gave students passages to read in which the middle paragraph had deliberately confusing features such as inconsistent information, an unclear reference or an inappropriate connecting word. A large proportion of these confusions (62 per cent) seemed not to be detected by the students even after they had been specifically asked to search for them. However, asking them afterwards about what they had been thinking while reading suggested that many of their failures to report confusions were due to their use of 'fix-up' strategies for resolving comprehension problems. They often, for example, made inferences from what they read in order to make up for the omission of information in the passage. With other text problems, they seemed to make a rapid assessment that the problem was unimportant and then ignored it.

Baker and Anderson (1982), also working with undergraduate students, used a computer terminal to present texts for evaluation. Passages containing inconsistencies were presented one sentence at a time on a computer, under the reader's control. Records were kept of the total time spent reading the passages, of the time spent on each sentence and of the amount of looking back. The readers did seem to spend more time reading inconsistent paragraphs than consistent paragraphs and they also looked back at previous information more frequently when inconsistencies were present. A full third of the inconsistencies, however, seemed to go undetected but, of course, there are several possible explanations for this. They may really have been undetected; they may have been detected and 'fixed'; or they may have been detected and ignored.

However, it does seem that, in general, mature readers evaluate their own understanding during the actual process of reading. If they encounter a confusion they give extra time to studying it and they reread previous sentences in an effort to clarify their understanding. They also seem to be prepared to make allowances for the fact that the problem might lie in the text rather than in themselves. This comprehension monitoring behaviour implies an active approach to gaining understanding from texts. How and when does this develop in younger and less experienced readers?

Numerous research studies have examined children's monitoring of their own comprehension and there has been a remarkable consistency in the findings of these studies. The two most replicated results have been that:

- 'younger and poorer readers have little awareness that they must attempt to make sense of text; they focus on reading as a decoding process, rather than as a meaning-getting process' (Baker and Brown, 1984, p. 358); and
- 'younger children and poorer readers are unlikely to demonstrate that they notice major blocks to text understanding. They seem not to realise when they do not understand' (Garner and Reis, 1981, p. 571).

These findings have emerged from studies using a range of methodological approaches and it must be admitted that methodology has always been problematic. It is no easy matter to discover what is going on in the minds of even highly articulate adults, let alone those of young children and children with reading problems. Studies have focused on interviewing children (asking what they do when they read), measuring the eye movements of young readers for signs of their responses to lack of comprehension, asking readers to make a judgement about how certain they are that they understand a text and then to compare their judgements with their actual comprehension as measured by a test, examining children's self-corrections as they read, and the use of distorted texts (texts containing inconsistencies of various kinds or other deliberate errors).

While there are problems with each of these research approaches and there also remain several unanswered questions about comprehension monitoring in reading, it is possible to draw some fairly firm conclusions from the extensive research in this area. Garner (1987) sums these up well:

> The convergent findings from recent research can be summarised: Young children and poor readers are not nearly as adept as older children/adults and good readers, respectively, in engaging in planful activities either to make cognitive progress or to monitor it. Younger, less proficient learners are not nearly as 'resourceful' in completing a variety of reading and studying tasks important in academic settings. (p. 59)

It appears that 'planful, strategic behaviour' (Brown, 1978, p. 457) in the face of the kind of reading tasks likely to be encountered in school learning does not develop until relatively late in children's school careers, and for those children who find reading difficult, this may be very late indeed. This is important because this kind of awareness is an essential ingredient in success in school.

> Part of being a good student is learning to be aware of the state of one's mind and the degree of one's understanding. The good student may be one who often says that he does not understand, simply because he keeps a constant check on his understanding. The poor student, who does not, so to speak, watch himself trying to understand,

does not know most of the time whether he understands or not. Thus the problem is not to get students to ask us what they don't know; the problem is to make them aware of the difference between what they know and what they don't know; the problem is to make them aware of the difference between what they know and what they don't. (Holt, 1969, p. 23)

This, of course, begs the question of how teachers might help children to develop the monitoring of their own understanding while reading; the next section of this article will examine some teaching approaches to this.

Teaching approaches to comprehension monitoring

Several teaching strategies have been suggested as beneficial in developing children's comprehension. Most, however, have not yet been subjected to objective research assessment and conclusions about them must remain tentative. (See Wray, 1994 for a more extensive discussion of teaching approaches.) A major problem which has emerged in work on teaching awareness and strategy use has been that of transfer of learning. Children who demonstrate that they have learnt to act in a particular metacognitive way in the context of the training they have been given often seem not to maintain this way of acting in other situations or over the longer term. Brown, Armbruster and Baker (1986) suggest that, in order to overcome this problem, children need to learn strategies rather than particular techniques, strategic understanding involving a knowledge of not just what to do but of when, where, how and why to use particular techniques.

One relatively simple strategy with some history of success is that of teacher modelling. Tonjes (1988) discusses metacognitive modelling as a way that teachers demonstrate to children the monitoring strategies they use in their own reading, and Duffy, Roehler and Herrmann (1988) similarly discuss the idea of the teacher modelling mental processes to children. They argue that teachers using this approach should concentrate upon transferring metacognitive control from themselves to their children and should model mental processes (what they think as they read or write) - rather than simply procedures (what they do). Only in this way, they suggest, can children learn strategies which they can apply across a range of situations rather than which are limited to the context in which they were encountered.

Another apparently beneficial strategy is that of teaching children to ask themselves questions as they read. Miller (1985) reports on a study in which 8- to 10-year-olds who were explicitly taught a self-questioning procedure to accompany their reading were better able to identify inconsistencies and errors in texts (that is, according to Miller, to monitor their comprehension) than other children, who were directly told to look for these inconsistencies. The self-questioning procedure these children were trained to apply consisted of the following points which they had to raise for themselves as they read.

1. I am going to decide if this story has any problems in it, like if one sentence says one thing and another sentence says something different or opposite.

2. As I read I will ask myself, 'Is there anything wrong with the story?'

3. I will read two sentences and stop and ask if anything is wrong.

4. So far, so good, I am doing a great job. Now I will read the whole story and decide if there are any problems in the whole story.

5. Did I find any problems in this story?

It should be noted that this study does not provide evidence that the effects of the training would transfer to other, more self-sponsored reading tasks. It is perhaps not so surprising that children trained to alert themselves to the presence of text inconsistencies should become fairly good at spotting them. This does not necessarily mean, however, that they will have improved their abilities to monitor their own comprehension when reading texts in which there are no deliberate errors or inconsistencies.

Tregaskes and Daines (1989) report on their research into the effectiveness of the direct teaching of strategies to monitor comprehension to 12-year-olds. These children were taught the following metacognitive strategies.

1. *Visual imagery (Stewart and Tei, 1984):* The children were asked to visualise selected passages as the teacher read them, then to share their images by discussing and sketching them.

2. *Summary sentences (Stewart and Tei, 1984):* The children were taught to omit trivial and redundant information in order to identify the main ideas of a text.

3. *Webbing (Clewell and Haidemos, 1983):* The children were shown how to make concept maps of the ideas in a given passage.

4. *Self-interrogation (Brown, 1978):* The children were encouraged to ask themselves questions about what they already knew about a topic and what they expected to learn from the new passage.

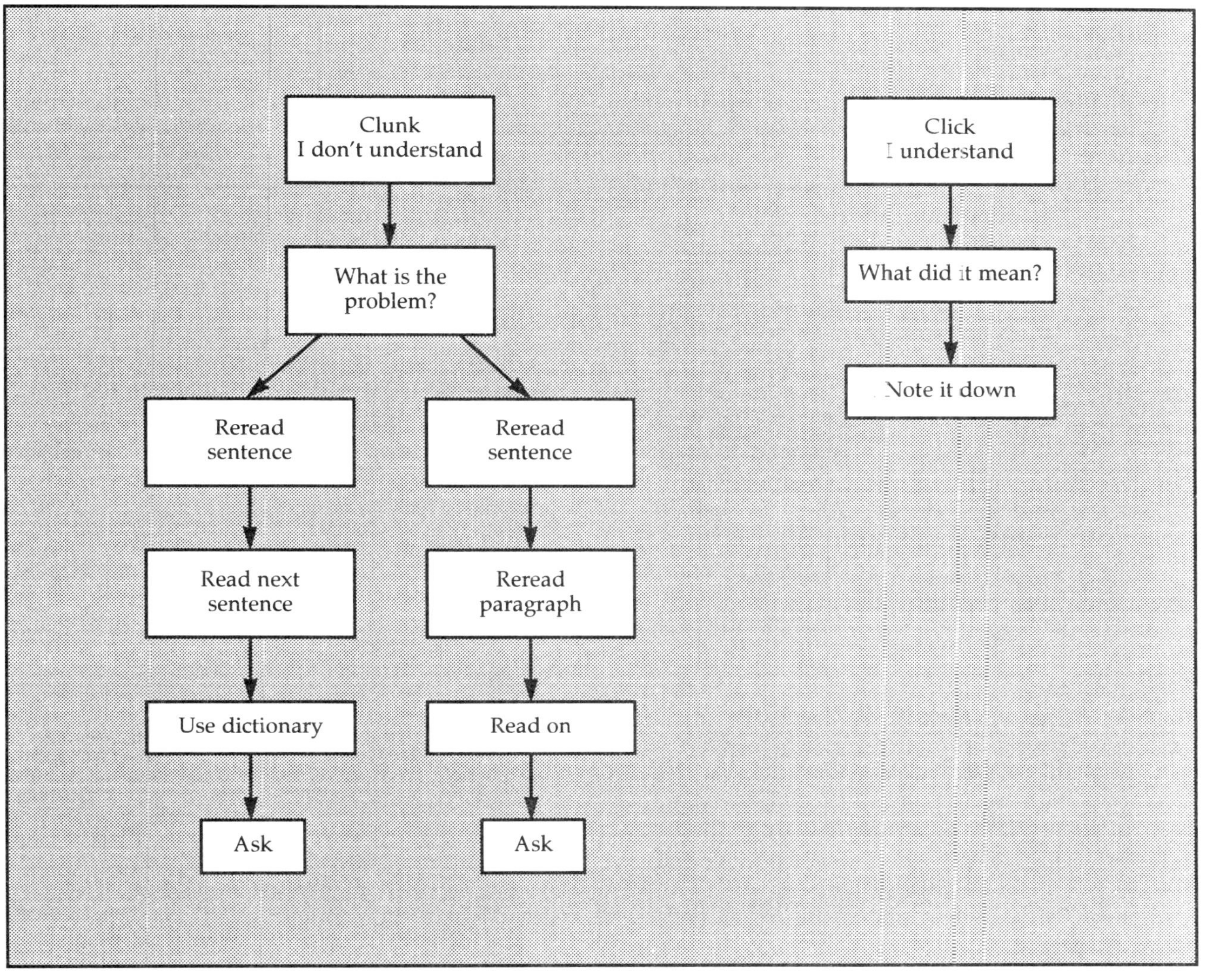

Figure 7.1 - 'Clunk Click' cards (from Babbs, 1984).

5. *'Clunk Click' cards (Babbs, 1984):* The children were introduced to a monitoring procedure outlined for them on a personal card. A copy of this card is shown in figure 7.1.

Groups of children were directly instructed in these strategies over a 12-week period. After that time they were found to perform significantly better on the testing measures than children who had not been taught the strategies. Again, however, it needs to be pointed out that these testing measures were less than satisfactory, involving, firstly, cloze tests in which the children received a mark only for each word they got exactly right, and, secondly, an error detection test in which children had to underline words or sentences in passages which did not make sense to them. This seems a limited method of measuring improvements in comprehension and in comprehension monitoring. No attempt was made to assess whether the children's command of comprehension-monitoring strategies extended to other contexts or indicated a lasting improvement.

Studies such as these give some hope, albeit tentative, that beneficial effects might arise from the direct teaching of metacognitive strategies. Approaches such as the modelling of mental processes by teachers, the encouragement of children to ask themselves questions about their own understandings and intentions and the setting of this kind of work into collaborative contexts may all be useful procedures for teachers to adopt.

Larger-scale research has been carried out on one teaching approach which is currently receiving major worldwide attention. It will be useful to explore this in greater detail.

Palincsar and Brown (1984) begin by arguing that most training studies have produced rather discouraging outcomes, with little real impact on children's use of strategies and, particularly, on the transfer of these to activities outside those directly experienced during the training context. They attribute this failure to effect real change in learners' approaches to dealing with text to a model of learning which sees learners as simply responding, relatively passively, to instruction without really being made aware of just what they are learning and why. They claim that training, to be successful, needs to encourage learners to be active in their use of strategies and to understand why, and when, they should use the strategies to which they are introduced. The model of learning they propose as an alternative is based upon the twin ideas of 'expert scaffolding' and what they refer to as 'proleptic' teaching: that is, teaching in anticipation of competence. This model arises from the ideas of Vygotsky (1978), who put forward the notion that children first experience a particular cognitive activity in collaboration with expert practitioners. The child is firstly a spectator as the majority of the cognitive work is done by the expert (parent or teacher), then a novice as s/he starts to take over some of the work under the close supervision of the expert. As the child grows in experience and capability of performing the task, the expert passes over greater and greater responsibility but still acts as a guide, assisting the child at problematic points. Eventually, the child assumes full responsibility for the task with the expert still present in the role of a supportive audience. Using this approach to teaching, children learn about the task at their own pace, joining in only at a level at which they are capable - or perhaps a little beyond this level, so that the task continually provides sufficient challenge to be interesting. The approach is often referred to as an apprenticeship approach, and many teachers will be familiar with its operation in the teaching of reading (Waterland, 1985). The distance between the level at which children can manage independently and which they can manage with the aid of an expert is termed by Vygotsky 'the zone of proximal development' and it is, according to the model, the area in which the most profitable instruction can proceed. Vygotsky (1978) claimed that 'what children can do with the assistance of others might be in some sense even more indicative of their mental development than what they can do alone' (p. 85).

Palincsar and Brown (1984) designed their comprehension monitoring teaching procedures around this apprenticeship model of learning. Their approach used what they termed 'reciprocal teaching' to focus upon four activities:

1. *summarising:* asking children to summarise sections of text, thereby encouraging them to focus upon the main ideas in a passage and to check their own understanding of these;

2. *questioning:* getting children to ask questions about what they have read, which again encourages them to attend to the principal ideas and to think about their own comprehension of these;

3. *clarifying:* asking children to clarify potentially problematic sections of text, requiring them to critically evaluate the current state of their understanding;

4. *predicting:* getting them to go beyond what the text actually says to make inferences which they have to justify by reference to what they have read.

Each of these activities had a cognitive and a metacognitive dimension in that not only were the children working upon their comprehension of the texts (comprehension fostering) but they were also having to reflect upon the extent of their comprehension (comprehension monitoring).

The reciprocal teaching procedure involved an interactive 'game' between the teacher and the learners in which each took it in turns to lead a dialogue about a particular section of text. The 'teacher' for each section first asked a question, then summarised, then clarified and predicted as appropriate. The real teacher modelled each of these activities and the role played by the children was gradually expanded as time went on from mostly pupil to mostly teacher.

This procedure was tested on a group of 11-year-olds with reading difficulties. These children did initially experience some difficulties in taking over the role of teacher and needed a lot of help in verbalising during summarising, questioning, clarifying and predicting. They did eventually, however, become much more accomplished leaders of the comprehension dialogues and showed a very significant improvement on tests of reading comprehension, an improvement which seemed to generalise to other classroom activities and did not fade away after the completion of the research project. Palincsar and Brown attribute the success of their training programme to the reciprocal teaching procedure, suggesting that it involved extensive modelling of comprehension fostering and monitoring strategies which are usually difficult to detect in expert readers; that it forced children to take part in dialogues about their understanding, even if at a non-expert level, and they learnt from this engagement.

Gilroy and Moore (1988) report on the results of their replication of the Palincsar and Brown reciprocal teaching procedure with 9- to 13-year-olds in New Zealand. They found that positive gains in comprehension test scores were made by these children. In a review of research on the reciprocal teaching approach, Moore (1988) agrees with the Palincsar and Brown analysis of the strengths of the approach and suggests that it has a great deal to offer, particularly to children with identifiable weaknesses in reading comprehension.

Conclusion

Although there are several caveats to be made about the quality of the research evidence, in particular about the methods typically used to ascertain children's comprehension monitoring performance, it does seem that there is reason to focus upon the development of this ability as one possible way forward in developing reading comprehension, particularly in poorer readers. It may be that the key to enhancing children's understanding in reading is to develop their abilities to be more 'aware' of their reading.

If this is the case, then teachers need to consider carefully how they will set about doing this. Although, again, the research evidence is as yet incomplete, there do seem to be several teaching strategies which might be beneficial in this area. Reciprocal teaching is certainly creating a great deal of interest, especially among teachers of children with reading problems (see, for example, McGowan and Bell, 1993), and this procedure currently seems to offer the greatest hope in terms of a well-founded, systematic approach to teaching. Its components, however, such as teacher modelling, encouraging self-questioning and explicit discussion of comprehension processes, are all beneficial teaching activities in their own rights. The teaching of reading comprehension would undoubtedly benefit from wider use of such approaches.

References

Alessi, S, Anderson, T and Goetz, E (1979) An investigation of lookbacks during studying. *Discourse Processes,* 2, 197-212.

Anderson, T (1980) Study strategies and adjunct aids. In R. Spiro, B. Bruce and W. Brewer (eds), *Theoretical Issues in Reading Comprehension.* Erlbaum: Hillsdale, N J.

Babbs, P (1984) Monitoring cards can help improve comprehension. *The Reading Teacher,* 38, 200-4.

Baker, L (1979) Comprehension monitoring: Identifying and coping with text confusions. *Journal of Reading Behaviour,* 11, 365-74.

Baker, L and Anderson, R (1982) Effects of inconsistent information on text processing: Evidence for comprehension monitoring. *Reading Research Quarterly,* 17, 281-94.

Baker, L and Brown, A (1984) Metacognitive skills and reading. In D. Pearson (ed.), *Handbook of Reading Research.* Longman: New York.

Brown, A (1978) Knowing when, where and how to remember: A problem of metacognition. In R. Glaser (ed.), *Advances in Instructional Psychology.* Erlbaum: Hillsdale, N J.

Brown, A (1980) Metacognitive development and reading. In R. Spiro, B. Bruce and W. Brewer (eds), *Theoretical Issues in Reading Comprehension.* Erlbaum: N J.

Brown, A, Armbruster, B and Baker, L (1986) The role of metacognition in reading and studying. In J. Orasanu (ed.), *Reading Comprehension: From research to practice.* Erlbaum: Hillsdale, N J.

Clewell, S and Haidemos, J (1983) Organisational strategies to increase comprehension. *Reading World,* 22, 314-21.

Duffy, G, Roehler, L and Herrmann, B (1988) Modelling mental processes helps poor readers become strategic readers. *The Reading Teacher,* 41, 762-7.

Garner, R (1987) *Metacognition and Reading Comprehension.* Ablex: Norwood, N J.

Garner, R and Reis, R (1981) Monitoring and resolving comprehension obstacles: An investigation of spontaneous text lookbacks among upper grade good and poor comprehenders. *Reading Research Quarterly,* 16, 569-82.

Gilroy, A and Moore, D (1988) Reciprocal teaching of comprehension-fostering and comprehension-monitoring activities with ten primary school girls. *Educational Psychology,* 8, 41-9.

Holt, J (1969) *How Children Fail.* Penguin: Harmondsworth.

McGowan, J and Bell, G (1993) *Learning Difficulties and Classroom Support: Reciprocal teaching (Primary English Notes 90).* PETA: Newton, New South Wales.

Miller, G (1985) The effects of general and specific self-instruction training on children's comprehension monitoring performances during reading. *Reading Research Quarterly,* 20, 616-28.

Moore, P (1988) Reciprocal teaching and reading comprehension: A review. *Journal of Research in Reading,* 11, 3-14.

Palincsar, A and Brown, A (1984) Reciprocal teaching of comprehension-fostering and comprehension-monitoring activities. *Cognition and Instruction,* 1, 117-75.

Stewart, O and Tei, E (1984) Some implications of metacognition for reading instruction. *Journal of Reading,* 27, 36-43.

Tonjes, M (1988) Metacognitive modelling and glossing: Two powerful ways to teach self responsibility. In C. Anderson (ed.), *Reading: The abc and beyond.* Macmillan: Basingstoke.

Tregaskes, M and Daines, D (1989) Effects of metacognitive strategies on reading comprehension. *Reading Research and Instruction,* 29, 52-60.

Vygotsky, L (1962) *Thought and Language.* MIT Press: Cambridge, Mass.

Vygotsky, L (1978) *Mind in Society.* Harvard University Press: Cambridge, Mass.

Wagoner, S (1983) Comprehension monitoring: What it is and what we know about it. *Reading Research Quarterly,* 18, 328-46.

Waterland, L (1985) *Read With Me.* Thimble Press: Stroud.

Whimbey, A (1975) *Intelligence Can Be Taught.* Dutton: New York.

Winser, B (1988) Readers getting control of reading. *Australian Journal of Reading,* 11, 257-68.

Wray, D (1994) *Literacy and Awareness.* Hodder and Stoughton: Sevenoaks.

(First published in *Support for Learning,* Vol. 9, No.3, 1994.)

8 - Making reading for information more accessible to children with learning difficulties

MAUREEN LEWIS, DAVID WRAY and PATRICIA ROSPIGLIOSI

The following scene might have occurred in many classrooms.

The learning support teacher arrives to find that Zoe, along with the rest of the class, has been asked to 'find out about whales and dolphins'. The child is working diligently. The outcome of her 'research' is the writing given in figure 8.1.

She cannot read this work back to her support teacher and has only the vaguest understanding of what she has written. Of course, we all recognise what has happened. Zoe has copied, word for word, from a book. Why is this? Our earlier research (Wray and Lewis, 1992) has suggested that most children are aware that they should not copy directly from books. Many can give sound educational reasons for not doing this (such as 'you learn more if you put it in your own words'), and yet they continue to do so. There appear to be several reasons underlying this but figuring largely amongst them must be the nature of the task the child has been given to do and the type of text with which s/he is asked to engage when reading for information.

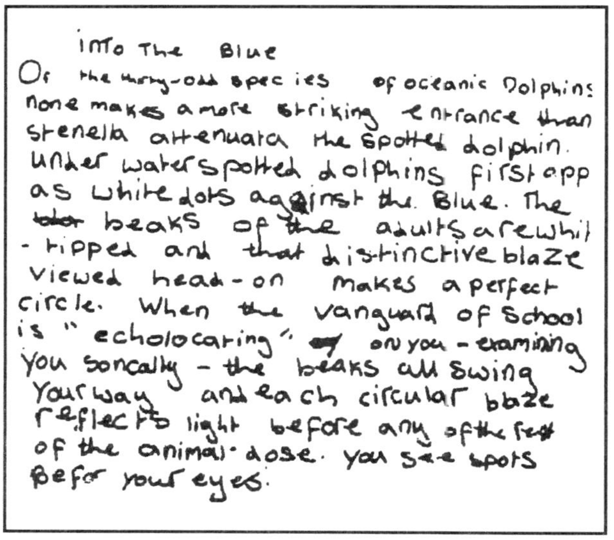
into The Blue
Of the thirty-odd species of oceanic Dolphins
none makes a more striking entrance than
stenella attenuata the spotted dolphin.
under water spotted dolphins first app
as white dots against the Blue. The
beaks of the adults are whi
-tipped and that distinctive blaze
viewed head-on makes a perfect
circle. When the vanguard of school
is "echolocating" on you - examining
you soncally - the beaks all swing
your way and each circular blaze
reflects light before any of the feat
of the animal dose. you see spots
befor your eyes.

Figure 8.1

The purpose for 'finding out' may not be clear to the child and how to begin to 'find out' may seem difficult and daunting. Having located a book on the required topic, the child might still find the text difficult to deal with. Children in primary classrooms tend to lack experience of the different genres of non-fiction and their organisational structures (Littlefair 1991, Winograd and Bridge 1986). They find the linguistic features (vocabulary, connectives, cohesion, register) more difficult to comprehend than those of the more familiar narrative texts (Anderson and Armbruster 1981, Chapman 1983, Halliday and Hasan 1976, Littlefair 1991, Perera 1984) and this textual inexperience affects their writing of non-fiction as well as their reading. In the case of Zoe, the problem was further compounded by the child's poor literacy skills (relative to her age). Her diligent copying was the only strategy she had for coping with the demands of the task.

The Exeter Extending Literacy (EXEL) in the Junior School Project is a 2-year research project based at the University of Exeter School of Education and funded by the Nuffield Foundation. In the course of the project we have been working with groups of teachers throughout the country to develop a model to describe the process of children's interactions with texts, especially non-fiction texts. We call this model the EXIT model - *EX*tending *I*nteractions with *T*ext. Alongside this model, and integral to it, we have been developed classroom strategies with which teachers might help their pupils to become more skilful researchers. Although our work has been largely focused on 'average' children, several of the teachers who have worked with us are individual learning support teachers or teachers with responsibility for special needs in their schools. These teachers have reported that they have found the process model and its linked strategies very useful for their pupils. The complete model has ten stages, ranging from the activation of children's prior knowledge about a topic they are to research, to their final presentation of what they have found, in whatever format. However, it is on just two of those stages, which suggest ways of helping children with learning difficulties get *started* on research, that we now wish to report. These stages help make the reading task children are faced with more accessible by providing a logical scaffold that children can apply for themselves.

Moving children on

Zoe's support teacher has been working with the EXEL project and she decided to introduce Zoe to a different way of approaching her task. At the end of their hour together Zoe had produced a different piece of writing about dolphins and whales (see figure 8.2).

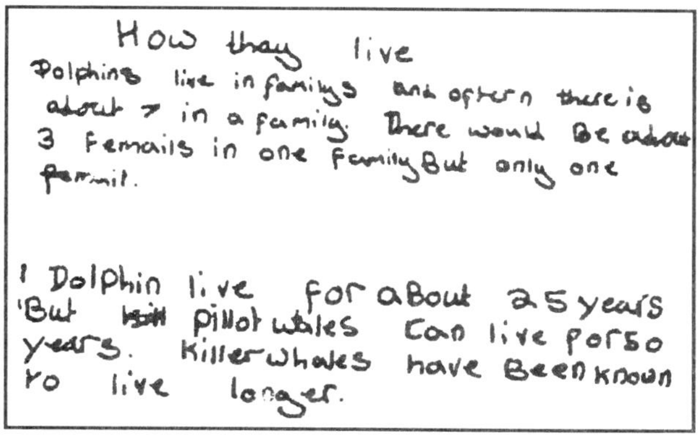
How thay live
Dolphins live in familys and oftern there is about 7 in a family. There would Be about 3 femails in one family But only one permil.

1 Dolphin live for aBout 25 years But pillot wales can live perso years. Killer whales have Been known to live longer.

Figure 8.2

Let us examine how this support teacher moved Zoe on from passive copying to undertaking her own research. The first step was to close Zoe's library book. Zoe was then taken through two of the stages in the EXIT model and taught strategies to help her use these stages before she returned to looking for information in books. These stages, with their linked teaching strategies, are given in figure 8.3).

Activating prior knowledge ('What do I know?')

There is now a great deal of research which indicates the importance of children's prior knowledge in their understanding of new knowledge (for example, Anderson 1977, Anderson and Pearson 1984). Furthermore, it appears to be important that this prior knowledge be brought to the forefront of the learner's mind - that is, made explicit - if it is to be useful (Bransford 1983). Schema theory suggests that our brains are not a random ragbag of knowledge but that knowledge is structured and categorised into schema, organised cognitive 'maps' of the parts of the world we know about. The concepts that constitute a schema can be said to 'provide slots that can be instantiated with specific information' (Wilson and Anderson, 1986). When we encounter new knowledge we incorporate it into our existing schema either by accretion (adding detail to the map) or restructuring (altering the map to fit the new information). If we have already activated our prior knowledge (schema) we are more ready to deal with new knowledge.

Many teachers already use discussion to activate prior knowledge but research has shown that this can be an ineffective way of enhancing comprehension unless it is undertaken carefully (Alvermann, Dillon and O'Brien, 1987). If prior knowledge is to be made explicit, it may be helpful to record it in some way. This has the added advantage of giving the teacher some record of the child's knowledge and, importantly, access to gaps in that knowledge and any misconceptions the child may hold.

Much interest has been apparent in recent years in the use of brainstorming, semantic mapping (Johnson, Pittelman and Heimlich, 1986) and concept mapping (Champagne and Klopfer, 1991) and these are all strategies we have used successfully within the EXEL project. They are, however, already familiar to many teachers (although they may be known by different names; concept maps are, for example, often referred to as topic webs). We wish therefore to concentrate here on another strategy that we have found specially useful with children with learning difficulties, that of Know, Want, Learn (KWL) grids.

The KWL grid was developed as a teaching strategy in the USA (Ogle 1986, 1989) and is a simple but effective strategy which both takes children through the steps of the research process and also records their learning. It gives children a logical structure for tackling research tasks in many areas of the curriculum, and it is this combination of a simple but logical support scaffolding that seems to be so useful to children with learning difficulties. A KWL grid consists of three columns as shown in figure 8.4.

Process stage	*Question*	*Teaching strategies*
1. Elicitation of previous knowledge	**What do I already know about this topic?**	**Brainstorming; concept mapping; Know, Want, Learn (KWL) grids**
2. Establishing purposes	**What do I need to find out and what will I do with the information?**	**Question-setting; KWL grids; Question, Answer, Debit, Source (QUADS) grids**

Figure 8.3 - Helping children get started on research.

Zoe's support teacher introduced her to the strategy by drawing a KWL as three columns in Zoe's jotter. She then asked Zoe what she already knew about whales and dolphins, and acted as a scribe to record Zoe's responses. What Zoe knew can be seen in the 'K' column of figure 8.5. In the introductory stages of teaching the strategy, as for most new strategies and skills, teacher modelling is very important. Only when the child is thoroughly familiar with the strategy should s/he be encouraged to attempt it independently.

Not only did the activation of prior knowledge have a vital role to play in helping Zoe comprehend the texts she was to read, but it also gave her an active role in the topic right from the beginning. By being asked what she knew, her self-esteem and sense of 'ownership' of knowledge was enhanced and she was not faced instantly with the (for her) negative experience of tackling a text without knowing quite how she was to make sense of it. This activity prior to reading is not text avoidance but text preparation. As one teacher put it, the whole of our process model can be described as 'before the eyes meet the page, when the eyes are on the page and after the eyes leave the page'. Each of these plays a vital part in the process of understanding text.

The discussion between Zoe and her teacher was crucial at this stage and the activation of prior knowledge should always be an active social process. Sometimes we do not actually know what we know until it is triggered for us by discussion. This discussion could, of course, also take place in partnership with another child or in groups with other children rather than with a teacher.

Establishing purposes ('What do I want to know?')

The next stage helps focus the subsequent research. The usual formulation of the task, as in 'find out about', is far too broad to be useful and can be interpreted as requiring enough information to fill a postcard or to fill a book. Discussing and recording what she already knew was enough to generate further questions for Zoe - question which she would be interested in researching. These were again scribed by the teacher (see figure 8.5). It is tempting here to talk about giving the child some ownership of the work she is to undertake.

In this case Zoe easily generated her own questions but there are also various question-setting strategies that can be introduced:

- Turning 'What I know' statements into questions; for example, 'Whales are hunted by fishermen' can become 'Why are whales hunted by fishermen?'

What I Know	What I Want to Know	What I've Learnt

Figure 8.4

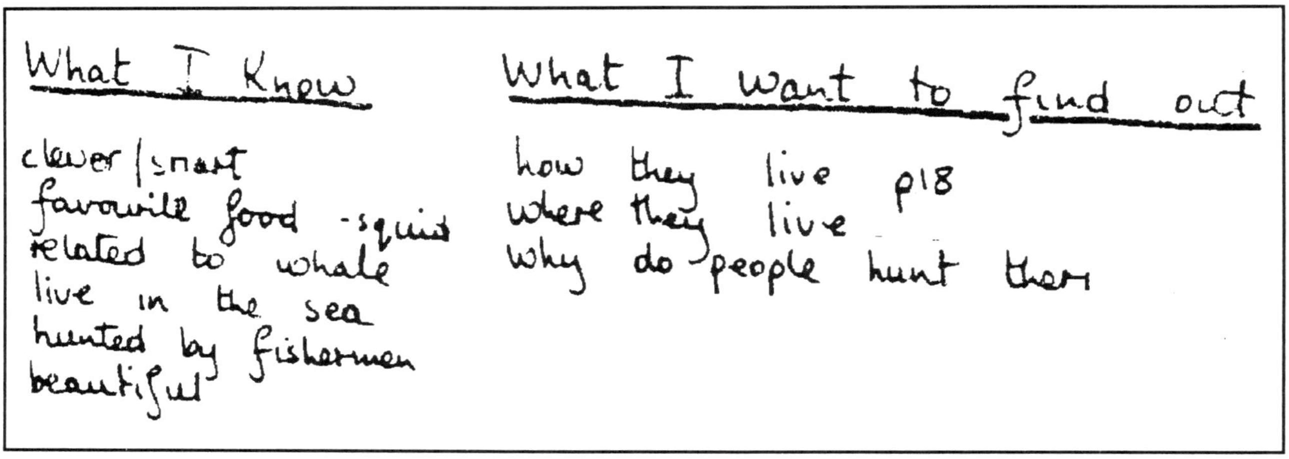
What I Know
clever/smart
favourite food - squid
related to whale
live in the sea
hunted by fishermen
beautiful

What I want to find out
how they live p18
where they live
why do people hunt them

Figure 8.5

- Using question words such as *what, where, when, why, who,* and *how.*
- Using various graphic forms such as question trees, question hands and question wheels to add child appeal, with question on each branch, finger and spoke.
- Using pictures or artefacts to trigger questions.
- Using Question, Answer, Detail, Source (QUADS) grids.

It may be necessary for the teacher to set questions at this stage. If, for example, there was incorrect information in the 'What I Know' column then the teacher would wish to direct a question to lead to further investigation in that area. There may be content details dictated by the National Curriculum that the teacher regards as vital to include and these could form the focus of questions. There is the opportunity at this stage for the teacher to intervene as little or as much as their professional judgement deems appropriate.

On this occasion Zoe and her teacher decided to concentrate on just one question (they had only an hour together) and she was encouraged to brainstorm around her 'How do they live?' question. Again her teacher scribed and the resultant concept map can be seen in figure 8.6.

The sub-questions generated by this procedure were numbered to keep the process clear and manageable and at this point Zoe was ready to return to her library books to try to find the answers to her questions. Now Zoe also had key words which she could use to search the index and contents list. Sometimes her teacher wrote the word on a piece of card for her so that she could run it down the index or page and match the word. This gave her practice in scanning. We can see from the writing she had completed by the end of the session (figure 8.2) that she was working her way logically through the questions (she had completed 1 and 2) and not only had she learnt something about dolphins but she had also had a powerful lesson on how to begin research.

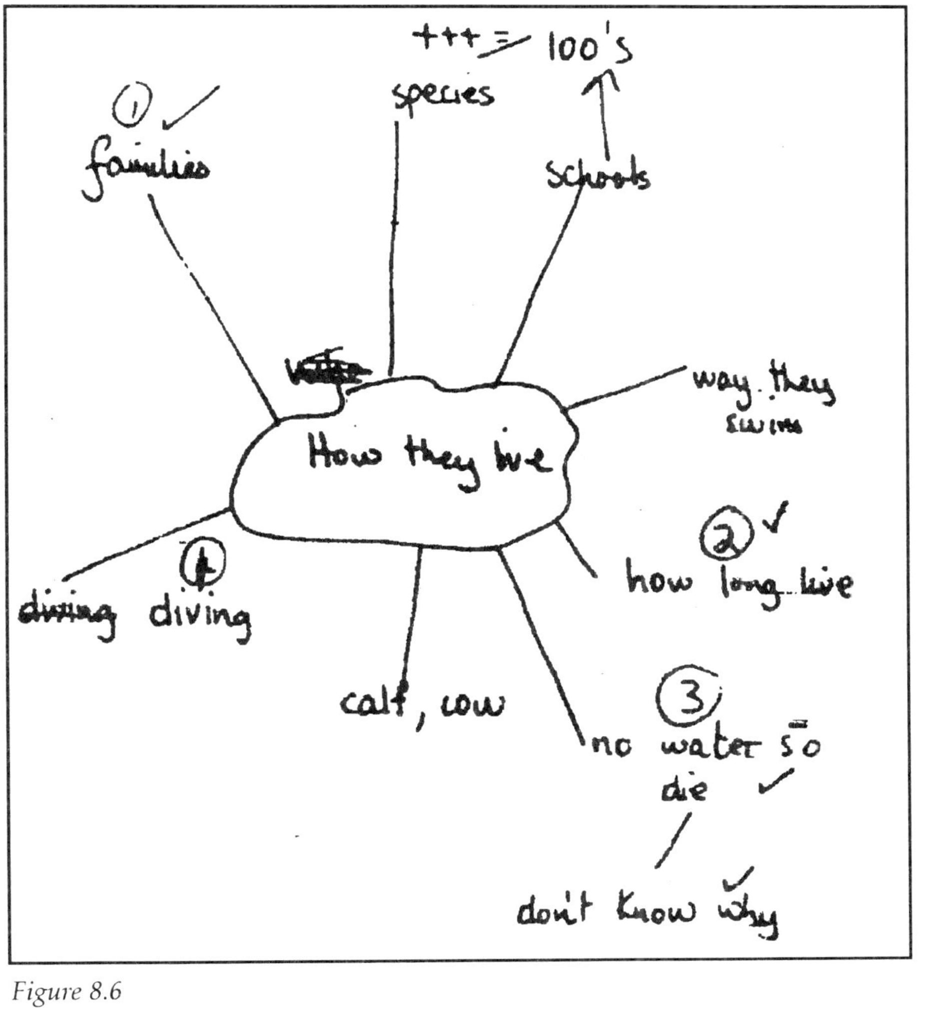

Figure 8.6

Another important aspect of establishing purpose is in deciding what the information is for. Is it just to be for the child, is she to share it with a wider audience, is it to be part of a wider piece of research? The answer to such questions should be discussed explicitly before the actual research begins. The purpose will, for example, influence which questions seem appropriate. For example, if the research was just for Zoe, she could choose just those questions which interest her, but if it were to find information for a group project on conservation she may have needed to concentrate on the hunting of whales. Such information about purpose will also influence how the information is recorded.

From external to internal scaffold

Perhaps the usefulness of this process of making research accessible to less able children can be judged by whether the children, having been introduced to it by their support teacher, choose to use it spontaneously when their support teacher is not with them. Baker and Brown (1984) have suggested that students do not gain any long-term benefits from study strategies until they start to incorporate these strategies spontaneously for themselves, signalling that they understand how and why they work.

An example of this happening is the case of James. He was introduced to the two process stages and the use of KWL by his support teacher when working on the topic of Ancient Greece. Notice how his listing of what he knows (figure 8.7) also enables his teacher to see his misconceptions (medals were not given at the Olympic Game in Ancient Greece) as well as things he does know. His KWL grid, scribed by his teacher, then served as the basis for his subsequent writing on the topic (see figure 8.8) which was a very extensive piece of work for James.

James had obviously found the strategy useful because the following week his support teacher returned to find that he had spontaneously used it

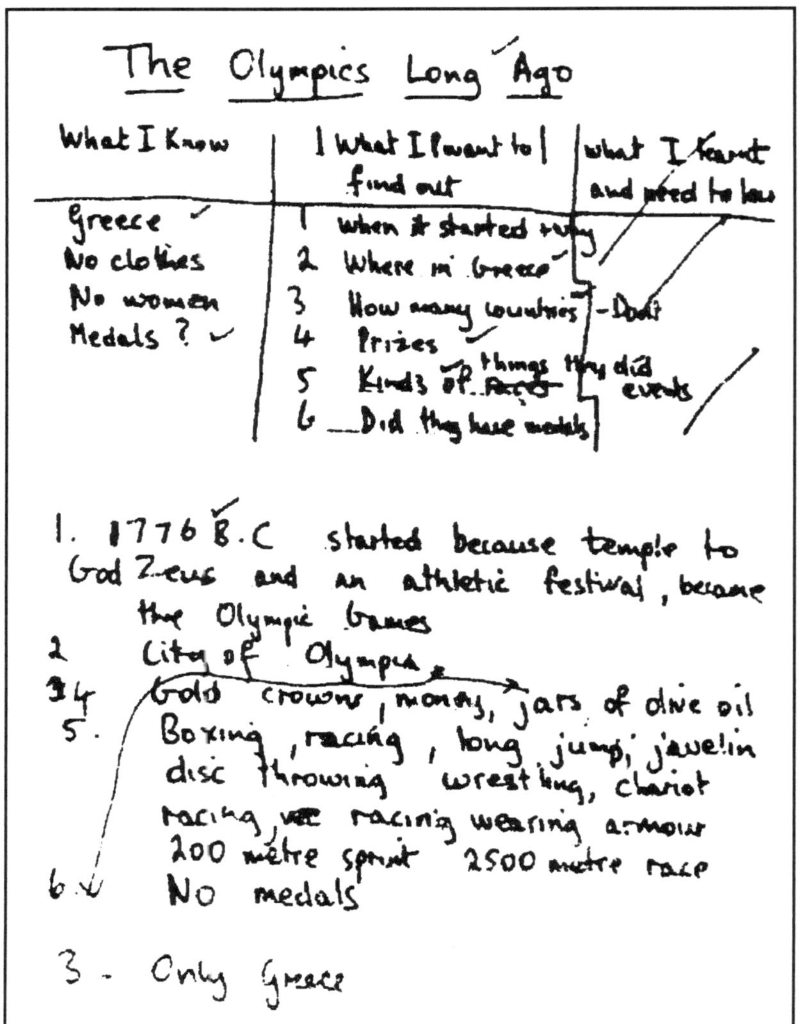
The Olympics Long Ago

What I Know	What I want to find out	what I learnt and need to learn
Greece No clothes No women Medals ?	1 when it started [illegible] 2 Where in Greece 3 How many countries 4 Prizes 5 Kinds of things they did events 6 Did they have medals	- Don't

1. 1776 B.C started because temple to God Zeus and an athletic festival, became the Olympic Games
2 City of Olympia
3 4 Gold crowns, money, jars of olive oil
5. Boxing, racing, long jump, javelin disc throwing wrestling, chariot racing, [illegible] racing wearing armour 200 metre sprint 2500 metre race
6. No medals

3. Only Greece

Figure 8.7

again in his next piece of topic work. This time the class was finding out about the home life of Athenians. James had drawn three columns in his jotter and although he hadn't labelled them - why give yourself extra writing if writing is a problem? - he had used the middle column to set himself four questions and was ticking these off as he gathered the information to answer them (see figure 8.9a). His subsequent writing indicates how the questions may also have suggested the structure of the finished piece (figure 8.9b).

Conclusion

Activating prior knowledge and establishing purposes are obviously only two stages in the process of becoming a researcher and they are stages that may be returned to at various points throughout the research process, not just at the start of the process. It is important that the work these children undertook was in the context of their class topics and was not as the result of some decontextualised attempt to teach them study skills. The concept of situated learning (Lave and Wenger, 1991) convinces us that this contextualised approach to teaching is likely to be much more effective than decontextualised approaches.

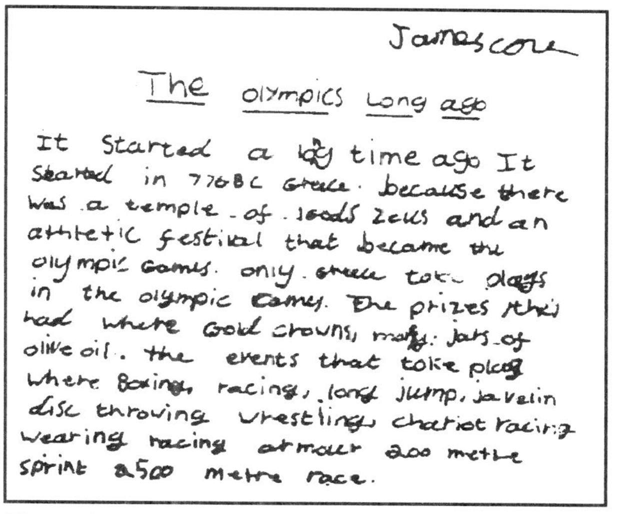

Figure 8.8

As we have already mentioned, the process model is much fuller than the two stages we have described here, but we can see clearly how breaking a complex process down into manageable stages and providing supportive strategies that children can apply themselves can provide a helpful and rewarding way into research tasks for children with learning difficulties.

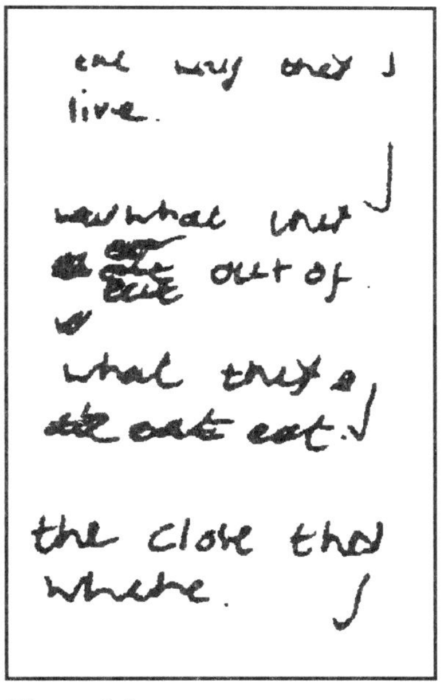

Figure 8.9a

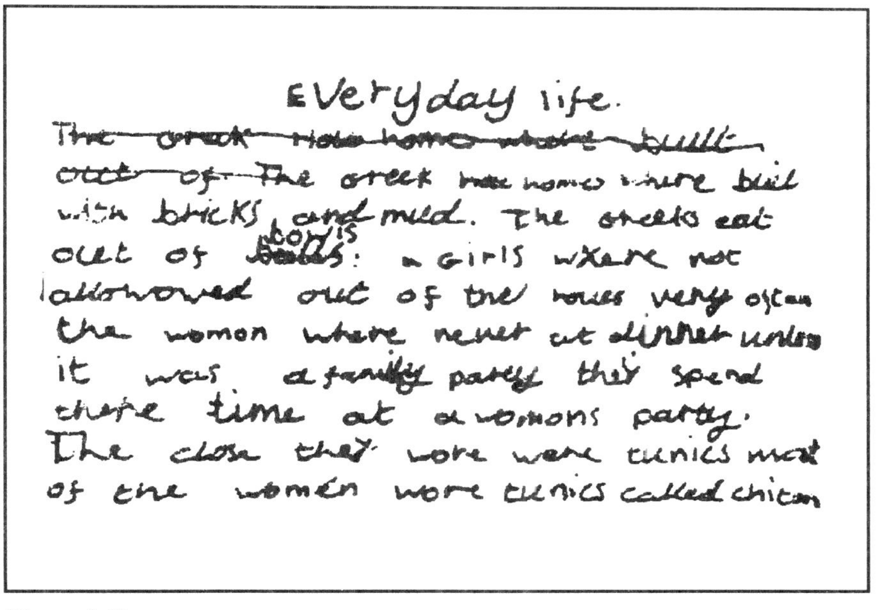

Figure 8.9b

References

Anderson, R C (1977) The notion of schemata and the educational enterprise. In R C Anderson, R J Spiro and W E Montaque (eds), *Schooling and the Acquisition of Knowledge.* Lawrence Erlbaum: Hillsdale, N J.

Anderson, R C and Pearson, P D (1984) A schematheoretical view of basic processes in reading comprehension. In P D Pearson (ed.), *Handbook of Reading Research.* Longman: New York.

Anderson, T H and Armbruster B B (1981) *Content Area Textbooks* (Reading Education Report No. 24). University of Illinois Center for the Study of Reading, Urbana, Ill.

Alvermann, D E, Dillon, D R and O'Brien, D G (1987) *Using Discussion to Promote Reading*

Comprehension. International Reading Association: Newark, Del.

Baker, L and Brown, A L (1984) Cognitive monitoring in reading. In J Flood (ed.), *Promoting Reading Comprehension.* International Reading Association: Newark, Del.

Bransford, J (1983) Schema activation - Schema acquisition. In R C Anderson, J Csborn and R J Tierney (eds), *Learning to Read in American Schools.* Lawrence Erlbaum: Hillsdale, N J.

Champagne, A B and Klopfer, L E (1991) Understanding science text and the physical world. In C M Santa and D E Alvermann (eds), *Science Learning: Processes and applications.* International Reading Association: Newark, Del.

Chapman, J (1983) *Reading Development and Cohesion.* Heinemann: London.

Halliday, M A K and Hasan, R (1976) *Cohesion in English.* Longman: London.

Johnson, D, Pittelman, S D and Heimlich, J E (1986) Semantic mapping. *The Reading Teacher,* 39 (8), 778-83.

Lave, J and Wenger, E (1991) *Situated Learning.* Cambridge University Press: Cambridge.

Littlefair, A (1991) *Reading All Types of Writing.* Open University Press: Milton Keynes.

Ogle, D M (1986) K-W-L: A teaching model that develops active reading of expository text. *The Reading Teacher,* 39 (6), 564-70.

Ogle, D M (1989) The Know, Want to Know, Learn Strategy. In K D Muth (ed.), *Children's Comprehension of Text.* International Reading Association: Newark, Del.

Perera, K (1984) *Children's Reading and Writing.* Blackwell: Oxford.

Wilson, P T and Anderson, R C (1986) What they don't know will hurt them: The role of prior knowledge in comprehension. In J Orasanu (ed.), *Reading Comprehension: From research into practice.* Lawrence Erlbaum: Hillsdale, N J.

Winograd, P and Bridge, C (1986) The comprehension of important information in written prose. In J F Baumann (ed.), *Teaching Main Idea Comprehension.* International Reading Association: Newark, Del.

Wray, D and Lewis, M (1992) Primary children's use of information books. *Reading,* 26 (2), 19-24.

(This article was first published in *Support for Learning,* Vol. 9, No. 4, 1994.)

9 - Getting into the rhythm: Children reading poetry

MICHAEL LOCKWOOD

When the role of literature in children's reading development is under consideration, the discussion most often focuses on novels, short stories and traditional tales. Each of these represents an important element in that range of literature which the present National Curriculum suggests children should experience. However, the list leaves out one important area of literary experience for children: poetry. Sometimes poetry is seen as the icing on the cake of children's reading experience (if not the decoration on the top) rather than the essential ingredient it can be.

Reading poetry at age 11

The evidence is that the primary years are a more fertile ground for poetry reading than the secondary school. The Assessment of Performance Unit's surveys of children's attitudes to reading, carried out between 1979-83, consistently show a more positive response to poetry from pupils at age 11 than at age 15. In the 1979 Primary and Secondary Surveys, for example, the most detailed of the APU reports, the responses to the statement: 'I like reading poems' were as follows:

	Totals		Boys		Girls	
	% Yes	% No	% Yes	% No	% Yes	% No
Age 11	59.5	36.9	50.0	46.0	68.8	27.9
Age 15	32.4	67.0	23.6	75.4	41.5	58.3

The percentage of 11 year olds professing to like reading poetry seems to have remained stable or risen slightly across the years of the survey from the (incomplete) figures available:

	Total	% Yes	Boys	% Yes	Girls	% Yes
	1979	1983	1979	1983	1979	1983
Age 11	62[sic]	65	53	57	71	72

Predictably girls were consistently more positive than boys in their attitudes to poetry reading throughout the surveys.

The picture of poetry reading in the primary school presented in the APU surveys is not all rosy. To put the above figures in context, 80.5% of the 1979 sample said they 'would rather read stories than poems', given the choice and 82% of the same sample agreed that they 'prefer funny poems to serious ones' when they do read poetry (no significant differences between the sexes in either of these). Humour and rhyme were the features of poems mentioned most often by children who said they liked reading poetry. In the 1982 Primary Survey, where pupils were asked about the kinds of poems and poets they liked. 'Spike Milligan was the versifier referred to most frequently by pupils in the sample', to use the loaded words of the report.

From the evidence, the picture seems to be one of a receptive audience for poetry at age 11, without the assistance which seems to have set in by the early years of secondary school, but also of a limited range of experience of poems and poets and an overwhelming preference for reading narrative.

One other, more unexpected finding of the APU reports is worth picking up also at this point. Taking an overview of 'reading as a source of pleasure and enjoyment' for 11 year olds over the years of the surveys, APU concludes:

> There were clear indications that some pupils whose reading performance was lower than the average nevertheless enjoyed reading poetry and preferred it in some cases to other kinds of reading.

If we reflect on this, it is less surprising. Research by Bryant and Bradley (1985) and more recently by Goswami and Bryant (1990) has shown the importance of poetic language in the initial learning of reading. It should come as no surprise then that less fluent older readers often prefer the experience of reading poems to that of reading prose.

It is ten years now since the APU's monitoring of language performance ended, a period which has seen the introduction of the National Curriculum in English and what seems like an explosion in the number of poetry books being published for primary and middle school children. What is the position now as far as the reading of poetry is concerned at age 11?

HMI's report on the second year of implementation of English in the National Curriculum suggests an increase in the amount of poetry reading in schools at KS 1, 2 and 3 ('poetry received more attention in the classroom than has been customary recently'), but gives tantalizingly brief glimpses of its findings.

The middle school

I talked to some 10 and 11 year olds in a primary, a junior and a middle school to try to get some idea of attitudes to poetry in English classrooms now, and also to try to find out just how pupils approach poems as a reading experience. I had in mind a remark by Michael Benton that 'Reading a poem is different from reading a story or any other text ... [it is] a reading process that is more varied and unpredictable than any other'. My group of Y6 middle school pupils were a teacher-selected cross section of readers. Moira enjoyed writing poems but said she only read them if they were exciting; Sarah loved reading poems but couldn't write them, although her mum did; Eleanor used to like poems, but didn't now; Max didn't find poems at all interesting to read or write; Tom liked books but didn't choose to read or write poems much; and finally Russell found poems OK, but wasn't particularly interested, preferring stories ('You get more involved in it in a book ... character and things ... than in a poem').

I would like to concentrate on the comments of Sarah, as the only reader in the group who sometimes preferred a poetry book to stories. For Sarah, how she read a poem was important:

> I think it's much better if you read the poem aloud ... I find it difficult to read poems in my head because it's much nicer if you read them aloud and listen to your own voice.

This led Sarah to choose other poetry than the 'comicky sort of poems' which were the only ones Max and Eleanor liked reading (though Eleanor didn't really think these were 'proper poems'):

> I like poems that you have to use a lot of voice expression for ... like if it's a dark poem then you have to lower your voice down.

Sarah's reading practice with poems was different from the other members of the group. Her response to the question 'do you read poems differently from stories?' was: 'I actually read poems slower ... because I like trying to listen to the sound and the rhythm.' Some members of the group said they read poems faster than stories. Max, who didn't generally read poems, read them more slowly if he had to but for reasons of comprehension, 'so I can actually make most out of it and hear what it's saying.' In contrast to Sarah's savouring of the poem's music, Max and Russell said they would never read a poem twice except 'if it was really complicated and you rushed through it'. Max made a comparison with films, which he said he *did* often watch twice: 'you have to put effort into reading but a film you just stick it in the video and watch.' Poetry reading was equated for them with having to work hard at understanding something difficult.

Sarah's response to the question 'what is a poem?', following the reading of a shape poem, revealed a relaxed and tolerant attitude. Whereas Tom and other members of the group were anxious to define formally what is and isn't a poem, trying out formulations such as:

> This is a poem
> Do you think it is?

Sarah's feeling was that:

> There is no actual definition. Lots of people think lots of different things about poems so it's your definition for your personal liking.

The personal nature of poetic enjoyment posed problems for the classroom, according to Sarah:

> Some teachers make you read poems but you can't be forced to read a poem ... it's just something you like or don't like ... you can't be forced to write or read a poem because you won't enjoy it.

As an enthusiastic reader of poetry, Sarah reminds us of the importance of letting children read poetry aloud, of allowing children the time to choose what poems they would like to read and of giving them the time to read them effectively.

The primary school

Bearing in mind the comments made by this keen poetry reader, when I talked to another group of 10-11 year olds in the top year of a primary school I tried to find similarities of approach in those who enjoyed reading poems. The second group I talked to were again teacher selected but this time they were *all* children who were enthusiastic about poetry. Thomas expressed the group's feelings about the kinds of poems they liked when he commented:

> I don't really like poems that are long and well they just go on a bit ... and they don't rhyme ... I think I like the shorter poems better really.

Discussing the difference between reading stories and reading this kind of poem, Emily expressed her experience of the two in this way:

> A story has a start, a middle and an end - well most stories do - and ... a poem ... can be a start of a story or a middle or an end or just, you know, whatever you want ... and also a poem is sort of a way of expressing your feelings sometimes.

Thomas mentioned this expressive quality of poetry too when he commented: 'Poems are sort of a better way of expressing things than a story really.'

As far as actually reading poems was concerned the group as a whole did feel they read them in a different way from narrative. Emily felt it depended on the type of poem as to how slowly or quickly she read it, but Christine gave this very clear description of her own practice which the entire group greeted with a 'Yeah!' of approval:

> In a poem you stop for a while afterwards, longer than you do when it's just a full stop ... you stop and then go on to the next line and you stop, go on to the next line ... and you read it slowly (...) you need more time to think with a poem ... 'cos stories you just read it through and get it all into your head but a poem you need to be reading it quite slowly to take it all in.

Here Christine seems to echo the kind of approach to reading poems Sarah described.

The junior school

My third group of 10-11 year olds were drawn from a Year 6 class, this time in a Junior school. Of the group of 8 picked for me by their class teacher, 6 were positive towards the reading of poetry, one was 'so-so' about it, and one, Jeremy, was emphatically hostile ('If it was the last book on Earth I might read some poems'). In general the group preferred stories to poetry ('stories take me into a place,' said Matthew), as with the children in the APU sample, and there was again a dislike of 'really long poems' and of 'descriptive poems', as with the children in the previous school. Roald Dahl was as popular for his poetry as for his fiction, a view echoed by all the groups I talked to, and other poets mentioned by this group were Brian Patten and Edward Lear.

With this group, when I asked about how they read poems they stressed to me the importance of rhythm. 'It depends what the rhythm is how fast or slow you read it,' said Jeremy, the non-reader of poetry, and Cheryl felt that the crucial thing was 'if you can get into the rhythm'.

We read together Brian Patten's poem 'The Newcomer' (which Jeremy liked!) and had a vigorous discussion about what or who this newcomer was ('it's about us,' said Matthew; 'a mythological creature,' said Jeremy). Keeping in mind the comments made earlier to me about reading poems more slowly than stories, when I read the poem aloud to the group, after their own initial silent readings, I consciously slowed down my reading and tried to bring out the poem's rhythm and metre. The group's reactions were mixed:

> 'You read it much more slowly ...'
> 'It sounded a bit more interesting ... I couldn't get into it.'
> 'It sounded very, very different when you read. I read it much faster.'
> 'I preferred my reading to myself.'

At this point I asked the group whether they had ever been given any guidelines for reading poems, and the reply was that they hadn't but had 'just picked up' how to do it. I asked then whether they felt these sample guidelines would have been useful to them as poetry readers:

Reading poems

1. Choose any poem in the book. You don't have to start on the first page and you don't have to read the poems in any order.

2. Read the poem quickly to yourself. It doesn't matter if you don't understand it all.

3. Read it again more slowly to yourself.

4. Read it aloud, so you can hear what it sounds like.

5. Share it with someone else. Read it together and talk about it.

6. If you really like it, remember where to find the poem so you read it again to yourself or someone else later.

The reactions to these guidelines were again mixed ('All poems are different,' Cheryl rightly pointed out), so I asked the children to produce their own advice to give to beginner poetry readers. Their main recommendation for younger readers was to try to hear the rhythm of a poem:

> 'I'd say read it slowly a few times. Try to make it sound more exciting.'
> 'It's important to get the rhythm of a poem.'
> 'Read it carefully and slowly to yourself. If you don't understand it get someone to help you.'

Conclusions

Talking to these children at the primary/secondary divide in a number of different schools confirmed my belief in poetry as an essential reading experience for the less fluent and also the independent older reader. I felt there were lessons to be learnt from those readers such as Sarah, Christine and Cheryl (all girls!) who were committed poetry readers and likely to continue to be so into secondary school and beyond.

As well as promoting and supporting poetry as a reading experience and widening children's awareness beyond humorous poetry (but not excluding it), it seems helpful to talk about the actual process of reading poems. This may mean keen readers sharing their practice with others, or groups of children suggesting advice for younger readers on 'how to read poems', as distinct from prose stories or information books.

Almost certainly it will mean children discovering or rediscovering the music of poetry through reading aloud themselves as well as hearing poems read. As my third group reminded me, the single most important thing for children reading poetry is 'getting into the rhythm of it'.

References

APU (1981) *Language Performance in Schools: Primary Survey Report No. 1.* HMSO: London.

APU (1982) *Secondary Survey Report No.1.* HMSO: London.

APU (1984) *1982 Primary Survey Report.* DES: London.

APU (1988) *Review of APU Language Monitoring 1979-83.* HMSO: London.

Benton, M (1992) *Secondary Worlds. Literature Teaching and the Visual Arts.* Open University Press: Buckingham.

Benton, P (1986) *Pupil, Teacher, Poem.* Hodder and Stoughton: London.

Bryant, P and Bradley, L (1985) *Children's Reading Problems.* Blackwell: Oxford.

Goswami, U and Bryant, P (1990) *Phonological Skills and Learning to Read.* Lawrence Erlbaum: London.

HMI (1992) *English Key Stages 1, 2 and 3: A Report on the Second Year 1990-91.* HMSO: London.

Patten, B (1985) *Gargling with Jelly.* Viking Kestrel: London.

10 - The quintessential quartet: Parent, teacher, child, book

ANGELA REDFERN

The early years: what parents know and do well

Parents from all social and cultural backgrounds take a delight in singing to their newborn babies, chanting nursery rhymes, finger rhymes, doing action songs and then adding ring games and verbal games of ever increasing sophistication as the months and years go by. Parents do not need the Kingman report to tell them that they should encourage their offspring to develop an ear for language and build on their children's innate interest in the rhymes and rhythms of language - they know all that (whether they can articulate it or not) and they just get on and do it: they sway with Piggy on the railway, they stomp with the Grand old Duke of York and they lean this way and that as little teapots.

One of the most treasured possessions in a colleague's classroom was a tape of lullabies recorded by families in the community in all the languages spoken in our school. Not only did it make clear our stance on language diversity but it was also a symbol of the power of that early rapport of parent and child through language ... the first ever story that the two would share. For me, it signalled in no uncertain terms that we saw shared stories as the heart of the matter.

Parents talk freely to their offspring long before there is a hope of any reply in kind. Chatting as you go about your business keeps infants' interest engaged and is one way of involving them in the daily events of family life. Recounting to recently returned members of the family what's been going on in their absence is another family ritual - where we went today, what we did, who we saw and so on. Long journeys become bearable because everyone is included in the fun of retelling favourite family anecdotes. Valuing family members' personal stories in this way and responding to them wholeheartedly is a most powerful demonstration of our belief in the central importance of storying in all its many guises.

But most precious of all perhaps is the final shared emotional experience of the day as parent and child snuggle down together in a secure loving environment to share a well-loved tale - the bedtime story. Sometimes it is from a book but at other times it is an oral tale that has been handed down from generation to generation. It comes in all dialects, all languages and is a vital bond between the generations. Older siblings enjoy sharing again in the tales when they come round a second and third time with the next new baby. Children join in the end-of-line rhymes as they learn the text off by heart, they chip in with what's coming next, they remonstrate when two pages get turned over at once and a favoured bit is missed out, they create images in the mind and greedily feed the imaginative impulses as they laugh with you at Hairy McLary, make friends with Frog and Toad and weep with you when Charlotte dies.

Research has shown that it is not only the traditional middle classes who engage their children in these special moments but *all* parents, though the stories will differ from home to home along with the flavour of the language. And there is an added bonus since a great deal of incidental learning takes place: children learn how to handle books and care for them, they learn that print goes from left to right in English and from top to bottom, they learn the language for talking about books e.g. author, title, chapter, they learn to distinguish print from pictures, they may even begin to notice individual words and letters, they learn literary vocabulary and they learn about narrative structure. Most importantly, love of story and storying is there at the centre from the very start and, if we want to hook children on books for life, there it should stay. But, does it?

At school

Everyone knows that literacy counts. More than anything else in the modern world, literacy counts in educational terms. It is the foundation for all learning, the master key that can open up all doors. In Britain, children are channelled into compulsory schooling at the age of five. Classrooms all over the country are filled with books of every shape and size. Teachers are at the ready to teach children to read with 'independence, fluency, accuracy and understanding' the minute they cross the threshold of the school. The English National Curriculum document spells out an important requirement for the teaching of reading: 'Individual response to literature is fundamental to the programmes of study for reading'. Indeed, programmes of study and non-statutory guidance are full of references to a varied reading diet of all types of fiction, poetry and non-fiction books, rich and stimulating good quality texts from a range of different cultures to deepen children's understanding of themselves and their world. They stipulate that children regularly hear stories and poetry read aloud and that they retell loved stories, talk about books, and the characters in them, ask and answer questions about books.

So the evidence is there in the English document to support the continuation of the kinds of experiences that children have already learnt to love at home, in playgroups and in nurseries. Teachers are fully aware of the vital role that stories have to play in all our lives. Storytime has a hallowed place in classrooms around the country and, along with USSR, library sessions, bookshares, paired and shared and group reading, offers rich opportunities for children to engage in an active dialogue with a book or about a book. Sadly, however, in 1990/1 teachers took a battering from the popular press that undermined their confidence in what they knew to be effective practice. Cries of falling standards and calls for a return to a golden age that had never existed naturally threw an already demoralised profession into a state of increased anxiety. The first round of officially reported and published SATs results were badly (maliciously?) misinterpreted in the press which did nothing to help the situation nor to restore teachers' faith in their own expertise.

It is the attainment targets and not the programmes of study or the non-statutory guidance that get press attention and which are, therefore, best known to the population at large. You only have to look at the terminology of those attainment targets to realise why parents and teachers are getting more anxious. Statements of attainment are set out in *levels* - and which parent or teacher is not going to want their children to reach the highest level? The race is on for Level 3 at Key Stage One and nothing less will do or what chance will the children have of success in the future? And so the temperature rises. A closer look at the SATs for 7 year olds reveals that reading the words with complete accuracy is the key to achieving a high score. As we all know, to be awarded Level 2 children have to

- read 3 signs around the classroom
- show they know how to use a dictionary.

When reading a continuous piece of text they have to

- use a phonic clue or a wordshape clue
- use a meaning clue
- have no more than eight words supplied by the teacher
- reach a specified accuracy grade on a count of 25 stipulated words.

There is then a check that smacks of the old style comprehension tests to ascertain whether the child can recount two main points from the story and make a sensible prediction about how the story will end.

It is clearly the sub-skills that count highly, not the engagement with the text, not the affective response that avid readers all run to a book expressly to experience. Of course children need to have a battery of cueing strategies to call upon in order to become fluent readers - no-one would deny that - but the essential reason for reading in the first place must not be forgotten in all this: to find out what the author has to say, to respond in our individual way to that message and to share our ideas, thoughts and emotions with fellow readers; to feel Anne of Green Gables' pain when Matthew dies, to wince with the collective guilt when the Iron Man is deliberately trapped, to ache with misery as Sonny recounts in the letter home the fateful incident that brought him to his cell. Teachers *know* what counts as reading and it is not just word for word accuracy. It is very much more than that! It is about getting the story, not the words, right because, as Margaret Meeks points out, although 'it is useful to get information, it is crucial to grow as a person'. Perhaps we need to proclaim in letters six feet high in every classroom in the land that stories:

- help us all make sense of our own lives
- give us greater knowledge of others
- let us stand in someone else's shoes and see the world from a different standpoint
- have the power to project us into new worlds in different places, different eras, different cultures from our own so that we gain understanding of how others live, have lived or might live in the future
- encourage us to grapple with social and moral issues
- force us to negotiate new thoughts, new ideas
- broaden and deepen our imaginative experiences
- teach us how narrative works so that we gain increasing pleasure from our dialogues with authors as we read

- increase our store of literary vocabulary and our knowledge of the rhythms and rhymes of languages.

Yes, stories engage us totally as thinking, feeling human beings because as James Britton so rightly observed, 'We never cease to long for more lives than the one we have; in the role of spectator we can participate in an infinite number'.

Home and school together

Parental involvement is rightly acknowledged as a highly significant factor in children's learning. Countless schemes sprang up nationwide in the 1980s to link Home and School in the teaching of reading in an effort to ensure that no child would slip through the net and leave school without becoming a proficient and avid reader. It even became big business: shop shelves filled with allegedly helpful little books destined to support parents as they joined in the task of teaching their children to read. The HMI report of 1990/1 pointed out that schools which were successful in teaching reading all had excellent links with the home and drew on parent participation. From schools all over the country plastic folders go home night after night, parents and older siblings listen to the requisite passages each evening, notes are written back and forth between parents and teachers about the successful outcome of the reading. But what happens to all those good reading habits that parents had instinctively cultivated from early childhood, long before their children got to school? Where is the emphasis placed now when all these hundreds of books go home each night? Is it on the fun and the delight in sharing and responding to the tale? A look at a few of the notebooks travelling to and fro would suggest that this is no longer so. What everyone now seems to be looking for with an eagle eye is how well the child is reading the words; how accurate the reading is, which cueing strategies the child has at her finger tips ... in other words for all those points which will count for SATs. I was in the children's section of a local bookstore one day and watched a three year old having immense fun telling herself made-up stories from all the books that appealed to her until her seven year old sister came along and burst the bubble:

> 'No. No, that's no good at all. When you go to school you have to do it *properly.*' Grabbing an early One, Two, Three and Away book she held it up and continued:
> 'What does this say? ... Say yellow.'
> 'Yellow' dutifully repeated the three year old.
> Page turned.
> 'And what does this say? ... Yellow, say yellow.'
> 'Yellow.' Page turned.
> 'And what does this ...'
> 'Yellow,' interrupted the three year old in a loud bellow, 'yellow yellow yellow yellow yellow yellow!' then she yawned with a great gaping wide mouth!

I chortled to myself from behind a book display but, really, it was no laughing matter. Presumably the older child had been bubbling over with excitement about books when she was three, just like her sister. What had happened to all her enthusiasm since then? At seven she'd lost it all and now professed to know what *proper* reading was all about ... getting the words right however tedious they might be!

One of the saddest things for a teacher to witness is the tension and anxiety about success at SATs that is flooding into parents when their children start school. It militates against the very goal they are after. And, like a disease, it spreads to infect the children themselves. Yet schools can do much to alleviate the situation by harnessing parents' natural talents and keeping the emphasis on the real values of reading rather than allowing it to shift to a tense struggle to notch up all the subskills in the hope of reaching the highest level of attainment.

Teachers simply need to endorse parents' instinctive belief in the immense power of literature to ensure that we grow into fully enriched human beings by articulating clearly for them exactly how we grow when we engage with a book - as a person in our own right, as a social being, as an intellectual being, as a political being and as a fluent reader. For a rattling good story is the biggest and juiciest carrot of them all!

There is little that is more satisfying for a teacher than to forge strong links with parents so that the two major influences in a child's life, home and school, can pull together in the best interests of the child. Brochures and sometimes videos, too, are on offer that can reassure parents who are anxious or confused about current approaches that spring from the mass of recent information we have about the reading process. The pamphlets that most parents receive when their children start school could so easily include a model, step by step, of the pattern for hearing reading that is practised in reading conferences in the school. Then parents could mirror that pattern at home. Due consideration to reading strategies should be given but *not* at the expense of reader involvement. It is not an either/or situation. Both are essential and the vital area of response to text should also be included as a top priority.

Here is an extract from one Berkshire school's pamphlet for new parents:

Step 1: warming up to the read
Have a brief chat about

- the cover of the book
- the title
- the author, the illustrator

to set up expectations of what the story might be about. This is a powerful aid for a reader.

Step 2: supporting your child as she reads
What you do will vary according to how much experience your child has had with reading. It helps inexperienced readers if you

- sometimes read the story to them
- accept words that mean the same e.g. dad for father
- ignore minor errors that do not alter the meaning and when your child gets stuck try to find the quickest way to help her solve the problem successfully by
- pointing to a picture or
- asking an appropriate question or
- reading the previous words yourself with expression or
- saying the initial sound or
- pointing to the first letter or
- giving the word

And here comes the best bit ...

Step 3: talking about the book together
Try to avoid a feeling of a test with right answers! Remember it is a time for you to enjoy together. Encourage your child

- to tell you in her own words what she liked or disliked about the book
- to retell the story if she wants to
- to talk about how the events compare with your own family's experiences or with other books you've read together
- to think about why people acted the way they did or what they must have been feeling or thinking
- to tell you how she would have liked the story to end
- to look at any words or phrases that she particularly liked.

This sort of brochure helps parents to understand the importance of their natural forte - the shared dialogue about a story that's been read and enjoyed together.

Parents in school
Initiatives that encourage parents to play a part in the classroom, whenever they can, are gathering momentum. In some schools parents are welcomed into the classroom to work regularly with young readers as part of the school's programme of reading conferences. In other schools parents spend one morning a week in school working with their own child and part of that time will be spent on reading together. In such cases the teacher can model for new parents how to go about things, parents can support each other as they grow in confidence and become more relaxed in the classroom environment. Inevitably parents claim that the new skills learnt by working in this way stand them in good stead at home too.

Some schools have gone further and have established family reading groups where whole families meet regularly in school or in the local library. Grandparents, mums, dads, big brothers and tiny sisters can all be included. They share the pleasures of browsing and choosing books and everyone in the family has something to take away to read before the next group meeting. When they meet again, they will share their thoughts and feelings about the books.

Different language groups co-exist quite happily as talk about books can be in any language and bilingual speakers can translate across the language gaps. It is assumed right from the start that the feelings that books arouse are of the utmost importance and enthusiastic debates flourish once more as trust is established within the group. It is good for youngsters to realise that adults can occasionally make a wrong choice and have a disappointing experience for a change. It is also good for them to hear adults bursting with excitement at discovering a new author. It is very good for them to hear adults express their need to re-read old favourites to savour choice morsels once again or perhaps to discover some fresh details or insights that they may have missed on earlier readings. In just the same way, children learn to love particular books and clutch them to their bosom like long-lost friends and that, of course, is exactly what they are.

Wider horizons

As adults, we read at home, we read at work, we read at leisure and for pleasure, we read as citizens. In order not to be controlled by propaganda, as Freire feared, we need to exercise our autonomy over the printed word, to make choices and critically assess what is put before us whether it be a newspaper report, minutes of a meeting, an election pamphlet or a holiday brochure. Literacy is a source of power as well as pleasure. By encouraging children to respond with their full critical faculties to those early stories in the way I have outlined - comparing events to their own lives, characters to their own friends and relatives, dialogues to the authentic voices they hear around them, by giving vent openly to their feelings and opinions - they learn to become discriminating readers who can respond, in the first instance, to story then, subsequently, to all forms of print with a sharp questioning mind instead of being manipulated in later life by those who aim to sway us with empty rhetoric, false argument, half truths and biased opinions dressed up as facts.

So, away with books that 'make a narrative something apart from life as it is lived' and 'turn the food of story into a dry biscuit' (Barrie Wade). Since we know that what beginner readers read makes all the difference to their view of reading, then let's have the richest of chocolate cakes all round!

11 - Achieving more with less: Raising reading standards via parental involvement and peer tutoring

KEITH TOPPING

There are many different pathways to the goal of becoming a skilled and efficient reader. Individual children succeed best by different routes. Because of this the vast majority of primary school teachers give their pupils a range of types of professional reading instruction, rather than concentrating on one method. This simple reality seems to have largely escaped the politicians and the media, who, for their own different goals, have sought recently to distort public perceptions of these matters. Fortunately, the public are not as simple minded as either group imagine.

However, given the current burdens of curriculum change, assessment and record-keeping which are preoccupying many teachers, there is concern in schools that teachers are even less able than hitherto to 'hear children read' - and thus children are not having sufficient reading practice. Using the Government's own crude type of input-output analysis, at best the result is that as the amount of teacher contact time is reduced, both teachers and children spend less time 'on task' at reading. Clearly, this shortfall is likely to result in declining reading standards. There are no prizes for guessing who gets the *blame* for any decline in reading standards, though.

Some schools have adopted a policy of timetabling chunks of 'class reading', 'silent reading' or 'United Sustained Silent Reading' to try to ensure children obtain sufficient reading practice in school. However, this becomes increasingly difficult as the School Examination and Assessment Council enthusiasts try to cram more and more into an already crowded curriculum. It also militates against the (perhaps idealistic) notion of developing reading skills across the curriculum.

> The opinions expressed in this article are those of the author and have no representative implication. The facts are of course public property.

Most crucially, such activities are often monitored only superficially by harassed classteachers, with the result that some children may be staring at the book without interacting with it - weaker readers perhaps being particularly good at appearing to be on task while actually enjoying a rest. For efficient learning and skill development, readers need close monitoring, immediate rather than delayed error correction, and regular and frequent feedback about their efforts. That is, they need all the things for which teachers no longer have time. There was a hope some years ago that first teaching machines and later computers would get round these problems. In fact, as Bloom (1984) noted in a review of research, no methodology has been found which is as effective as one-to-one tutoring, the impact of which leaves computer-based teaching standing - even supposing you have enough computers.

Thus many schools have developed and co-ordinated arrangements for promoting non-professional 'hearing' or tutoring of reading in order to ensure pupils receive guided and monitored practice in reading to consolidate learning and increase fluency. Where parents are asked *into* school for this purpose, only a small proportion of parents can usually participate. This leads to the phenomenon of a small elite of middle class 'trustees' being allowed into school as a token gesture towards parental involvement. By contrast, schemes to promote reading at home typically involve many more families. Increasingly, schools are also experimenting with 'peer tutoring' of reading, which has been found to increase the reading age of *both* the tutoring child and the tutee if it is properly organised.

Research has shown that in parental involvement and peer tutoring projects, well-structured and organised schemes involving clear advice and training for the participants, together with some follow-up or monitoring, tend to produce the best results. In the past, far too many schools professing to have a parental involvement scheme kept the superficial control firmly in the hands of the teachers but paradoxically offered little to parents by way of practical guidance other than middle class verbiage and airy fairy philosophy. Given little indication of just what they were supposed to do, for how long they were supposed to do it (*ad infinitum?*), and what the effects were except in terms of movement through the reading scheme, it was small wonder that many parents got themselves into difficulties and/or gave up.

The press, showing their usual high nasal sensitivity for 'knocking copy', have been quick to give many column inches to the occasional less than favourable report concerning parental involvement. This may have had the damaging effect of reducing the motivation of teachers who might otherwise have launched a project and were not sufficiently familiar with the research literature to realise that a small proportion of non-significant results are always expected in any series of studies, just by random chance.

Thus the failure in the Belfield project to demonstrate significant gains on reading tests in project children as compared to non-participants (given the research design adopted) received considerable media coverage. The press totally failed to set this in the context of all the other research on the subject, not least the Haringey project, which, using similar simple intervention methods, demonstrated in a deprived multi-ethnic area not only striking differences between project children and non-participants, but that these differences were still evident at follow-up four years later.

Not that the discovery of the effectiveness of parental involvement is particularly recent. In 1984 Walburg reported on a review of US research literature: 'School-parent programmes to improve academic conditions in the home have an outstanding record of success in promoting achievement. In 29 controlled studies, 91% of the comparisons favoured children in such programmes over non-participant groups.'

As noted above, well-structured and organised schemes are generally found to yield the best results - hardly surprising. Some parental involvement in reading projects merely ask parents to 'hear' their children read from a teacher-chosen book in a non-specified way. In fact, the research evidence on the effectiveness of this approach is surprisingly sparse in quantity and not always satisfactory in terms of quality (with the distinguished exception of Haringey and one or two other projects). By contrast, the more structured methods for parental involvement have tended to generate better quantity and quality of research. A recent interesting example is the study of Leach and Siddall (1990), who compared groups of parents using with their children:

1. The Direct Instruction (DI) programme for parents devised by Englemann and his associates

2. The Pause, Prompt and Praise (PPP) technique

3. The Paired Reading (PR) technique and

4. Traditional 'hearing'.

Further details of these will be found in Topping and Wolfendale, 1985). The highly structured DI approach did best on tests, although it was more expensive to implement, while the 'hearing' approach did worst. PR did significantly better than PPP.

Paired Reading (the specific structured technique, not a vague name for any old thing two people feel inclined to do with a book) has gained widespread acceptance throughout the world as a cost-effective approach, now being widely used on a mixed-ability basis across the whole age range. PR has been the subject of a great deal of research, recently summarised in Topping and Lindsay (1991). A PR research study especially large in scale has been undertaken by the Kirklees Education Authority Psychological Service. Reading test results on a sample of 2372 participating children showed marked gains in reading attainment as compared to non-participants. As in Haringey, these gains had not 'washed out' at long-term follow-up, which is more than can be said for many educational interventions. The Kirklees Service has since developed similar approaches to spelling and mathematics (see note on p. 115).

This is all very well, you may say, but if there's all this supposedly effective parental involvement going on, why are reading standards falling?

Well, firstly, well-organised parental involvement and peer tutoring is not as widespread as we might wish to believe. While some local education authorities (LEAs) have a majority of schools actively promoting parental involvement in reading (PIR), some other LEAs remain very much fallow ground. Even where a school claims to have a PIR scheme, it often proves to be poorly organised and structured, or to depend on the enthusiasm of just one or two teachers and does not impact all the children in the school - unequal opportunities indeed. So it would be unrealistic to expect the increase in parental involvement in the 1980s to be translated into higher reading standards across the board nationally as yet.

Secondly, are reading standards actually falling? And if indeed they are, why? Teachers interested in an objective viewpoint based on careful research can do no better than study the recent report on this topic from the National Foundation for Educational Research (NFER) (Cato and Whetton, 1991).

Commenting that there has been concern about supposedly declining standards for decades, this report notes that the consensus of academic research opinion is that there has been no significant change in reading standards throughout the 1980s, or indeed for the last 25 years, and that the Assessment of Performance Unit has in recent years reported evidence of *improved* reading standards among 11- to 15-year-olds, which is hardly compatible with supposedly declining standards among 7-year-olds.

The NFER gathered usable data from a small proportion of LEAs, who self-selected to respond to the enquiry. In contrast to the evidence cited above, a majority of the LEAs did report a fall in reading standards among 7-year-olds. However, this amounted to only two points of standardised score over the whole decade, an insignificant shift in view of the increasing inappropriateness of the tests in use. (In any event, reading standards cannot meaningfully be measured by norm-referenced reading tests alone.) Furthermore, apparent overall decline was most usually hiding a specific increase in the number of weak readers at the bottom end of the spectrum. And, most pointedly of all, what decline *was* evident was mostly associated with certain years - (1985) (onset of teacher industrial action) and 1988-90 (onset of the National Curriculum etc.).

Even supposing this constitutes evidence of any decline in reading standards, which is extremely doubtful, how can we tell if this is due, as has been claimed in the press, to the abandoning of phonic instruction in favour of the 'real books approach'? The NFER report concludes that there is no evidence that any decline in reading standards is attributable to the deployment of a 'real books' approach, or indeed to any other methodology. Other plausible explanations, if any are needed, include the effect of teacher turnover, increases in the proportion of children from backgrounds where English is a second language, changes in pupil/teacher ratios and other forms of resourcing, and so forth. To disentangle the relevant factors at work is virtually impossible.

Of course, the vast majority of teachers do not see phonic instruction, look and say approaches and the use of 'real books' as in any way incompatible or conflicting. Indeed, teachers have no choice in this, since the National Curriculum attainment targets clearly make reference to all three. Nor is there any evidence from elsewhere that the real book approach results in declining reading standards; indeed, a review of forty research studies by Tunnell and Jacobs (1989) reported that in twenty-four cases the outcomes favoured the 'real books' approach, in only one case did the outcomes favour reading schemes, and in the remaining studies there was no significant difference. (We may speculate that the 'real books' approach might be more fragile than methods showing greater structure - it might be easier for the ordinary teacher to make a mess of it than phonics - and that the research might be unrepresentative of real life everywhere. But this is merely speculation.)

So what might our end of term report on the Government and the media be like? Perhaps 'Attainment very poor and frequently disruptive - would benefit from placement elsewhere'! However, the reality of the situation is that teachers will have to do more with less, or *we* will get the blame. Certainly a radical reappraisal of our own practices is essential, preferably *before* this is forced upon us. Running very fast just to stand still will do nothing except wear us out quicker - so we must look to doing something different and more cost-effective with the same time and resources.

Which gets us back to parental involvement and peer tutoring. These approaches are of proven cost-effectiveness, strongly supported in the research literature by the overwhelming majority of studies - provided structure and organisation are good. Time devoted here places the teacher in the role of the professional manager of the child's learning, rather than trying to do all the teaching personally. This expanded role can prove to be more potent and less stressful - the latter consideration being of high relevance in these distracting times. Furthermore, parental involvement in reading brings many parents into a closer relationship with their neighbourhood school, in a real working partnership which will do a great deal more to create a positive attitude to the school in the local community than any number of Parents' Meetings or other bureaucratic nonsense.

However, it is extremely important that such schemes are seen as a supplement and complement to the professional teaching of reading in school, and not as a substitute. It would be most unfortunate if any school were to seek to operate such a scheme in order to raise reading standards where the low level of such standards was mainly due to deficiencies within the school, such as the lack of a clear and effective whole school policy on teaching reading or a lack of necessary resources.

References

Bloom, B S (1984) The search for methods of group instruction as effective as one-to-one tutoring. *Educational Leadership*, 41 (8), 4-17.

Cato, V and Whetton, C (1991) *An Enquiry into LEA Evidence on Standards of Reading of Seven Year Old Children.* National Foundation for Educational Research: Windsor.

Leach, D J and Siddall, S W (1990) Parental involvement in the teaching of reading: A comparison of Hearing Reading, Paired Reading, Pause Prompt Praise and Direct Instruction methods. *British Journal of Educational Psychology,* 60, 349-55.

Topping, K J and Lindsay, G A (1991) Paired reading: A review of the literature. Submitted for publication.

Topping, K J and Wolfendale, S W (eds) (1985) *Parental Involvement in Children's Reading.* Croom Helm: London and Nichol: New York.

Tunnell, M O and Jacobs, J S (1989) Using 'real books': Research findings on literature based instruction. *The Reading Teacher,* 42 (7), 470-7.

Walberg, H J (1984) Improving the productivity of America's schools. *Educational Leadership,* 41 (8), 19-27.

The Paired Reading Training Pack, and other information about similar approaches to spelling, writing and mathematics with applications in parent and peer tutoring and in adult literacy, is available from the Paired Learning Project, Oastler Centre, 103 New Street, Huddersfield HD1 2UA, West Yorkshire, UK.

(First published in *Support for Learning,* Vol. 6, No. 3, 1991.)

12 - A school policy for reading

JANE MEDWELL

Introduction

As the language co-ordinator in a primary school one of my chief objectives was to review our school reading policy both for itself and with a view to creating an overarching language policy throughout the school. This policy was arrived at as a product of a whole school in-service programme, spread over a year. The policy was drafted by a working party and amended in the light of feedback from the rest of the staff. It is offered here not as a new or original statement (indeed it cannot but be derived from the work and reading undertaken by the staff) but as a reference point for others who may be involved in similar, seemingly endless tasks. I hope it may be useful as a starting point for discussion although, of course, as with all learning and development, the process of arriving at a product is of more value than the product itself.

The policy

Introduction

The ability to create meaning from a written text is probably the most useful skill a child can develop during the school years. Our teaching of reading is based upon a number of assumptions about reading:

- reading should be an enjoyable experience. We should encourage children to get pleasure from stories and other forms of literature. Reading itself can be a pleasure, alone or with others.

- children come to school with a variety of experiences and understandings about readings. Our early teaching of reading should use and build upon these and offer a continually expanding range of reading experience.

- readers do not read in only one way but rather they use a range of strategies for making sense of a text. Children need to acquire the ability to use and orchestrate these strategies in a flexible way.

- becoming a reader is not merely acquiring a level of skill but developing a knowledge of texts, stories and purposes for reading.

- as readers develop they become more able to reflect on their reading and offer personal and critical responses to what they have read. We must support children in this reflection and offer opportunities for response.

The teaching of reading at our school

Our policy, based upon the above assumptions, can be summarised as a set of aims:

1. to provide a wide variety of reading material: fiction, non-fiction, plays, poetry, teletext etc.

2. to help children develop and expand the skills of reading.

3. to offer opportunities and real purposes for a wide range of reading activities.

4. to encourage children to become confident and independent in their reading, both for pleasure and as a tool for other work across the curriculum.

To achieve these aims we have created a set of guidelines which can be briefly summarised as follows:

1. We recognise that there is no one method of teaching and that different children may need different approaches as they develop as readers.

2. It is vital that we give literacy a high profile in our school. This involves creating the right environment in class, both in terms of organization of resources and of time.

3. Reading with a supportive adult is at the centre of our reading instruction and we must use each shared reading or reading conference in a way most suited to the needs of the individual child.

4. We recognise that reading can best be learned with the support of both school and parents. This support works effectively only if we communicate well with our parents and encourage them to take an active part in their children's learning.

5. Assessment, for formative and diagnostic purposes as well as statutory assessment, is the basis of our teaching and must be continuous and systematic. This can be achieved through efficient record keeping.

6. It is important to choose books with care and offer our children the best quality fiction and non-fiction books. These are broadly graded for ease of choice, but children will need to learn to choose appropriately.

7. All children need to learn to use reading strategies like skimming and scanning as well as information skills. They should also be confident with the alphabetical and Dewey classification in the school library. These skills can best be tackled as an integral part of thematic work.

Guidelines for the teaching of reading

A general approach to reading

Different children learn to read in different ways, and the way an individual reads depends on the nature of the task. It is obvious, therefore, that we need a variety of approaches if we are to help all our children become flexible readers.

Word recognition

Whilst reading is not just a case of recognising words this can be a useful strategy. Word recognition is best developed in the context of whole texts such as story books or big books.

Sound-symbol correspondence

We would not want our children to try to decode every sound (only the poorest readers do this) but recognising letters and the sounds they represent is a very important part of reading (particularly the initial and final sounds). If phonic knowledge is to be used it is best learned in the context of stories and whole texts. Pointing out and talking about sounds and letters is a natural part of our handwriting, spelling and writing work and can be done in shared reading time or using big books. This can be extended using games (such as 'my aunt went to town ...').

Using the context

All children need to be able to use the pictures and their understanding of the text so far to guide their guesses. It is likely that many children will need to discuss this in shared reading sessions.

Prediction

The ability to predict is a basic part of reading. Readers are constantly using their expectations as a basis for their guesses of words. We need to encourage prediction by using predictable texts, and discussing what will come next. Sequencing activities and cloze procedures encourage children to predict as well as use the sense of the passage.

The ability to use all the available cues efficiently is not the end of reading development. Children need to adapt the way they read to the needs of the task. This means learning to skim and scan. Children also need to learn information and library skills. This can best be taught through the thematic work of the class.

The right environment

In physical terms we aim to create classrooms which encourage children to use reading as part of their daily lives. This involves notices, instructions and displays both by and for the children. Classes for younger children use reading materials such as newspapers, magazines, timetable, directories etc in the dramatic play areas. Older classes will need these reference materials for use in their thematic work.

Reading areas are a crucial part of class organisation. These areas can offer an attractive display of fiction and topic related non-fiction from which children can choose. Learning to choose is an essential part of becoming a reader and should be fostered at all ages and stages. Reading areas offer our children the opportunity to browse regularly among good quality books and seek guidance from teachers.

Reading areas are enhanced by displays of relevant pictures, dust jacket designs and reviews. Groups of children may be able to take responsibility for such displays.

The teacher's planning of reading time is also important in creating a reading environment. Time for browsing needs to be planned. If 'spare minutes' are used there will be some children who will rarely have this time. All children need to have stories read to them, preferably every day, but at least three times a week. These might be picture books or more sustained stories. It can sometimes be useful to read the first story of a series (such as the Happy Families Books, Paddington or Anastasia books) and make the rest of the series available for the children to read. In addition to story reading it may be appropriate to read from non-fiction books for thematic work.

A silent reading time (USSR - uninterrupted sustained silent reading) can be established on a regular basis for any age group. Teachers should also try to read at this time - children rarely see us enjoying books.

Reading is intimately related to writing and children can benefit from writing their own books to read to others or to add to the class book stock. These can be used by other children but must be treated with the respect accorded 'real' books.

Many planned reading activities will take place as part of normal class activity. This might include using language master cards to read maths instructions, reading big books as a group, skimming and scanning as part of topic research or doing topic related cloze, sequencing or modelling tasks. At the heart of our reading instruction is the time spent reading with adults, and this must be skilfully used.

Reading with an adult

Young readers are moving from dependence on adult help to independence as readers and the support offered to them in the infant and early junior stages is important. Shared reading has been adopted in our school as a term to cover a range of ways of reading a text with a youngster. This might take the form of

- reading the book to the child and talking about the pictures
- adult and child reading in unison
- the adult doing most of the reading and the child supplying words
- the child reading with the adult there to provide support.

The type of support will depend on the way that child is reading. Some children will need to work on phonic cues, others may need to make more use of the sense or the sentence structure to guide their guesses.

A child might do any, or all of these activities with the same book. Sharing a book in this way allows the adult to discuss the story with the child or develop such strategies as word recognition, sound symbol correspondence and prediction. All these strategies are more likely to be used effectively if they are learned in the context of a story rather than as a separate exercise.

Time must be set aside for shared reading and evidence suggests that regular sessions of ten to fifteen minutes are more useful for teaching than daily sessions of a few minutes.

As children gain independence they will move on to silent reading. Shared reading or simply reading to the teacher will be less useful than a reading conference. This conference might include a number of ingredients such as

- listening to the child read a passage to monitor reading performance
- discussing what has happened so far in this particular book, or what might yet happen
- discussion of the 'best bits' of this story, such talk allows children to develop the ability to talk about plot, character, themes etc
- discussion of the type of books the child has been reading recently, as evidenced from entries in the reading diary
- a more formal analysis of reading behaviour such as miscue analysis
- the child re-telling stories which have been read.

In addition to individual reading, group reading can be a very supportive reading experience which is easily organised with multiple copies of a single text. Group reading for younger readers might involve discussing the text and pictures and reading with an adult initially, then reading silently, or reading a page each aloud or even reading all together. For independent readers, group reading might involve reading in turn and predicting what will happen or discussing the book, with or without an adult. For independent readers, poetry and plays are popular texts for group reading. Multiple copies of some texts are available in the school library.

Regular individual shared reading and reading conferences are at the heart of the reading programme, but other reading experiences are also valuable. These might include using listening centres to listen to taped books, perhaps following the text, or reading with peers, reading to younger children, reading with other adults in school and reading at home.

Parents and reading

Parents share our concern to develop readers and are usually only too keen to support school efforts at home and at school. It is important that children realise that school and parents are working together. To maximise this support we must communicate with parents in a number of ways.

Before children start at the school the class teacher will make a home visit and this is an ideal opportunity to discuss early language with parents. Most parents will also bring their children into school to the pre-school link group before the child starts school and teachers will be able to explain the school's approach to reading to parents and show them the materials currently in use.

At the start of each year all parents are invited into school, and this is a useful time to discuss school policy on reading, and how parents can best help.

All children are encouraged to take their school books home and read them with parents.

At the start of the academic year each child is given a reading diary (a Shared Reading Record for infants or Personal Reading Record for juniors) and a pamphlet of advice for parents which is appropriate for the child's reading level. Some parents may wish to discuss this further, either individually or at a parents evening.

Reading diaries are used primarily as a record for use by child, teacher and parents, but may also be a vehicle of communication with busy parents. If a particular strategy is being stressed it may be useful to note this in the diary for parents to pursue. Similarly parents may make a note of their worries in the diaries.

Some parents may be willing to come and work in school with children on a regular basis, and this extra attention is of great benefit to all children. They may do shared reading with younger readers, or read and discuss books with older readers. Other parents may be able to do group reading sessions with children and help them choose books either from the school or class library. In either case they will probably expect the teacher to clearly discuss what is required with them before they start. Some parents will be happy to work in class whilst others will prefer to use the library, when that is possible. There may be some parents who cannot offer a regular commitment of time, but are happy to undertake tasks at home such as recording taped books for class use.

Parents also support school reading in other ways, by discussing book club leaflets with children and bringing them to book fairs. Most importantly by taking their children to the public library and encouraging them to join schemes like Booktrack. Library membership is an important part of becoming a reader.

Some contact with our parents will be through the school brochure, newsletters and letters from individual teachers, but just as important is the day to day end of school contact we establish.

Assessment of reading

As teachers we must consider and assess the following aspects of each child's development as a reader.

- acquisition of a growing range of strategies for making sense of a text, their ability to orchestrate these strategies and use them appropriately and flexibly,

- enjoyment of books, story and reading, which gives them the confidence to tackle new texts and so leads to growth in independence,

- different kinds of reading experiences, at home and at school, which leads to expanding range as a reader,

- increased ability to reflect on reading, and respond critically or personally to what they read.

Our assessment of these factors, which work together in the developing reader, are the basis of our teaching, the way we ensure progression, as well as the content of statutory reported assessment.

Most assessment can best be done through teacher observation. This takes place at each shared reading session, in group reading sessions and as the teacher observes children in the class. Some systematic record of this should be kept. The reading diary is a record which teachers, children and parents can contribute to and discuss. This could be supplemented with observation notes of other reading experiences (the Primary Language Record handbook is helpful). Both diaries and notes eventually pass into the child's language profile file with other samples of work, to accompany the child through the school.

Occasionally teachers will wish to use more formal procedures such as running record (early years) and miscue analysis (for further details consult the Primary Language Record handbook). These error analysis techniques offer insight into the reading strategies children use and are a basis for further, or remedial teaching. The analysis should be briefly included in observation notes.

Some children may experience reading difficulties to the extent that they require extra support. The teacher can call on the support teacher and devise an individual plan to address particular difficulties.

Reading resources

In choosing books for our children we need to consider three main criteria: content (topic and language), attractiveness (visual and handling appeal) and ease of reading (difficulty and legibility of text).

Children learn to read by reading what they enjoy, and this may not always be what we think is good for them. However, we can attempt to choose a wide range of quality books which include humorous books, favourite characters and series of books with familiar characters.

In considering content, relevance is important. In terms of fiction this includes relevance not only to the child's daily life, but to the inner life of the imagination. This type of fiction helps children to explore worries and fears safely. Non-fiction should initially relate to the child's world and go on to expand in scope and widen the child's world view. Hopefully reading will encourage understanding of one's own and other people's problems. To do this we must avoid sexism, racism or class bias.

The attractiveness of books depends on their age and the quality of materials and content. Children will not want to handle old and tatty books, and these will not teach children to respect books. Illustrations in books are important as they offer clues to the meaning of the text and often extend it. We try to have picture books suitable for older children as well as beginners.

Some types of texts help young readers to learn. These are texts which are interesting to youngsters and have a high degree of predictability. Repetition, where it is a natural part of the text, is also helpful for early readers. Books with unnatural sounding language or forced repetition should be avoided.

When choosing non-fiction, content and attractiveness are important, but we must also consider the way children will read these books. Most non-fiction is not designed to be read from cover to cover. As a rule non-fiction books should contain a contents page and index, and in some cases a glossary.

Ease of reading must also be considered for those who have made a start on reading. This is not to say that children can only read books in which they can decode all the words, this is often not the case, but that teachers and children must recognise that some books will require a higher level of adult support than others. Likewise, the choice of 'easy' books from time to time is not a cause for concern, but a normal part of reading behaviour.

Grading books

The books in class libraries have been chosen for their high quality and attractiveness. They include both scheme and trade books and should provide a choice to suit all tastes. We have graded the books into broad categories based on reading and interest level. These categories are intended to contain a wide range, but are not intended to limit the choice of the individual. They are a guide for teachers and children.

It is to be hoped that in the next few years our book stock will be gradually enriched, and new books will be incorporated into these levels as they are acquired.

Sets of group reading books are being compiled and graded according to the same scale. These are stored in the school library to allow access to all.

The school library

The school library is a resource available to the whole school. It contains both fact and fiction books. The fiction books are organised alphabetically by author and by the junior level all children should be learning how to select and replace books in this way. Non-fiction is organised on the simplified Dewey system. There are guidance pamphlets available for use in the library, and all our junior children should be familiar with the system and make use of it for thematic work.

SECTION 3

Dealing with Reading Failure

13 - Literacy and teacher assessment at Key Stage 2

LOUISE POULSON

The complex nature of literacy in the closing decade of the twentieth century is widely acknowledged. The report on Primary education produced by Alexander, Rose and Woodhead for the DES may have been controversial in some respects, but certainly not so in stating the following:

> ... it is clear that to function effectively in the 21st century, our children will need higher standards of literacy and numeracy than ever before. (DES, 1992 III.24).

Public awareness of the need for a literate population is often manifested in concern that standards of literacy may be falling; a concern which is not limited to any particular moment in history. Indeed, it seems to have recurred with some regularity since the middle decades of the nineteenth century. However, evidence from reasonably reliable sources, such as HMI surveys, indicates that there has not been a significant decline in UK literacy standards in recent years. A problem in assessing the extent of literacy within a society at any given time is that a common source of data is the results from standardized tests of reading ability. The use of such data to give information about the extent and degree of literacy is based upon the premise that a more literate school population will be indicated by higher standardized test scores. This is, however, a fallacy. Standardized tests of reading ability show only a very limited range of competence in literacy (Dombey, 1991). First of all, they are concerned only with *reading* ability and, secondly, they are concerned with the ability to read a limited range of text types in an artificial context. In examining the standardized tests of reading ability used by LEAs, the NFER found that none of them assessed how competent readers actually read in real life (NFER, 1991). Nevertheless, the media debate on reading standards has rested entirely upon the premise that standardized tests indicate the extent of literacy within a population.

Whist there has been some questioning of what standardized tests *actually* show as opposed to what it is *claimed* they show, there has been little analysis of what is to be fully literate in the closing decade of the twentieth century. Nor have we devised the means by which a more complex version of competence in literacy might be assessed. There is no doubt, however, that the human ability to understand and use writing as a means of representing the world symbolically offers potential freedom from the restrictions of making sense of experience only within the immediate context. Thus, writing allows that which is known to be separated from the knower and, therefore, allows for the formulation of an abstract, and more generalised view of the world.

The establishment of a statutory National Curriculum and associated assessment procedures might have gone some way towards clarification of these problems. Unfortunately, this seems not to have been the case: more problems have been generated than have been solved. Nevertheless, assessment has become an obsessive concern in British education; so much so that clichés about the relationship between teaching, learning and assessment have become established as self-evident truths (Desforges, 1992). Yet, as Desforges argues, there is little, if any, empirical evidence to illuminate the part that assessment might play in teaching and learning.

How can a wider conception of literacy be assessed?

It was the aim of a recent research study conducted at the University of Exeter School of Education to examine practices in the teaching and learning of literacy at Key Stage 2. An aspect of this work was concerned with the *process* of assessing literacy. We wanted to establish what teachers actually did in the classroom context, interacting with pupils and, furthermore, when and how assessment occurred in the classroom. Our concern was to identify the integrated aspects of formative/diagnostic assessment of reading and writing in the Key Stage 2 classroom. A particular difficulty in researching teacher assessment was that much of the advice given by SEAC tended to suggest that it was something done apart from ongoing classroom activity. Whilst there seemed to be many recommendations as to what teachers should do, there were relatively few accounts of what they actually do in order to gain knowledge of pupil abilities and achievements, or even of how they gained information to inform future teaching decisions. We were concerned to find out not so much how teachers record or report achievement, but how they assess and provide feedback to pupils on work in progress. It seemed that this aspect of the assessment process had been overlooked and yet it was, potentially, the point at which assessment connected most closely with teaching and learning.

In concentrating on teachers of Key Stage 2 children, it was felt that although there was probably an increased awareness of assessment because of the National Curriculum legislation, there was not the immediate pressure, as with Key Stage 1 teachers, to fulfil the formal assessment requirements in order to report results. Furthermore, it was felt that if Key Stage 2 teachers were not subject to the immediate pressures of reporting, then they might be more inclined to develop practicable teacher assessment strategies in their classrooms.

We worked in three Primary schools, diverse in location, size and social composition, but all within the same LEA. In each school, we observed part of a normal day's work with a class engaged upon literacy activities and then the same teachers working closely with individual or small groups of children. Finally, the teachers were interviewed about their attitudes to and practices in assessment and the ways in which these had changed since the inception of the National Curriculum. The findings reported here aim only to give an impression, albeit a limited one, of what teachers are doing in terms of giving formative/diagnostic feedback on literacy at Key Stage 2.

Formative assessment in the teaching and learning of literacy in Key Stage 2 classrooms

The classroom observation of interactions between teachers and pupils revealed a pattern common to all three schools: the assessments which took place were not distinct in procedure from other forms of interaction between teacher and pupils in the classroom. The critical factor in distinguishing an interaction as assessment was that it provided feedback and comment on work completed or in progress. In providing such feedback, the teacher held, in his/her head, a complex and detailed pattern of information about children's achievements and difficulties in literacy. This will be no radical revelation to most teachers, nor is it intended to be. It is, rather, an attempt to make explicit what may previously have been known only implicitly. Indeed, teachers in this study reported that the effects of the National Curriculum were both positive and negative in this respect. On the one hand, there was a fear that teachers' judgements would not count unless they were formalised by being written down. But also, as a consequence of having to be more explicit about what was being assessed and in having to find evidence to support their judgements, teachers felt that they had become more reflective about their own practices. They also reported making fewer assumptions about children's achievements and considering with more care what counted as evidence of progress in learning:

> There's a big danger, particularly in a small school, that because you know the children very well, you can think you don't actually need to record the day-to-day things because you're going to have them for four years - that's an awfully long time. (This was in a small rural school with 2.5 teachers, including the Head.)

The teachers in this study used continuous records, frequently in the form of notebooks, in which events regarded as significant might be written. Significant events were defined by the teachers as: (i) those which indicated that a pupil recognised a problem, or was thinking in a different way about something which had previously caused difficulty; (ii) which showed pupils beginning to overcome difficulties which previously would have led them to abandon a task or approach; (iii) those which showed that a pupil was able to approach and complete a task independently where once he/she had needed substantial help; (iv) those which showed that a pupil could complete a task easily where once he/she had struggled.

It was clear that the Primary Language Record (ILEA/CLPE, 1988) had been a strong influence on practice, even if used in a modified form. Even so, all the teachers identified the importance of information and evidence about children which he/she held in his/her own head:

> I suppose really most of the assessment is done directly from their work ... it's internalizing again ... and jottings ... and talking to them about their writing in the conferencing ... and listening to them talking to each other.

The impossibility of writing down all observations of events identified as significant by teachers was pointed out. Nevertheless, the teachers in this study felt a covert pressure to make a written record of as much as possible; in that such written records would provide proof of professional judgements made in the classroom. It was clear from classroom observation that teachers' judgements and interventions were embedded within a framework of contextual knowledge. This framework included knowledge of the history of a particular event judged as significant, and its relationship to other events in the classroom. However, as Donaldson (1978) has pointed out, in relation to children's thinking, knowledge embedded within a specific context may be both fragile and, ultimately, limiting.

The challenge with which teachers are faced is the disembedding of knowledge of children and their achievements from a specific context and its communication to others.

Pupil and teacher perceptions of feedback

At the conclusion of each pupil-teacher interaction, both were asked for their perceptions of the value of the exchange. Even where teachers had not made a written record of the interaction, they were usually able to recollect an exchange when interviewed and to indicate why they felt it to be significant. An example of this was when a pupil initiated an exchange by approaching the teacher; she had previously received help with the beginning of her story. The child was asked to share the beginning of the story with the rest of the class. Encouraged by the teacher, she read the beginning of her story aloud whilst the rest of the class listened intently. At the end, the teacher commented positively, as did other children in the class. Interviewed afterwards, the class teacher said that initially the child had not been happy with the beginning of the story. She had spent the previous two weeks concentrating on ending stories and was finding it difficult to focus on beginnings. Recognising that the child had managed to do something with which she had been struggling, the teacher asked Hannah to share her writing with the rest of the class; firstly, to encourage her and, secondly, to offer a model to everyone else. In this instance, the child's perception of the interaction with the teacher was positive, she commented to the observer:

> I thought it wasn't any good. When Mrs J. read it out I was embarrassed at first ... but I'm happy with it now ... I won't alter it ... I'll correct the spelling at the end.

Although no written record was made of the event, it was regarded as worthy of note by both pupil and teacher.

A further example was when the class teacher had initiated an interaction with a pupil having difficulty in getting beyond the introduction to a story.

> You need to get more organisation into your notes ... and story-file ... it's a bit too disorganised ... you don't know what you're doing. I'll write down in my diary to have a good look with you on Monday and that gives you a chance to have a good sort out. Right, I've made a note ... let's look at what you've done today.

After listening to the boy's ideas for the story and discussing how these could be developed from the introduction, the teacher ended the interaction saying:

> Now you've sorted out the beginning, stick to it. Don't tie yourself in knots ... don't try to do them all at once. I'll come back and look at the content when you've got a bit more.

The pupil's perception of this exchange was that it had helped to clarify what he was doing and what he should do next:

> We've sorted out the introduction a bit ... it was muddled up ... so it helped me sort it out.

Pupils reported that interactions with the teacher had been useful and had helped with their writing or reading. Several emphasized that the teacher was the best person to comment on their work. Whilst peers or paired partners were regarded as useful for discussing books or ideas for writing, pupils were afraid that their peers lacked the teacher's expertise:

> ... but they might get it wrong ... tell you the wrong thing to write.

However, many commented on the usefulness of peer-feedback in the initial stages of structuring the plot of a story. We were aware, in soliciting pupils' comments on the value of interactions with the teacher, that there might be some distortion: pupils might tell us what they believed we wished to hear. Or, equally, that we might convey comments back to the teacher. The form of questions, therefore, did not require direct comparisons to be made.

In many instances, the teachers' interventions served to help children to focus more closely on their task and, if necessary, to reorientate them to its demands (in this case, letters of thanks following a visit):

> It (interaction with teacher) made me get on ... and I altered the capital letters.

> She reminded me how to start ... I'd have forgotten the date (on a letter).

> It helped with the spelling ... Miss wants us to get it right because we're going to send them (the letters) off.

Some children were more sceptical about the value of interactions with the teacher, as the following comments reveal:

> Asking what I'm going to do doesn't alter what I'm going to do.

> I've learnt how to spell 'learnt', that's all really.

> You feel relieved when she says 'good, fine, good boy' ... it means I don't have to write it out again.

In all three schools, observations showed examples of teachers giving feedback to children - an aspect of formative assessment - which were not separate in procedure from the rest of the teaching and which were not planned beforehand. In each case, interactions which could be categorized as assessment were most successful where the teachers' assessment system was in accord with their teaching aims. In short, where teachers gave comments and feedback on the features of writing or reading which the pupils had been actually asked to focus upon in the task. Desforges (1992), and Bennett, Desforges et al. (1984) have documented examples of where the rules for assessment and the feedback given to children are not in accord with what is overly demanded when a task is set. As Bennett, Desforges et al. show, where there is such a mismatch, pupils quickly learn the covert rules and consciously aim to meet those requirements in their performance in spite of what the teacher might say he/she wished them to do.

> ... regardless of the teachers' expressed aims ... (the children) were clear about what would please their teachers. They recognised and were able to rate neatness as an important criterion. (Bennett, Desforges et al. 1984. 102)

The findings of the study reported here accord with those of Bennett & Desforges, although we generally found a positive correlation between the teachers' stated aims in task-setting and the assessment system which was actually operated in the classroom. Whilst all the teachers maintained that assessment was an ongoing feature of their classrooms, they were not necessarily confident in identifying specific examples out of context. In many instances, the teachers in this study did not immediately identify an interaction as being a part of the assessment process. It was only on reflection, in explaining reasons for actions, that they recognised them as such. This implies that teachers may need to gain confidence in identifying their own assessment system and strategies as well as adopting externally-devised models such as those suggested by SEAC.

Teachers' assessment and evaluation of pupils' progress on a one-to-one basis

The observation of teacher and pupil interactions in a classroom setting provided an overview of the teacher assessment system in operation during a normal day's activity. In addition, the study aimed also to examine planned and sustained examples of teacher assessment. The teachers themselves chose the particular form and content of the assessments to be observed. Interestingly, all chose a form of conferencing with children. In one school, this was an established part of assessment procedure and the Primary Language Record (ILEA/CLPE, 1988) was used in an unmodified form. In another, conferencing with children was practised by the teacher who took part in this study, but not necessarily by other teachers in the school. In the third, the class teacher was developing a version of the teacher-pupil conference, although she admitted that it was a relatively new practice to her. The topic of the conferences covered both finished and draft pieces of writing and also reading.

The conference on reading was for the purpose of gaining information and an agreed teacher-pupil comment for the Primary Language Record. The teacher lead the individual children into talking about their recent experiences of reading and asked them to reflect upon these. Questions covered such areas as:

- choice of books being read at the time.
- what the book was about; what had happened in the plot so far (if a narrative).
- evaluation of beginnings and endings of stories.
- comparisons with other books/authors.
- ways of reading: individual/partnerships with other children.
- when reading is done: home/school; specific times/places.
- relationship between reading and writing (and other forms of representation): how reading influenced pupils' own writing; getting ideas from other writers; ways of telling and structuring a narrative.
- reflection upon pupils' own achievement in literacy and areas for further development.

It can be seen from the range of topics covered that the discussion between teacher and pupils was searching. It emerged very clearly that the children were able to articulate their practices in reading and to identify aspects of the relationship between reading and writing. This was not only with reference to a small sample of reading matter, but across a wide range of texts and genres. The teacher was enabled an insight into the social practices of reading in her classroom and factors influencing the pattern of children's reading.

Children most frequently referred to the visual/graphic dimensions of a book as being the most influential in their choice of a text by an unknown author. Furthermore, their appraisal of the graphic aspects of texts was not superficial: sophisticated observations were made of the relationship between the written and the visual text, as the following extract from a conversation about a book by Sheila Lavelle shows:

> The illustrations are good too ... she doesn't just put things in straight ... she puts things in the background ... he *looks* sly (pointing to picture of boy and written text together).

Connections were made between the children's own writing and the books which they had read with a conscious focus upon the constructedness of written text:

> I'm interested in the way they end books. A lot of stories end with something like 'they lived happily ever after' ... I don't like that ... you have to have something to think about ... with a good ending you can keep people hanging on ... and maybe write a sequel.

Children's familiarity with inter-textual reference was shown in drawing upon their own and other children's experience of texts to inform understanding of the ways in which books work. They made comparisons between ways in which stories were narrated by different authors, drawing distinctions between the order of events and the ways in which these are disclosed - Genette's (1980) concepts of histoire and recit. This has already been identified in relation to younger children's understanding of narrative structure (Poulson, 1991), but in the instances of older children outlined in this study, there was an explicitly articulated understanding. There was, in fact, a network of information in this particular class about books and reading; which of the children's own books were being circulated; who had read which books; which were the currently popular texts; where to go for advice on choice of book; whose recommendation and opinions counted.

The teacher-pupil conferences on children's writing generated evidence of an equally sophisticated awareness of text construction. One in which the two dimensions of writing identified as secretarial and compositional in the National Curriculum English document (HMSO, 1989) were interwoven. The National Curriculum for English allocates a much greater weighting to the compositional aspects of writing, but much research evidence (e.g. Britton et al. 1976; Kress 1982; Bennett, Desforges et al. 1984) has revealed the limited extent to which children are taught, and presumably, assessed in this aspect of writing. Most attention tends to be paid to the surface, orthographic features of children's writing, in spite of the rhetoric about current practice. In observing teacher-pupil conferences, we found examples of both aspects being interwoven in written text construction.

The assessments made by the teacher in this instance included the contribution that orthographic features of writing made to the composition of a text. For example, how the inclusion of commas to mark off main and subordinate clauses would contribute to overall coherence. Additionally, how the use of quotation marks and other conventions for distinguishing between direct speech and reportage actually signalled and marked out category boundaries and discourse shifts within a text. In one instance, the teacher showed the child an example of this from a familiar book, requiring the pupil to shift her perspective from that of writer to that of reader of her own text.

The need for cohesive devices within written text and how inconsistency, or a lack of cohesive signalling might make reading difficult, was explained in several of the writing conferences. One such example was in the use of the conjunction 'but', normally used to indicate contrast or concession between propositions, but in this case used to indicate a relationship of reason-result and, therefore, confusing to a reader. Another example was when the conjunction 'but' had been omitted and, therefore, the relationship of concession between two propositions was unclear. When this was pointed out, the pupil remarked that: '... the 'but' takes it back ... in the story.'

The instances described above indicate that the teachers were concerned with more than the ability to decode print, or to construct neat and correctly spelled examples of written text. Each, in different ways, was attempting to encourage children to solve problems in literacy. They were not only concerned with the child's mastery of particular aspects of reading or writing, but also with the identification of patterns and relationships within written texts. Thus, evidence of achievement or progress might include mastery of a particular aspect of reading or writing, or equally, might be the beginning of a child's recognition of the necessity of particular features of text organisation in the construction of meaning.

Conclusion

It is clear that the teachers in this study made judgements about and provided feedback on a wide range of literacy events. Even so, these interactions may not have been viewed explicitly as assessment. No pre-devised assessment instrument was used, but evidence of pupil achievement was being gathered. Not only was evidence being gathered of pupil achievement at a particular moment in time, but also the teachers were often aware of what pupils might achieve in the future.

We had started the research with an implicit hypothesis: that specific examples of assessment by teachers would be detectable from observation. The hypothesis was only partly supported and further questions were raised, these included: how these particular instances of teachers' practice in providing feedback to children on literacy events might be recognised more clearly, by the teachers themselves, as contributing to formative assessment. Equally, how teachers might be encouraged to identify and articulate their own, often implicit, assessment systems and to relate these to other, less individual and idiosyncratic models of assessment. Furthermore, the question was raised of how the evidence of children's achievement generated in the classroom might be validated and, where necessary, be made reliable. If, as Desforges (1992) suggests, the key question in establishing the validity of assessment is the extent to which a particular procedure or system promotes quality learning, then that must be the dominant criterion by which to judge the evidence presented in these examples. It is a critical question, but one which is seldom asked when the focus of assessment becomes the reliability of results found in large samples of children engaged in a limited range of literacy events.

For literacy to be understood as a complex activity, then it is necessary to understand the range of literate practices with which children are familiar. It is clearly not enough to focus upon the teaching and learning of grapho-phonemic or, for that matter, graphomorphemic features of written text nor upon the syntactic structure of small segments of text. This is not the sum total of literacy, nor should it be represented as such, but there is, however, a danger of it coming to be the sum total of literacy *assessed*. In identifying, if not defining, quality learning in literacy, it is necessary to return to the importance of representing not a narrow conception of literate competence, but one appropriate to the complex demands of the late twentieth century. One which fully acknowledges the cognitive demands of reading and writing as inter-related dimensions of the same cultural process.

References

Alexander, R, Rose, J and Woodhead, C (1992) *Curriculum Organisation and Classroom Practice in Primary Schools.* DES: London.

Barrs, M, Ellis, S and Thomas, A (1988) *The Primary Language Record.* ILEA/CLPE: London.

Bennett, S N, Desforges, C et al (1984) *The Quality of Pupil Learning.* Lawrence Erlbaum Associates: London.

Britton, J et al (1975) *The Development of Writing Abilities 11-18.* Macmillan: London.

Desforges, C (1992) 'Assessment and Learning.' In *Forum,* Vol. 34, No. 4.

Dombey, H (1991) 'Testing time for infant reading'. In Wray, D (ed.) *Standards in Reading.* Perspectives 44. University of Exeter School of Education: Exeter.

Donaldson, M (1978) Children's Minds. Fontana: London.

Genette, J (1980) Narrative Discourse (trans. J. Lewin). Blackwell: Oxford.

Her Majesty's Inspectorate (1990) *The Teaching and Learning of Reading in Primary Schools.* DES: London.

Kress, G (1982) *Learning to Write.* Routledge & Kegan Paul: London.

NFER (1991) *An Inquiry into LEA Evidence on Standards of Reading of Seven Year-Old Children.* NFER: London.

Poulson, L (1991) 'Narrative in the infant classroom.' In *English in Education,* Vol. 25, No. 1.

SEAC (1989) *A Guide to Teacher Assessment: Pack C.* SEAC: London.

14 - Accessing the curriculum: How well do they need to read?

CHRIS SAWYER, VAL POTTER and TRISH TAYLOR

The vast majority of what we expect children to read in school should be readable by the vast majority. If not, we are in danger of artificially creating an increased number of pupils who are seen as having special needs in the area of reading skills and so adding fuel to the debate concerning deterioration of reading standards. Teachers have less time than ever to evaluate the books they expect pupils to use in class and, in any case, the National Curriculum limits their choice. It is therefore important to know the range of reading material used and how good a reader a pupil needs to be to access this material unaided.

With the advent of the National Curriculum, much has been made of each pupil's right to have full access to all the subjects the curriculum contains at the appropriate levels. If pupils are unable to read at an adequate level, however, their ability to access the curriculum is likely to be severely impaired. This becomes increasingly important as pupils progress through the school system, as the delivery of the curriculum relies more and more on pupils being able to read text books, work sheets and resource materials.

It is important, therefore, to identify those pupils whose reading ability is insufficient for them to have adequate access to the curriculum and to ensure that their needs are met through differentiation and remediation. Class teachers in the primary sector will be aware of some of these children but there may be other pupils who seek the help of fellow pupils and thus hide their problems. What is really required is knowledge of the range of text material used in schools at various ages and some way of quantifying the level of difficulty. This information, together with the reading age necessary to read the material concerned, would enable objective identification of pupils needing help and may highlight curriculum areas where the reading level of the material used is too high.

Several formulas for grading text material exist. Known as readability formulas, they are based on the average sentence length, number of syllables in a 100-word sample or, in some cases, the number of words not found in a list of 'easy' words. The result is usually a readability age level indicating that the text would be suitable for pupils of that age. As it would be too time-consuming to apply the procedure to a whole book, several samples of 100 words are selected and the results are averaged, then transformed into a readability age level. This includes the ability to understand what is read as well as reading it accurately in the first place and so does not seem to correspond too well with the reading ages of pupils. These usually measure how accurately the pupil can read, with comprehension being given as a separate age score by a few of the tests.

Some surveys of textual material in schools have been attempted but these few studies are somewhat limited in the range sampled and do not attempt to find the equivalent reading age based on pupil reading tests. Harrison (1980), for example, using the Flesch formula, surveyed 53 passages of text material used with year 7 to obtain an average readability level of 12.73 years and 71 passages of year 10 text material to obtain an average readability level of 13.6 years. These show a very small increase in difficulty level between the two and a dubiously high readability age level for year 7.

One study has attempted both to survey textual material and to find the reading age on a pupil reading test which would be necessary to enable pupils to be able to read the majority of text material surveyed. Sawyer, Ferguson, Hayward and Cunningham (1991) used the Fry readability formula to survey GCSE examination papers. They found that the highest average sample, a level which included about 90 per cent of the text material used, was at the 13 year, 10 month level and that examination candidates with a Neale revised accuracy reading age of 9 years, 10 months were expected to be able to read the examination questions.

Sawyer et al. have therefore shown that it is possible to equate text readability level with a pupil's reading age from a particular test. The study reported below sought to build on that work, extensively sampling the textual material found in schools from year 2 to year 10 and finding the equivalent reading ages necessary for pupils to access this textual element of the curriculum.

Sampling the text materials in schools

The survey of text materials read by pupils in schools covered all areas of the curriculum. The sampling was limited to alternate years - that is, years 2, 4, 6, 8 and 10. Over 80,000 words were sampled, on as near a random basis as possible, in 100 word blocks of text. Six schools were used for each year and, although all were in the same authority, they were chosen to give a mix of large, small, rural and urban schools.

In each case, teachers were asked what pupils in the year in question were being asked to read and several children were questioned as to what they had read recently. Textbooks, workcards and worksheets were sampled, but text presented on computer screens and blackboards was not. Where a reading scheme was being used, a number of books were sampled from the middle of the range in use by the children. Resource material was included if at least one of the children questioned had been using it. A particular problem became apparent with year 2. Teachers were aware of the difficulties which some of the text material imposed on these 6- and 7-year-old children. They therefore tended to preread aloud or explain instructional or informative text before children read and used it themselves. The decision was made to include such material in the sample as it would not have been possible to ensure such material had been fairly excluded or to judge how effective this prereading approach was in giving access.

With so many blocks of text to analyse, a fast, computerised method of calculating the Fry readability level was used as described in Sawyer and Knight (1991). This had the additional advantage of allowing comparison with the work undertaken by Sawyer et al. (1991) in establishing reading levels for GCSE examination papers. The Fry formula is based on the number of syllables and number of sentences in a 100-word block of consecutive text material and gives readability age levels from 6 years to 22 years.

As can be seen from figure 14.1, the 'All areas' means for years 2, 4 and 6 are above the chronological ages of at least some pupils in the year. Whilst this may cause concern, a more worrying piece of information is that some samples of text were dramatically higher. The highest 100-word sample for each year was identified and the readability level was, on average, found to be 6.75 years higher than the age of the pupils expected to read it.

When the means are broken down into curriculum areas as in figure 14.1, then a pattern of difficult text, particularly in the humanities, emerges. Science and other categories are, however, not much lower overall. The 'Other' category included subjects such as music, PSE or health education, economics and drama. No text in this category was found to be in use with the year 2 groups of pupils whose reading material was sampled. Note was made at the time of the survey that the majority of the most difficult texts was found in the resource material arising out of the demands of the National Curriculum, particularly in the humanities. Such material is often an article or similar passage extracted from a reading source intended for adults. It is important, therefore, that schools should be aware of this problem and take steps to make access to this material easier.

Figure 14.2 shows a sample of text taken from a book found to be widely used by year 4 pupils as resource material. The sample was chosen as it illustrates text with an inappropriately high readability level. The series of books it was taken from varies in readability between about 12 and 16 years, though the readability age level of the sample in figure 14.1 is well in advance of this. Some teachers appeared to be aware of the difficulty and were using the series of books for illustration only or pointing the children to certain parts of the text. Other teachers, however, gave no such instructions.

Archaeological evidence from the Athenian dockyard at Piraeus shows that triremes were about 41 metres long and 6 metres wide. Experts think that in good sea conditions they could reach speeds of around 16 kilometres per hour over short distances.

Figure 14.2 - Extract from an illustrated world history used with Year 4 pupils. The reading level is well in advance of 16 years.

	Year 2	Year 4	Year 6	Year 8	Year 10
Maths	6.52	7.78	8.12	9.38	10.79
English	6.67	8.84	9.91	10.71	10.96
Science	7.54	9.07	11.85	11.09	12.75
Humanities	7.45	10.87	11.86	11.69	13.67
Other	-	8.95	10.33	12.47	12.47
All areas	6.90	9.15	10.20	11.13	12.38

Figure 14.1 - Mean Fry readability age levels for samples of text in curriculum areas.

Producing Fry test sentences

Sawyer et al. (1991) produced passages of about 100 words from the text of the examination question papers themselves. Text was chosen to give a predetermined readability age level. About 90 per cent of all their samples from question papers were below or at this level. Pupils were then given a passage-reading test as well as two of the 100-word text samples. A similar procedure was adopted in the present study. For each of the 5 years the text samples were ranked on the basis of the readability age level. The age level at or below which 90 per cent (90th centile) of the text samples fell was then identified. These age levels were 8.80, 11.95, 13.50, 13.75 and 15.75 for school years 2, 4, 6, 8 and 10 respectively.

The results caused some concern. In year 4, the youngest pupil would be just 8 years of age on 1 September. The 90th centile age level was almost 4 years above that. By comparison, the 90th centile age level was only 1 year, 9 months above the youngest pupils in years 8 and 10. In addition, the 90th centiles for years 6 and 8 showed an increase in readability age level of 3 months only. In the interests of even progression across the years, a decision was made to use the 90th centile age level or the age level 2 years above the chronological age of the youngest child in the year, whichever was the lower. Opting for even progression across the years allowed a table of equivalent ages to be produced more reliably (see figure 14.4). The age levels used still covered at least two thirds of the text material sampled: 83rd, 66th and 76th centile for years 2, 4 and 6 respectively with years 8 and 10 remaining at the 90th centile.

Three English and three science text samples of about 100 words each were produced for each year at the relevant Fry readability age level (8.00, 10.00, 12.00, 13.75 and 15.75 for years 2, 4, 6, 8 and 10 respectively). Five complete sentences were selected from the text material found in schools, each sentence having the appropriate age readability level. They were photocopied to retain the original print size and type, and were arranged to form a block of text, similar in format to a sentence-reading test. English and science were used because they were the core subjects from the National Curriculum with the most text available to construct these Fry test sentences.

Method: Equating reading ages to readability age levels

A passage, a sentence and a word reading test were used to see how well each equated with the Fry test sentences. These were the revised Neale Analysis of Reading Ability (Neale, 1988), The Salford Sentence Reading Test (Bookbinder, 1976) and the British Ability Scales Word Reading Test (BASWRT; Elliot, Murray and Pearson, 1978). Only the reading accuracy test from Neale was given because of time constraints and comparability with the other two tests. Pupils of each age group were asked to read aloud one English and one science set of Fry test sentences, chosen at random from the three sets available for each subject. The pupils were judged as being able to read the text adequately if no mistake was made which critically affected the meaning. Pupils who read one passage successfully but failed the other were counted as being at the threshold of that reading level. Such pupil were then given the three reading tests.

Schools were asked for their weaker readers in the years from which the Fry test sentences had been drawn. In all, 459 pupils were screened on the Fry test sentences. Screening continued until at least 30 pupils were found at the threshold level for each year group, able to read one passage but not the other. In the total sample of 157 given the full battery of tests, 82 were boys and 75 girls.

Results

The mean and median reading ages for the group of pupils at the threshold level, determined by the use of the Fry test sentences, are given in figure 14.3. The ceiling effect is shown quite clearly in the Salford results, results for years 8 and 10 being considerably depressed by the maximum age score of 10 years, 6 months. The Neale ceiling of 13 years may have had a depressing effect on the year 10 result but the test does discriminate beyond 13 years in terms of raw scores. Taking this into account, together with the fact that the result fits well with the overall pattern of results, it is likely to represent a reasonably accurate average reading age for the group.

Taking the 90th centile readability age level, or 2 years above the chronological age of the youngest pupil in the year, gave a reasonably even spread of five age levels used. The gap between the age levels used then approximated the gap between the chronological ages for pupils in the years concerned. This spread allowed scattergrams to be produced to illustrate the relationship between each of the reading tests and the Fry test sentences. Age scores were used in all cases. The scattergram for the Salford, and to a lesser extent for the Neale, showed a flattening of the distribution at the ceiling of the test. Curved lines were then drawn on the scattergrams, estimating the line of best fit, as this was considered to be more accurate then using linear regression equations. These lines were used to produce the reading test equivalent scores for a range of Fry readability age levels given in figure 14.4.

	Year 2	Year 4	Year 6	Year 8	Year 10
BASWRT	7:2 (7:2)*	8:6 (8:6)	9:1 (9:6)	11:12 (11:4)	12:9 (12:9)
Salford	7:6 (7:5)	8:9 (8:9)	9:6 (9:6)	10:1 (10:3)	10:5 (10:6)**
Neale (Accuracy)	6:9 (6:8)	8:2 (8:2)	9:7 (9:5)	10:11 (11:0)	12:9 (13:0)**

* Figures in parentheses indicate median reading ages.
** Effective test maximum score.

Figure 14.3 - Mean reading ages for groups at the threshold levels.

As can be seen from figure 14.4, producing equivalent age scores between the Fry ages and the three reading tests implies what the equivalent age scores would be between the three reading tests themselves. The three scattergrams and lines of best fit were therefore also drawn to show the relationship between the Neale, Salford and BASWRT to check on the accuracy of these implied equivalent age scores. No evidence was found to suggest any adjustment should be made to the implied equivalent age scores. Although all six scattergrams appeared to indicate that all four sets of age scores were strongly related, the correlations between them were also calculated and are given in figure 14.5.

Fry	BASWRT	Neale	Salford
16.00	12.10	13.00	10.06
15.09	12.08	12.11	10.06
15.06	12.06	12.09	10.06
15.03	12.04	12.05	10.06
15.00	12.01	12.02	10.06
14.09	11.11	11.11	10.05
14.06	11.09	11.08	10.05
14.03	11.07	11.05	10.05
14.00	11.05	11.02	10.04
13.09	11.03	11.00	10.03
13.06	11.00	10.09	10.02
13.03	10.10	10.07	10.01
13.00	10.08	10.04	10.00
12.09	10.06	10.02	9.11
12.06	10.04	10.00	9.10
12.03	10.02	9.09	9.09
12.00	9.11	9.07	9.08
11.09	9.09	9.05	9.06
11.06	9.07	9.03	9.05
11.03	9.05	9.01	9.04
11.00	9.03	8.11	9.02
10.09	9.01	8.08	9.01
10.06	8.11	8.06	9.00
10.03	8.08	8.04	8.10
10.00	8.06	8.02	8.09
9.09	8.04	7.11	8.07
9.06	8.02	7.09	8.06
9.03	8.00	7.07	8.04
9.00	7.10	7.05	8.02
8.09	7.07	7.02	8.00
8.06	7.05	7.00	7.09
8.03	7.03	6.10	7.07
8.00	7.01	6.07	7.04

Figure 14.4 - Equivalent reading test ages for Fry readability age levels (years, months).

Discussion

Correlations between any adequate measures of reading accuracy are normally high as the validity and reliability of such measures are particularly good when compared with those of other assessment instruments. As the Fry test sentences, reflecting the Fry formula age levels, are not designed as a reading accuracy test for pupils, the correlations between that measure and the three reading tests are remarkably strong. This suggests that predicting the reading age that a pupil will need in order to read a particular piece of text material, from figure 14.4, may be undertaken with some confidence if its Fry readability age level is first obtained. As mentioned above, the Fry readability formula is likely to contain an element of reading comprehension as well as reading accuracy. Neale (1988), comparing comprehension on one test form with accuracy on another, obtained correlations of .88 and .87. It is not so surprising, therefore, that a combined measure of reading accuracy and comprehension (Fry) correlates so well with reading accuracy measures.

The equivalent reading age scores detailed in figure 14.4 seem to be in conflict with the results obtained by Sawyer et al. (1991). They equated a Fry readability age level of 13 years, 10 months with a

	Fry	BASWRT	Salford
Neale	.94	.96	.93
Salford	.92	.90	—
BASWRT	.90	—	—

d.f. = 155

Figure 14.5 - Correlations between the measures of reading ability used.

Neale Revised reading accuracy age of 9 years, 10 months, some 14 months lower than the Neale equivalent given in figure 14.4. Text for GCSE examination papers is subject to simplification techniques to try and enhance readability. The effect of this sort of alteration is reported in Hartley, Williams and Trueman (1980). They found that such simplification (reducing the Flesch readability level for a text passage by 3 1/2 years) had no direct effect but interacted with pupils' ability in measures of comprehension and memory of what had been read. Adapting the language of a subset of text material and expecting that it will relate to another measure in the same way seems analogous to genetically altering a subgroup of the population and then expecting them to perform on standardised tests in the same way as the rest of the population.

A note of caution should be sounded from the above, however. Textual material which has been systematically changed may well have different reading test ages equating to its readability level than those given in figure 14.4. The wide sampling of school-based text material (over 800 samples of 100 words each were used) suggests that the reading test ages equating to the readability age levels given above are likely to be reliable for material which has not been artificially adapted on the basis of sentence length, grammatical structure or replacing difficult or long words.

Because of the difficulty of the range of text, the 2 years above chronological age cut-off point was used for years 2, 4 and 6. In the case of year 4, if the 90th centile level had been used instead, then figure 14.4 indicates that a BASWRT reading age of 11 years, 11 months would be needed to read such material. Based on an average chronological age for that year, only 15 per cent of the year would be able to access the reading material used in the curriculum. So what is a reasonable level to take? The 90th centile age level for year 2 is only 9 months higher than the age level used. This is despite the teachers recognising that they need to undertake pre-reading of material with the pupils in many cases. Years 2, 8 and 10 appear therefore to have some consistency, all within 12 months of the 2 years above the chronological age mark. It is years 4 and 6 which appear out of line. The 'age levels used' (10.00 and 12.00 years) do therefore seem to have some reasonable validity provided that teachers are aware that there is a higher incidence of difficult-to-read material in years 4 and 6.

Having proposed the reading age levels necessary to enable adequate access to the textual part of the curriculum, certain implications would seem to follow. As pupils at or above the threshold reading age levels shown in figure 14.3 are deemed to be able to read adequately, this implies that pupils with lower reading ages will not be able to read what is required. Some pupils just below the threshold level, however, may not be found to have a significant problem and the majority falling in a range immediately below the threshold may only need some support in the form of differentiation, or perhaps just help with the occasional word. Those whose reading ages fall some way below the threshold are likely to need more intensive support, varying in degree according to individual needs. Thus the threshold levels should be seen in terms of guidelines indicating groups of children educationally at risk, rather than rigid criteria to be applied on an all-or-nothing basis.

Who is to blame, then, for the unacceptably high level of some of the reading material in schools, especially in years 4 and 6? The National Curriculum, in so far as it restricts the choice that teachers can make, may be partly responsible but, as more published material comes onto the market, teachers must make choices based, in part, on readability levels. Publishers could help considerably by publishing the readability levels of what they produce. Ultimately, however, it is the class teacher who must choose what to use, what preparation to make for difficult material and how to differentiate it appropriately.

With only an estimated 15 per cent of pupils in year 4 able to read the range of material found to be in use in that year, it may be that the difficulty of the reading material in schools is adding to the number of pupils who are identified as having problems with reading. Once they have graduated from a graded reading scheme, and sometimes even when they have not, pupils will not make progress if they are presented with reading tasks which are too hard for them. Such experiences of failure will not only stunt progress in reading ability but may in some cases lead to disenchantment with the reading process itself. Such a situation may well be responsible, at least in part, for the much-debated apparent decline in standards of literacy.

Conclusions

In all the years surveyed a significant amount of reading material was found to be too difficult for the vast majority of pupils in that year.

Humanities and science were found to have the highest levels of readability, particularly in years 2, 4 and 6 (see figure 14.1).

Children need to read to a level approximately commensurate with their chronological age if they are not to experience difficulty with the text material they are expected to read (see figure 14.3). In years 4-6 , this will only be true for the majority of textual material (66-76 per cent) rather than the vast majority as for years 2, 8 and 10 (83-90 per cent).

At least one readability measure relates well to standardised reading tests and can be used with some confidence if equivalent ages are known (see figure 14.4).

The difficulty of the reading material in schools may be a factor causing the apparent decline in standards of literacy and increasing the number of pupils identified as having special needs.

While teachers must take some responsibility for what they expect children to read, both the National Curriculum (which has restricted choice) and the lack of information from publishers on the readability levels of books have hampered teachers trying to fulfil this responsibility.

References

Bookbinder, G E (1976) *The Salford Sentence Reading Test.* Hodder and Stoughton: Sevenoaks.

Elliott, C, Murray, D J and Pearson, L (1978) *The British Ability Scales.* NFER: Windsor.

Harrison, C (1980) *Readability in the Classroom.* Cambridge University Press: Cambridge.

Hartley, J, Williams, C and Trueman, M (1980) Choosing textbooks: The readability factor. *Head Teachers Review,* April, 2-4.

Neale, M D (1988) *The Neale Analysis of Reading Ability.* NFER-Nelson: Windsor.

Sawyer, C, Ferguson, I, Hayward, M and Cunningham, L (1991) On reading and the GCSE. *The Psychologist,* 4, 221-2.

Sawyer, C and Knight, E (1991) A fast method for calculating text readability levels. *Support for Learning,* 6 (2), 90.

(First published in *Support for Learning,* Vol. 9, No. 3, 1994.)

15 - Closing the gap: Compensating for literacy delay in children with specific learning difficulties/dyslexia

CYRIL HELLIER

It is a fundamental paradox that the poor or delayed reader is doubly disadvantaged by both his (the literature suggests that it is far more likely to be a boy) inferior literacy skills and the compounding factor of cumulative lack of experience of reading as a meaningful and rewarding activity.

It is my contention that, in contrast, the majority of skilled and unhindered readers spend considerable periods of time applying, practising and developing their skills in their own time and outside of school settings. The poor reader lacks the skills and, often, the confidence to spend time in unrewarding activity and so the *experience gap* develops. This is particularly the case for the child with specific learning difficulties/dyslexia. The literature on this group makes for confusing reading, given the differences in definition; incidence is dependent on differing parental, professional discipline, legal and political opinion. It is probably safe to conclude that the children experiencing severe literacy and other associated learning difficulties comprise 1-4 per cent of the pupil population. The literature suggests that many pupils with literacy difficulties remain unidentified.

My own view is that the question often asked by the practitioner, as to whom exactly we are talking about, can only be answered in functional terms, using a full description of the child's history and his strengths and weaknesses. Given that the practitioner's primary goal is to teach as effectively as possible according to the individual's needs, then the debate concerning definitions and labels can appear to be rather sterile at the coal face. In their wide-ranging inquiry into specific learning difficulties/dyslexia, Pumfrey and Reason (1991) provide backing for such a view:

> It is now better appreciated that studies using chronological age or mental age matched controls, as opposed to reading age matched controls are confounded by intractable 'chicken and egg' problems of interpretation concerning causality. Proposed symptoms and deficits could just as likely be a consequence of reading experience as a cause of reading difficulty.

Whatever the criteria applied in distinguishing those with specific learning difficulties from 'backward readers', it is most likely the case that all groups of poor or delayed readers share a lack of adequate and positive reading experience. The literature on teaching dyslexia tends to focus on cumulative multisensory programmes which aim to minimise the risk of failure, through a step-by-step approach. Such painstaking strategies (Lewis and Fowell-Jones, 1993) are designed to ensure that learning occurs successfully, albeit slowly.

One other factor is worth highlighting; namely, the predisposition of researchers to focus on reading age as the dependent variable. This reflects, to some extent, the preoccupation of those concerned with mainstream curriculum with particular subskills. In contrast, the global language approach, characterised by Marie Clay and commonplace in New Zealand and Australia, evidences a different focus on the wider concept of literacy. Current focus in the southern hemisphere is consequently on teaching methodologies which should help the vast majority of, it not all, potential readers. As a practising psychologist in South Australia in 1992, I was struck by the absence of usage of the term 'dyslexia'. Reading Recovery is an extension of mainstream teaching; it is the central plank of support delivered as early intervention to all unsuccessful children at the end of one year, and it is not focused upon any particular subgroup Further, it aims to teach individual children, concurrently, global understanding of the purposes of literacy as well as specific skills in reading, writing and spelling. I believe that the focus in the UK on mechanical reading skill, to the exclusion of wider pragmatic understanding of a child's situation, is at the very least ineffective and likely to lead to a less-supportive response from teachers and parents - although the child has particular difficulty in dealing with the mechanical aspects of decoding, it is important not to overstress this to the exclusion of focus on the reader's wider understandings and use of text.

As a practitioner working for 17 years, I have frequently received referrals of pupils experiencing specific learning difficulties. Children identified in this situation tend to share various similar attributes, including:

- varying degrees of *insight into their difficulties* such that they can talk about them; the intellectually more able child usually develops a greater degree of self-awareness earlier on;

- the growth of *defensive strategies* to protect themselves against the gradual awareness that they do have a problem;

- the expression of *frustration* often in an indirect manner; initially this is most apparent at home in the presence of family members, with whom they are less guarded and towards whom they are more inclined to express feelings.

Much remains to be written about the affective response to specific learning difficulties, as Biggar and Barr (1993) suggest in their plea for 'differentiation of the interpersonal to match differentiation of the curriculum'.

If genuine learning difficulties are left unrecognised and there is a lack in support to deal with them, secondary problems often arise, usually of a social nature. Peers may be unsympathetic, parents may exert undue pressure, and teachers may perceive their difficulties in inappropriate terms; these include explanatory hypotheses such as 'unrealistic' or 'overprotective' parents, 'lazy' or 'low potential' pupils. Interacting variables which affect the response of the child to his situation include:

- the age at which difficulties have been recognised and responded to,

- the degree of sympathy and understanding the child has experienced in coming to terms with his learning difficulties,

- the degree of parental support, as opposed to pressure,

- the teacher's attitude and response in terms of modified curriculum,

- peer responses and

- the child's developing self-image.

Presenting features

Following on from the variables outlined above, various presenting features may arise when pupils with specific learning difficulties are referred.

Significant literacy (and sometimes maths) skills gaps

Evidence for these gaps may be present, with no other obvious causal factor such as a sensory/medical impairment or a troubled home situation. One does have to be wary, as other contributory factors may co-exist and be viewed as the sole ones!

A discrepant skill profile

The student may appear to have adequate or good skills in areas including oral discussion, reasoning and artwork. When further assessed, he may reveal an uneven profile with a significantly depressed reading age and a relatively superior comprehension age - many referred pupils who struggle with analytic and phonological aspects of text still manage to extract a superior degree of meaning. Pupils scoring reading ages of between 6 and 7 years invariably display superior reading comprehension ages, by 6-24 months.

Bakker (1992) hypothesises two distinct groups of dyslexia, 'L' and 'R', mediated by left and right cerebral hemispheres respectively. My clinical experience is consistent with this view; pupils in the hypothesised L group may appear to read rather impulsively and to be desperately in search of meaning, making guesses based on approximations of the superficial aspects of each word. They *are* able to extract some meaning from context, utilising metacognitive strategies, but are held back from good performance by poor word recognition and word-attack skills. This inevitably also results in delayed spelling, with pupils lacking adequate phonic structures and decoding skills to differing degrees. In contrast, in the R group, children may read laboriously slowly using analytic strategies, decoding with the phonic knowledge which they have struggled to acquire; meaning is usually lost as a result of the processing demands of decoding. Spelling skills remain poorly developed. What distinguishes the two groups is the differing facility to use left-brain processes, to extract meaning over and above the right-brain ones which focus on letter and sound recognition.

A presentation where the child is cast as lazy or lacking in motivation

This is especially the case for the older pupil of the third year of schooling onwards.

Adjustment difficulties

These often figure at home initially; the school may or may not be aware of them. Some referrals are parent initiated against the wishes of the school, who may be unsympathetic. If they are present at school, adjustment difficulties can reflect the full range of diversionary and avoidance strategies, from withdrawal to active disruption. Over time, social problems may develop at school and these may be the first signs which alert teaching staff to make referral to outside agencies. At the earliest, these appear by the second year of school and may include word avoidance in specific tasks and/or minor social difficulties. In the most extreme cases, late referral of disaffected secondary pupils is the first indication to outside agencies. Referrals are on occasion made in the wake of a prolonged sequence of behaviour-management practices. When reading a pupil's school file, in such cases, a focus on learning issues, initially raised by relatively sympathetic class teachers, has often been displaced over time by focus on social and behavioural matters.

Implications for intervention

In aiming to close the gap as far as possible, my predisposition is towards a focus on functional aspects of a child's performance in areas of difficulty. Close scrutiny of strengths and weaknesses in the actual areas of skill application provide the best assessment, allowing intervention to follow directly on. Kemp (1987) typifies this approach. The typical scenario includes the situation where the child's functional literacy skills are matched by stage-appropriate material. This can result in an increasing gap developing between these and his interests and oral understandings. The challenge is to help provide experience as early as possible, to offset the cumulative losses which otherwise accrue. These may include lowered self-esteem, lack of general knowledge and failure to make adequate progress in the wider curriculum.

To minimise such effects, the student needs *early identification,* ideally by the second year at school. Although the literature is unable to define predictive measures to anticipate failure, it is the case that once difficulties are visible the experience of failure should be minimised for all children at risk. The need is for all involved to be aware; Pumfrey and Reason (1991) recommend that: 'Educational psychologists and teachers continue to develop skills and methods to effect early identification of children who are at risk of poor literacy development'. Clearly, mainstream staff need to receive in-service training, to make them more aware of these issues, and to help them to be more effective in identifying such pupils. Such support has been patchy to date (see, for example, Hellier, Kaye and Barron, 1991).

The student also needs *supported reading experiences* of preferred material, using a range of reading material consistent with the child's age and interests.

- Graded texts, although unfashionable in some schools of thought, do provide the opportunity to the student to experience relative success as an 'independent' reader. Pupils identified early on (by their second year at school) benefit from personalised 'organic' texts based around their world knowledge and language; these can include personalised reading material using photos of the pupil, familiar people, family, teaching staff and class peers, and familiar places and events. The tendency of teachers to structure and to limit experiences which may be perceived to be too difficult for the poor reader can result in very restricted experiences, especially if they are the main or the only intervention. Teaching only high-frequency words, for example, which tend to lack inherent meaning, fails to capitalise on a child's knowledge of the familiar and the idiosyncratic; such factors may help a pupil to maximise his learning.

- Graded and reduced-demand texts do not, however, provide adequate interest and information to older pupils and so it is essential to have regular experience of age-appropriate and interest-feeding material chosen by the pupil. The skill of actually choosing will not develop unless opportunities are made available to permit this to occur. Paired reading offers a stress-free and highly effective, research-validated methodology to provide supported reading experience which fulfils many of these needs. This well-documented technique, widely reported in the UK, was totally lacking in practice in South Australian schools - the bones of the technique called 'neurological impress' were in the literature (Kemp, 1987), but were not seen in the way I am outlining in this paper.

Supported reading experience needs to be made available daily; a range of different people might be able to provide it. Peers, either age equivalent or cross age, could be organised at school on a timetabled basis (see Thompson 1992, for example); if times are set aside for silent reading, then these would provide ideal opportunities. Settings could include reading centres in classrooms or resource libraries. The research evidence is clear that both tutors and tutees gain from such organised experiences (Topping and Lindsay, 1992). Tutors would need some training in these circumstances. Voluntary parental help could also be utilised, a further step being the training of parents themselves as part of a parental involvement programme.

The student with learning difficulties also needs *supported writing experiences,* which should be provided regularly, with the same aims - namely, to permit the pupil to experience personal written language at a level consistent with his age and abilities, rather than his skill level. Obviously, the child's age will determine the results expected of him, ranging from early literacy work in an infant department to examination performance in secondary education and beyond. Copying skills are usually relatively unimpaired (it may be a slow process), and are depended on by pupil and teacher. However, I am arguing for additional support, which may include the following elements.

- Paired writing - developing the theme so commonly associated with reading, an adult or peer can provide the role of scribe to ensure that the pupil's ideas are put down relatively quickly and spelt correctly.

- Use a tape recorder - through experience, a pupil can learn to express himself on audiotape, the results being subsequently written up by a third party (parental help could be enlisted on occasion). It would be possible in some situations for the pupil to copy the written work in his own handwriting. The end result would be for the pupil to experience the satisfaction of having his ideas well written-up for display purposes, to show to others. A folder of all such examples (photocopied) could then allow for a cumulative record of positive writing experiences.

- Computer technology - there are numerous opportunities to utilise new technology for pupils with severe literacy difficulties; these facilities include the following.

  - The concept keyboard with personalised vocabulary overlays of the child's own world knowledge and language. This technology is particularly appropriate for the younger child or for the more delayed learner, given its limitations on vocabulary size (up to 128 words/phrases per overlay). In effect, it allows a pupil to write using only word-recognition and discrimination skills. Spelling skills are not required; the advantage is that the technology is widely available in most schools.

  - Predictive word processors. Although these were originally devised to help those with physical disabilities, by significantly reducing the number of key strokes, they are also a boon to those with spelling difficulties. In effect, they provide a far more sophisticated form of the support provided by concept keyboards and are an extension to the increasingly prevalent spell checkers. The writer selects a word from a list on screen which is generated by his own initiative, for example by keying the initial letter of a word. The sophistication arises in the software's reference to past experience by that writer and to syntax, in offering choices. The word can be copied or printed directly on screen in mid-sentence depending on the pupil's choice. Pal (Booth, 1991) is the most commonly quoted program of this type.

  - Audio feedback built into word processors is rapidly becoming commonplace. As a result, attempts to write using available spelling knowledge can be checked against the sound of what has been written ('I drink m*u*lk'). If it sounds incorrect when read back by the computer, further attempts can be made until it tallies with recognised pronunciation ('I drink m*i*lk'). The advantages arising to assist reading do not need elaboration.

Conclusion

It is important to recognise the need for a balanced programme of response to a pupil experiencing considerable frustration in the face of severe literacy difficulties. The above strategies go some way to offset such frustrations through the provision of compensatory experiences, and although they are relevant to any child who is underachieving or delayed in reading acquisition, they are particularly relevant to those with specific learning difficulties/dyslexia. Each child facing the challenge of such long-term difficulties needs a balance of tuition which tackles phonological/analytical strategies (there are exciting new developments on the horizon; Hellier, 1993), and global understandings through delivery of the ideas in this article.

References

Bakker, D J (1992) Neuropsychological classification and treatment of dyslexia. *Journal for Learning Difficulties,* 25 (2), 102-9.

Biggar, S and Barr, J (1993) The emotional world of specific learning difficulties. In G. Reid (ed.), *Specific Learning Difficulties (Dyslexia).* Moray House Publications: Edinburgh.

Booth, L (1991) Having a Pal in the classroom. *TASK Magazine,* Spring, 13-17.

Hellier, C (1993) Reading unscrambled. *Times Educational Supplement,* 3 September, p. 14.

Hellier, C, Kaye, P and Barron, I (1991) *Specific Learning Difficulties/Dyslexia.* Introduction and background literature for TEPS in-service training session to mainstream staff. Tayside Region: Perth, Scotland.

Kemp, M (1987) *Watching Children Read and Write.* Thomas Nelson: Sydney.

Lewis, G and Fowell-Jones, M (1993) Dealing with dyslexia. *Special Children.* June/July, no. 67, 20-8.

Pumfrey, P and Reason, R (1991) *Specific Learning Difficulties/Dyslexia: Challenges and responses.* NFER: Windsor.

Thompson, P (1992) Raising reading standards: The reader-leader scheme. *Support for Learning,* 7 (2), 74-7.

Topping, K and Lindsay, G (1992) Paired Reading: A review of the literature. *Research Papers in Education 7.*

(This article was first published in *Support for Learning,* Vol. 9, No. 4, 1994.)

16 - Specific learning difficulty (dyslexia) and interventions

MICHAEL CONNOR

A rapid scanning of the nature of the research literature will demonstrate that there is a considerable discrepancy between work relating to the aetiology and form of dyslexia, and evidence concerning interventions. The emphasis is markedly biased towards efforts to understand, explain or define the condition, with limited information about the effectiveness of remedial approaches, such that one might question the extent to which the sheer quantity of published material on dyslexia has any impact on classroom practice. It is self-evident that research into the cognitive processes underlying learning to read, or failing to learn to read, is not the same as research into reading teaching methodology.

Reason et al. (1988) refer to different levels of investigation: *the instructional level,* which is relevant to teachers and educational psychologists, and examines a child's abilities in relation to stages in learning to read (such as a reading accuracy score); *the psychological level,* which concerns the way in which underlying faculties linked to reading (such as visual memory) may be different in the case of learning difficulties; and the *physiological level,* which is concerned with the location of the processes in the brain. The net effect may be to label a child as having certain deficits which are not linked to any intervention.

The review of evidence compiled by Seymour (1986) demonstrates the wide range of difficulties and characteristics that could all be subsumed under the heading of 'dyslexia', thus confirming that different children may learn to read, or fail to learn to read, in a variety of ways. Further, the link between specific characteristics or weaknesses and literacy difficulties may be bidirectional. For example, appropriate left-right orientation or phonemic awareness may develop as a *result* of reading experience.

It may not be possible to pinpoint evidence in respect of the ways in which differences between individual characteristics of dyslexic children (or between those of dyslexic and control children) are mirrored by differences in response to particular teaching methods. The lack of opportunity for classroom-based research may be exacerbated by a kind of ethical concern over experimentation. As perceived by the present writer, there is a feeling that all children deserve a share of the best available provision, and there is therefore some reluctance to set up experimental programmes where matched groups are given differential treatment. It may also be suggested that dyslexia is multifactorial such that it may be inappropriate to seek a single intervention style. Any given child likely to meet any criteria for dyslexia represents a unique interaction of personal, familial and experimental features. Further, there is always the possibility that a given approach is successful because child, parents and teacher have confidence in it.

The common emphasis upon the need for enhanced structure (notably in respect of phonic skill development) may be based upon observations that the prognosis for children with specific learning difficulty is poorer than that which applies to children with more general literacy or learning difficulties, hence the development of the 'multisensory' approaches which commonly contain a phonic framework for reading and spelling of regular words, and visual, phonic and kinaesthetic strategies for dealing with irregular words.

As a further justification for specialist teaching methodology, Frith (1985) argues that it is the very fact that difficulties may persist over a long time-scale and are not amenable to conventional teaching methods that provide the means of differentiating the specific from the general learning difficulty. A programme in which phonic skills are emphasised, and targets can be reduced to a series of smaller steps linked to increased reinforcement, assists the process by which reading moves from a logographic stage to an alphabetic stage, and eventually to an orthographic stage - the child is moved on from a whole-word memory approach through a phonic synthesis approach, to fluent reading using all or any of a range of cues.

According to the review of studies by Brooks (1993), there is much evidence for the benefits of a well-structured programme and a high level of reinforcement applied to the completion of targets. However, a consistent problem is that the studies concerned do not compare this method of teaching with alternatives, nor do they investigate differences in responding among different individuals or groups varying in cognitive skills, weaknesses, or experience of previous teaching and learning styles. In practice, therefore, one may try a range of approaches, sticking with that which brings about observable progress, with limited awareness of why it is successful or of whether other methods would be equally or more effective.

Effectiveness of teaching strategies (Non-differentiated pupil groups)

This section relates to those studies which have examined the effectiveness of a given teaching approach, but which have *not* related the level of effectiveness to particular pupil need - to cope with a general learning difficulty, mild learning difficulty, or specific learning difficulty (dyslexia) - or examined whether other approaches would have been as successful. Research evidence does strongly support the emphasis upon letter-sound correspondence as a significant and early teaching objective. For example, Adams (1990) concluded that reading methods that include explicit teaching of phonic synthesis, including the 'fixing' of letter sounds, and sound blending, 'are associated with higher achievements in word recognition and spelling among 6 year olds; and early benefits of this kind may lead, among 7+ year olds, to higher levels of competence in comprehension and rate of reading'.

However, there is an evident risk that one may be providing a child with tasks and goals of a similar kind to those with which there has already been experience of failure. Thus, one may seek to ensure that intervention and remedial approaches provide access to alternative cues for identifying unfamiliar words, and to constant reinforcement via task analysis. For example, the DISTAR (Directed Instruction Materials, Science Research Associates) materials may be effective because of the emphasis upon phonetic decoding strategies and the insistence upon mastery of each task. However, in the research completed by O'Connor et al. (1993), DISTAR did not appear more effective for use with young disadvantaged children than an alternative and less structured phonics programme, except that, for those with scope for the most progress, the DISTAR group showed larger reading gains.

It is, therefore, difficult to interpret results when heterogeneous groups of children are involved, even if they can be grouped within an ability band or under a descriptive label; it further implies that successful outcomes can only reflect the interaction of child, teacher and method factors.

Reason et al. (1988) highlight the significance of phonological awareness in young children, and note also the implication that children learn to read by reading, with the implication that research and instruction may be linked by the maximisation of oral work based on familiar rhymes with young children and for enhancing the time available for reading activities such as paired or shared reading. However, it would be dangerous to assume that teaching methods which are successful with children who do not experience learning difficulties will be equally successful for children who are learning disabled.

It is argued that one can reconcile the step-by-step approach to reading, involving the gradual build-up of skills, with the 'apprenticeship' approach which emphasises exposure to real books. For the reading-disabled child, it is particularly important to ensure access to elements of both these approaches. The important feature of any programme is that of balance: one does not abandon any effort to read for meaning if or when a structured 'bottom-up' approach is initiated.

The Barking Reading Project offers sets of material to improve subskills of reading such as sound blending, sequential memory and finding sounds in words. An evaluation sponsored by the Department of Education and Science (1983) used samples of children within the age range 6-9 and concluded that the material was valuable in providing a means of assessing performance within aspects of the early reading curriculum. However, using pairs of children matched according to reading age and skill profile, it was concluded that this methodology did not produce significant benefits. It was held that the project materials would best be regarded as components of general resources for the teaching of reading, and that they would be most appropriately 'dipped into' by the teacher, and not used as a total and mechanistic programme.

The Reading Recovery system was produced and monitored by Clay (see, for example, Clay 1987). In this system, the bottom 20 per cent of groups of 6-year-olds, in terms of reading, were identified and given concentrated attention for 30 minutes per day over a 20-week period. The content emphasised letter identification, use of cues, teaching to errors and writing a story (including the analysis of sounds in component words). Individual sessions and individualised programmes were arranged, and were followed up after a year. Outcomes revealed that 70 per cent of those taught were reading and writing at an average level, 25 per cent needed to continue the teaching and 5 per cent had failed to make positive progress. These generally positive results, however, were gained within a methodology which lacked control groups.

The evaluation of Reading Recovery in Surrey (and reported by Wright and Prance in *Support for Learning*, Vol. 7, No. 3) also demonstrated positive general outcomes but there remains the issue of the absence of control groups, and there may be some question about the maintenance of gains. Meanwhile, the perceptions of the Surrey teachers involved (as surveyed by the present writer; Connor 1991) emphasised:

- the considerable cost in terms of teacher time;
- the relatively small number of children involved;
- the status of other children with learning difficulties not included within the Reading Recovery Group.

A review of research evidence indicates that pupils exposed to Reading Recovery make impressive short-term gains in reading words in context. However, it may not be clear whether it is the model/material or the individualised attention which is the significant feature. Further, according to Glynn et al. (1992), the initial gains may have reduced by the time of follow-up. In any event, the greatest gains were found among pupils with the lowest reading levels at the start of the programme. It was suggested that one reason for the target children's losing their advantage over comparison children may have been the lack of direct communication between the Reading Recovery and mainstream classroom programmes, and a mismatch between the child's reading level and the level necessary for ease of integration within the mainstream demands.

The ARROW technique is described by Lane (1990). This involves listening to a recording of a word, repeating the word while looking at the written word, listening to a tape recording of this response, and then writing the word. This, then, is a multisensory technique involving the child's own voice. Children aged 9+ years were found to make significant progress after a year of daily 15-minute sessions, but no controls were involved and educational experience besides ARROW was not considered. Nevertheless, the basic ARROW method lends itself to many variations according to the needs and ability of each child, and it may enhance listening skills, short-term memory, speech, reading accuracy, reading comprehension and spelling.

Van de Leij and Van Daal (1987) described the effectiveness of repetition and practice in poor readers in the age range 8-13 in terms of enhancing reading accuracy and fluency, perhaps because of the compensation for verbally based deficits in many dyslexic children. The effects of repeated reading were investigated by means of computer-assisted instruction, and improvements were noted over twelve trials in accuracy and speed of reading practised words, and differences in reading high- and low-frequency words disappeared.

Moore (1988) referred to the benefits of Reciprocal Teaching for reading comprehension, through the interaction of good and poor readers, and emphasising the processes of summarising, predicting, clarifying and questioning. 'Neuro-linguistic programming' provides a model of good spelling performance, teaching children to visualise words and emphasising the upper left visual field. However, in all these approaches, there is a lack of clear data by which to determine the level of effectiveness.

The Haringey Reading Project sought to increase parental involvement in reading by means of promoting paired reading with children in the 6- to 8-year age range, and it was reported by Hewison (1988) that, 3 years after the project had been completed, those children whose parents had taken part were still reading significantly better than their counterparts without the experience of parental involvement. The outcome also suggested that its effects were better than those of extra teaching help during a similar intervention period. On the other hand, one can find evidence that other methods, such as the Pause-Prompt-Praise approach, or a less structured form of hearing children read, are able to achieve similar gains to a paired reading group.

What seems to matter with paired reading is:

- suitable choice of material such that the child can read independently a high proportion of words and
- parental willingness to allow children time to think or self-correct, and the ability to switch smoothly back to simultaneous reading after efforts in independent reading.

In respect of parental involvement, it is relevant to quote the work of Leach and Siddall (1990), who investigated the relative merits of training parents to work with their children on the following techniques:

- paired reading,
- Pause-Prompt-Praise approach,
- direct instruction, and
- the simple hearing of reading.

Parents of 6-year-old children were randomly assigned to an approach and given appropriate training.

Outcomes suggested that paired reading and direct instruction were associated with faster progress among the children. It was hypothesised that this reflected a greater instructional element rather than the relatively passive style of the other approaches.

Meanwhile, a form of multisensory learning, 'Simultaneous Oral Spelling', was investigated by Thomson (1991), who argued for its effectiveness compared with the outcome of using the 'Look, Cover, Write, Check' approach to spelling when working with dyslexic children. However, these studies, too, may need to be treated with caution in the light of limited control procedures.

Further to emphasise the issue over processes within literacy, one might return to the earlier work of Bradley (1982), who describes the confusion facing the teacher. 'Does one identify strengths and teach to those? Identify weaknesses and seek to provide compensatory activities?' Bradley argues for a significant relationship between auditory organisation and spelling/reading, and attempts were made to evaluate the effectiveness of remedial methods by an experimental procedure in which each child was her/his own control - that is, by learning some words under one condition and others under another condition. Three methods were involved, using subjects with a range of handicaps, where reading failure was a part:

1. a variation of simultaneous oral spelling (the child nominates a word; the word is written for her/him; the child names the word; the child writes the word saying each letter name as s/he writes it; the child names the word again, and checks that the word has been written correctly; the steps are repeated twice; the word is practised in this way for six consecutive days);

2. as above, but the writing was excluded: the child makes the word with plastic letters naming them as they are placed, and concludes by naming the word;

3. the words are presented, but not taught.

Results demonstrated that significantly better results were achieved by using the adaptation of simultaneous oral spelling with the effectiveness linked to the combination of visual, auditory and kinaesthetic memory cues, and to the reinforcement of the grapheme-phoneme connection through the multisensory image.

Teaching strategies (Dyslexic pupils)

The definition of, and criteria for, dyslexia may vary from one piece of research evidence to another. Further, in all or many cases, the evidence may not serve to determine whether the outcomes are specific to a dyslexic group (however defined) or are generalisable to other groups of poor readers and spellers not identified as dyslexic.

The present writer is also concerned that the merits of any method will interact with characteristics within the teacher, the pupil and the parent. For example, if a parent does not believe that her/his child will progress unless transferred to a specialist centre and taught by a teacher with specific training, then no method is likely to have a rapid, positive impact in the mainstream class. Meanwhile, one might be worried by the effect upon the child of constant reference to being dyslexic and unlikely to cope without specialist treatment.

Hicks (1986) investigated three 'levels' of intervention in the case of specific reading disabled children. Her review of findings and conclusions may be summarised as follows.

Process approaches (Subskills)

These methods attempt to develop visual or auditory subskills, and may take the form of such material as the Frostig programme or the Illinois Test of Psycholinguistic Abilities. However, it appears that efforts to remedy literacy failure by means of such training are misguided. This is largely due to the lack of a demonstrably clear relation between these skills and literacy, such that improvements in the skills, as measured, will have no impact upon reading or spelling.

Specialist approaches

By these, Hicks means those existing 'packages' which may be adapted for any child described as dyslexic, whatever the child's particular history and experience, such as the Orton-Gillingham approach, the Fernald approach and the Edith Norrie Letter Case.

One might summarise the findings as follows:

- Successes are noted but controls are lacking.
- The common emphasis upon a very repetitive or rigid procedure may be demotivating, and may not suit young children.
- Uncertainty about precisely what in the programme is the effective aspect.
- The threat to 'meaning' as a result of the bottom-up emphasis.

The implication is that the teacher should have access to arrange of materials, but should avoid reliance upon any one approach and offer a genuinely multisensory programme such that the benefits of a step-by-step structure are not outweighed by costs in terms of over-emphasis on phonics, a lack of experience of 'real reading', etc.

Modality preference methods

These are based on the assumption that each child will present a unique pattern of skills and weaknesses, and will require individualised intervention. However, these methods can be criticised on several grounds:

- claims that particular patterns can be identified may be based on unsystematic observations;
- more controlled studies have produced either no subtype patterns or patterns quite different from the auditory or visual categories hypothesised;
- the question of whether a visual problem (for example) is nothing to do with visual perceptual processing, but is actually a result of an inability to attach verbal labels to visual stimuli.

The work of Miles (1983), who observed the progress in multisensory teaching of children underachieving in reading, may serve to underline the significance of *early intervention* - that is, the need to offer enhanced support for children aged 7 or younger and the importance of the involvement of the parents. One implication of this work is that the phonological difficulty commonly observed among dyslexic samples will inhibit their progress through the alphabetic stage of reading and spelling development, hence early intervention with a multisensory approach is necessary.

Acknowledging that the results related only to single case studies of pupils in the early stages of secondary schooling, Brooks (1993) concluded that more effective than a clear structure per se or the teaching of rules to overcome specific weaknesses was the teaching to relative strengths, such as providing a visually oriented approach in the case of pupil(s) with a history of phonological deficits. An approach which encouraged the pupils to segment words into meaningful visual chunks (looking for words within words) was successful in reaching a pre-set criterion for word spelling, whereas there was limited or minimal progress using a phonic approach, a rules approach, a look-say (with or without tracing) approach, or a simultaneous oral spelling approach. (Interestingly, these older dyslexics improved significantly more rapidly when using the visual segmentation approach than when using a phonic approach; meanwhile, slower learning pupils - that is, those with moderate learning difficulties - showed the reverse and improved their word spelling using a phonic approach rather than a visual segmentation method.)

Emotional component

It should be noted that, alongside the issues of particular pupil profiles and histories, and the nature of remedial programmes, there remains the issue of the relationship between personality adjustment and the outcomes of interventions.

Emotional or personality problems may be perceived as primary and causal, or secondary and reactive, and the interpretation of cause and effect may depend, in part, on the examiner's orientation. However, it is acknowledged - for example, by Murray (1978) - that there is an association between emotional and personality variables and failure to learn to read. Further, there seems a link between successful remedial interventions and positive emotional adjustment, in that children with specific learning difficulties may show poor self-esteem, test anxiety and defensiveness. However, differences are not necessarily observed in respect of general anxiety or achievement motivation; the issue of self-esteem is concentrated upon school settings or academic-related demands. Given this, the learning-disabled child may be the more hesitant in admitting difficulties or accepting support. The implication is for remedial interventions to be linked to therapeutic input (counselling) with a view to reducing anxiety and enhancing self-esteem. The significance of early intervention is underlined by the common finding that the improvements linked to remedial teaching are negatively correlated with age, and this may be largely the result of motivational problems rather than of some firmer establishment of cognitive deficits - with age, there is that much more experience of failure and frustration.

Conclusions

1. There appears to be some risk that by concentrating upon psychological or physiological aspects, attention is distracted from the instructional aspect of specific learning difficulty. What matters is the problem that is located within the reading process, and interventions should be directed at enhancing this process rather than at over-narrow subskills. Reading is clearly more than the sum of its parts, even if one can be clear what those parts are. One might ask how an awareness of mixed laterality, familial incidence or other factor which may serve to identify the dyslexic child will inform remedial methodology.

2. One must not underestimate the issue of confidence and self-esteem in the children, nor the issue of parental support and appropriate parental aspiration. This being so, one would advocate an intervention which incorporates a number of features:

   Parental involvement

   - Pursuing complementary activities at home, such as paired reading
   - Participating in the setting of realistic goals and being seen to work consistently with the teacher(s)

A 'mixed' model within the remedial programme adopted for the child

- Therapeutic counselling and support
- A specific programme involving the establishment of attainable goals, to minimise anxiety and to maximise feelings of success
- Maximal exposure to meaningful and enjoyable reading (real reading)

3. In respect of the 'specific programme' element of the mixed model of remedial programmes, there appears to be converging evidence for the effectiveness of tackling the common cognitive deficit in phonemic awareness by means of activities such as simultaneous oral spelling, or variants thereof. Effectiveness may be enhanced by activities which will reinforce visual and kinaesthetic cues as well as the auditory-phonic cues. With different age groups, different emphases may be necessary; an emphasis upon a largely phonic approach may be less appropriate, and a visual-contextual approach more appropriate, as the pupil moves into the secondary age range.

In the light of the heterogeneous nature of presenting reading problems in school, and the wide individual differences in respect of the level of difficulty experienced, it is necessary to ensure access to a range of approaches. Given this, one might usefully quote the conclusion of Vellutino (1987), who stresses the need to be aware of individual learning style but also to focus on the nature of the learning task - that is, the instructional level. Given the early detection of difficulties, and access, where necessary, to individual support, it may well be that the dyslexic child can be helped by conventional methods, but Vellutino stresses that success may depend upon the combination of top-down and bottom-up approaches. Many 'specialist' approaches have principles in common with the teaching of literacy to any pupil. While the orientation of the specialist programmes tends towards a phonic emphasis (a bottom-up approach), the other differences from approaches for use with any child concern the degree of structure, detail, continuous assessment, systematic teaching, record-keeping and overlearning. Given that dyslexia is not a unitary condition, it is inappropriate to seek a unitary remedial approach or to suggest that a diagnosis of dyslexia would presuppose a teaching approach that is different in kind from approaches commonly used among children with reading difficulties, albeit not labelled as dyslexic. Therefore, one would seek a form of modified 'scatter-gun' approach (see Gittelman, 1988) to maximise parental involvement, ensure access to activities that will emphasise meaning and enjoyment and provide the teaching of specific skills based on an awareness of the child's experiences and current performance.

References

Adams, M (1990) *Beginning to Read: Thinking and learning about print.* MIT Press: Cambridge, Mass.

Bradley, L (1982) An experimental evaluation of effective remedial techniques for the learning disabled. *Thalamus,* 2, 43-59.

Brooks, P (1993) Diss., University College London, plus informal discussion, Helen Arkell Dyslexia Centre, Farnham, Surrey.

Clay, M (1987) Learning to be learning disabled. *New Zealand Journal of Educational Studies,* 22, 155-73.

Connor, M (1991) *Reading Recovery: An evaluation.* Surrey Educational Psychology Service, Kingston upon Thames.

Department of Education and Science (1983) *Evaluation of the Barking Project.* HMSO: London.

Frith, V (1985) Beneath the surface of developmental dyslexia. In Patterson, K, Marshall, J R and Coltheart, M (eds), *Surface Dyslexia.* Erlbaum: London.

Gittelman, R (1985) Controlled trials of remedial approaches to reading disability. *Journal of Child Psychology and Psychiatry,* 26, 843-6.

Glynn, T, Crooks, T, Bethune, N, Ballard, K and Smith, J (1992) Reading recovery in context. *Educational Psychology,* 12, 249-61.

Hewison, J (1988) The long term effectiveness of parental involvement in reading. *British Journal of Educational Psychology,* 58, 184-90.

Hicks, C (1986) Remediating specific reading disabilities. *Journal of Research in Reading,* 9, 39-55.

Lane, C (1990) ARROW - Alleviating Children's Reading and Spelling Difficulties. In P D Pumfrey and C D Elliott (eds), *Children's Difficulties in Reading, Spelling and Writing.* Falmer Press: London.

Leach, D and Siddall, S (1990) Parental involvement in the teaching of reading. *British Journal of Educational Psychology,* 60, 349-55.

Miles, T (1983) *Dyslexia: The pattern of difficulties.* Collins: London.

Moore, P (1988) Reciprocal teaching and reading comprehension: A review. *Journal of Research in Reading,* 11, 3-14.

Murray, M (1978) The relationship between personality adjustment and success in remedial programmes in dyslexic children. *Contemporary Educational Psychology,* 3, 330-9.

O'Connor, R, Jenkins, J, Cole, K and Mills, P (1993) Two approaches to reading instruction with children with disabilities. *Exceptional Children,* 59, 312-23.

Reason, R, Brown, B, Cole, M and Gregory, M (1988) Does the 'specific' in specific learning difficulty make a difference to the way we teach? *Support for Learning,* 3, 230-6.

Seymour, P (1986) *Cognitive Analysis of Dyslexia.* Routledge: London.

Thomson, M (1991) The teaching of spelling. In M J Snowling and M E Thomson (eds), *Dyslexia.* Whurr: London.

Van de Leij, T and Van Daall, V (1987) Repeated reading and severe reading disability. Paper presented to the 2nd European Conference for Research on Learning and Instruction. Tübingen, Germany, September.

Vellutino, F (1987) Dyslexia. *Scientific American,* 256:3, 34-41.

Wright, A and Prance, J (1993) The Reading Recovery Programme in Surrey Education Authority. *Support for Learning,* 7, 103-10.

(First published in *Support for Learning,* Vol. 9, No. 3, 1994.)

17 - Reading Recovery: What does it have to offer UK schools?

KATY SIMMONS

James, aged six, reads aloud to his teacher, who is carefully making notes before starting on the rest of a half-hour session of one-to-one instruction. At the other side of a one-way viewing screen a group of watching teachers, guided by an experienced tutor, discusses animatedly what is going on. The session is intense and energetic, the discussion increasingly searching. At the end of the half hour, the child goes off to play but the teachers return to their in-service afternoon, ready to relate what they have seen to their developing understanding of the reading process.

This session formed part of a Reading Recovery Programme that I observed last year [1990] in the State of Victoria, Australia. Now that Reading Recovery has reached the UK, it is important that teachers should be aware of what the scheme can offer and questions that might be asked before the scheme is adopted in UK schools.

What is Reading Recovery?

Reading Recovery is an early intervention programme providing long-term intensive help for children with reading difficulties. It was developed in New Zealand in the late Seventies by Professor Marie Clay and based on an extensive programme of research and development carried out by Clay at the University of Auckland and described by her in subsequent publications (Clay, 1985). The project began in New Zealand schools in 1978 and since 1983 has been nationally implemented by the New Zealand Department of Education. The programme is now widely spread throughout the country and as it continues to expand, it is predicted that up to a fifth of the targeted age group will be reached. Since then, Reading Recovery has spread to other parts of the world: it is now well established in the state of Victoria, Australia (Smith, 1986) as well as in Columbus, Ohio (Huck and Pinnell, 1985). Recently, nearer home, Surrey Local Education Authority has taken the initiative in introducing the programme into its schools: other Authorities look set to follow (Moore, 1991).

Reading Recovery is a systematic intervention programme targeted at children who, after a year in school, have not kept up with the reading progress made by their peers. The children who enter the programme are the poorest readers in their age group: Reading Recovery aims to tackle their problems before the gap between them and other children grows even wider and a pattern of continued long-term failure, such as that observed by Wells (Wells, 1986) sets in.

But Reading Recovery is not just aimed at children: it is also a well developed in-service programme for teachers. Reading Recovery teachers in Victoria, Australia not only worked with four children each day but also, once every two weeks, were released for a full day of in-service training in a local teachers' centre. In turn, the tutor who ran that course, and who went into school regularly to supervise teachers running the Reading Recovery sessions, was enrolled in a specially designed programme of study at a nearby University in Melbourne. The result was a sophisticated and well-monitored programme of in-service training which linked schools, teachers, advisers and teachers in higher education. This in-service programme for teachers is a key element in any Reading Recovery programme. Although it has clinical elements (in particular the use of the one-way mirror), it is fundamentally a practical, school-based training, with a strong theoretical framework: it involves the teachers and their school in a coherent, long-term programme of professional development.

Ideally, the teachers who train to implement Reading Recovery should be experienced, successful and highly competent classroom teachers who already know a good deal about the teaching of reading. They should be on the permanent staff of the school and should not hold another position of responsibility, since conflict of priorities is inevitable. Clearly, schools who want to participate in Reading Recovery need to have considerable commitment to it. Teachers should be free to work with a maximum of four children each day: they also need time for report writing and note keeping.

Before the programme starts

Once identified by their school as a candidate for the Reading Recovery programme, the child is thoroughly assessed, following the detailed, systematic procedures described by Clay (Clay, 1985). The testing process includes:

- text reading, during which the teacher keeps a 'running record' of the child's performance

- letter identification
- word test: the teacher tests the child's knowledge of basic words either from the Dolch list or from a reading scheme
- concepts about print: the teacher assesses the child's awareness of left to right movement in reading and awareness of words, letters and sentences
- writing: the child is given ten minutes to write all the words they know
- a simple dictation test which tests the child's sensitivity to letter/sound correspondence
- the Burt Reading Test; this test is used to measure progress as the programme continues.

After completing the initial diagnosis, the teacher develops a programme for each individual child.

The programme in action

The child stays on the reading Recovery programme for between 12 and 16 weeks. During this time, sessions of individualised instruction are offered for half an hour every day. The sessions are carefully structured and each one contains specific elements:

> Reading Recovery is based on the assumption that knowledge of reading and writing is acquired through immersion in literacy acts that are meaningful to the child. (Pinnell, 1989)

Consequently, in their Reading Recovery sessions, children read natural language stories and write stories based on their own language. Each day, the child reads again several previously read favourite books: as the reading progresses, the teacher makes a running record, noting errors and miscues and identifying the kinds of processes the child is using. This running record is one of the most important aspects of the Reading Recovery programme: learning to do it well is one of the most challenging parts of the training programme for teachers. The child then writes their own message or story and reads it with the teacher's support. The teacher will subsequently write out the story on a strip and cut it up for the child to re-assemble and read. At this point, the teacher may use magnetic letters on a board to demonstrate sounds or sequences. Each day, the child reads a new book that they will be expected to read without help the next day. Before the reading, the teacher talks to the child about the book as they look at the pictures. The books used in the scheme are drawn from many sources; the teacher selects books appropriate to the child's reading level from a list of over 350 books graded in difficulty from one to twenty. As part of their training, teachers become familiar enough with the available materials to be able to guide the child from one level to the next. For a child who cannot manage even the simplest reading book, teachers will use the language experience approach and make reading materials based on the child's own language.

The child's progress is continually reviewed until they have developed strategies for independent reading and are able to work successfully in their own classroom within an average group. Instruction is not prolonged indefinitely: a child may get an extra few weeks if necessary but in general, children who have not reached discontinuation point within the time allowed are then referred on to other sources of help such as the educational psychologist. As soon as one child leaves the programme, another enters.

Questions about the programme

Reading Recovery programmes have not been received with uncritical acclaim. One Australian teacher described the 'vehement opposition' she had encountered from critics (Richter, 1989). Criticisms of the programme often claim that Reading Recovery promotes a 'deficit' model of learning; even the name suggests illness from which the child must be 'cured' by an 'expert' practitioner who will 'diagnose' their problems then administer some sort of medicine before sending the child back to the otherwise healthy classroom. The deficit model has for some time been out of favour with those working in the area of special needs in the UK (Simmons, 1987); models of good practice now include much more collaborative kinds of working, with special needs teachers working alongside classroom teachers to support the child in the class and to offer advice on materials and approaches. Withdrawal of children out of classrooms for special help is often seen as undesirable. How compatible is Reading Recovery with the idea of in-class support?

Richter (1989) argues that the short-term intensive help offered by Reading Recovery enables children to return to their classrooms and gain maximum benefit from learning opportunities. The six year olds who enter Reading Recovery enjoy the extra attention and do not feel stigmatised by it: children actually clamour to be in the programme. She argues that Reading Recovery, far from focusing on weaknesses, actually starts from the child's strengths. The first ten days of the programme, for example, which are spent 'roaming round the known', establish what the child *can* do. Subsequent lessons always start from texts that the child can read or from the child's own language. The lessons focus on enabling the child to develop strategies for independent learning.

Other writers (Pinnell, 1989) have stressed that Reading Recovery is not a remedial programme. It is designed to run alongside the work of the regular classroom, not to replace it. It is 'something extra', additional to regular class activities. Children with specific or severe difficulties are quickly referred to other professionals: the programme is designed to give a 'second chance' to those who have fallen behind.

Another criticism of Reading Recovery is that it excludes parents. In the UK, parental involvement in reading has been a focus of development in schools for several years. How compatible is Reading Recovery, with its emphasis on classroom intervention by a highly trained professional, with schemes such as shared or paired reading? Again, exponents of Reading Recovery would argue that the programme does not replace existing approaches, it complements them. Once more it offers 'something extra'.

There is, however, one major area where queries about Reading Recovery are not so easily countered. Though it appears that the short-term effects of the programme both in New Zealand and Ohio are beyond doubt (DeFord et al., 1988; Pinnell, 1989), there is debate about how long children maintain progress once input is discontinued. Given the great cost of implementation of the Reading Recovery approach, it is important that long-term effects are also understood. It is in this area that research results have been inconclusive.

Bald (1991) describes two conflicting research reports, one based in New Zealand, the other in Ohio. While the Ohio study reported continued gains by the group of children who had been in Reading Recovery, the New Zealand study was less conclusive. The results were further complicated by administrative differences between the two programmes. The Ohio project, for example, had followed more closely the framework for Reading Recovery established by Professor Clay, particularly in the kind of teacher recruited for training.

Studies in Victoria, Australia, also produced differing results (Smith, 1986). Again, schools had not always implemented the programme in the recommended way and consequently some results were disappointing. For example, instead of training a permanent member of a school's staff, some schools had used peripatetic special needs teachers. Smith comments:

> The use of out-of-school personnel made communication difficult and seemed to take the responsibility of learning from the school.

Some children did not receive daily sessions, because of teachers' conflicting priorities. In other schools, inadequate supplies of books meant that progression of a kind intended by Clay was not possible.

Shortcomings in the early programme were largely rectified in the following year: Smith reports corresponding improvement in results and adds:

> Failure to adhere to requirements and recommendations may jeopardise the quality of the program and its effectiveness in a school.

It may be that administrative differences and failure to adhere to Marie Clay's original framework for practice have led to these inconclusive results. It is however, important to note that when Reading Recovery is done without coherent planning and effective resources, its impact is considerably reduced.

Reading Recovery is expensive. Glynn et al. (1989) estimated that the within-school salary costs alone amounted to between NZ$1300 and NZ$2500 per child (£450-£870), a substantial investment for a twelve weeks programme, especially when compared to the average cost of a year's education for children in ordinary classroom programmes. When long-term benefits are as yet not known, such a substantial investment cannot be made lightly.

Is Reading Recovery worth that investment? Teachers who have worked with the programme often become totally positive that it is. It is worth noting that the introduction to Richter's article (Richter, 1989) describes her as 'a firm believer': immersion in Reading Recovery often seems to have the effect of a conversion experience. Certainly, the programme offers a dynamic, energetic and well structured approach to reading difficulties.

As yet, we do not know conclusively whether improvements made while children are in the programme will be sustained. Results from the Ohio study suggest that where the programme is implemented in the way that Marie Clay intends, then they are. This point is an important one. It is not possible to have Reading Recovery 'on the cheap'. As the study in Victoria showed, deviations from the recommended format can lead to disappointing results. Reading Recovery cannot be partly implemented: any programme must have the complex components that make it a total package.

One of the most significant of these components is the in-service support and training for teachers which is a key part of the Reading Recovery programme. It demands extensive and intensive 'on the job' training of a kind not often seen in UK schools. Effective implementation of a Reading Recovery programme requires commitment to a continuing programme of teacher education, not only to long-term classroom support for children with reading difficulties. Teachers I have spoken to in this country are openly envious of the training opportunities offered by the Reading Recovery scheme as operated in Australia, comparing it favourably with the piecemeal in-service opportunities that have come their way. Evaluation of Reading Recovery needs to focus not just on the children but on the teachers involved in the programme. It would be interesting to learn more about the effects, for example, on self-esteem and morale of a year spent developing considerable professional competence and expertise as part of the Reading Recovery training programme.

If Reading Recovery helps children to become more effective learners, then perhaps it also helps teachers to give more effective help. It certainly encourages teachers to be accurate observers, to build a coherent rationale for the decisions they make and to engage actively in a process of systematic enquiry. It makes them more confident and aware of their own skills. It is maybe as a tool of staff professional development that Reading Recovery is at its most effective.

Reading Recovery raises many interesting questions. The programme was developed in a small country with a uniform approach to beginning literacy. Studies in Australia and elsewhere have shown that it *does* translate and can be successfully transferred from its original setting. But it remains a controversial programme. Its approaches and assumptions should be explored and debated fully before they are adopted as an answer to the questions currently challenging us in the UK.

References

Bald, J (1991) Roads to recovery. *Times Educational Supplement,* 19 January, 42.

Clay, M M (1985) *The Early Detection of Reading Difficulties (Third Edition).* Heinemann: Auckland, New Zealand.

DeFord, D E, Pinnell, G S, Lyons, C A and Young, P (1988) *Report of the Follow-up Study, Reading Recovery Project,* Vol. IX. Columbus, OH: The Ohio State University.

Glynn, T, Crooks, T, Bethune, N, Ballard, K and Smith, J (1989) *Reading Recovery in Context.* Department of Education, Auckland, New Zealand.

Huck, S and Pinnell, G S (1985) *The Reading Recovery Project in Columbus, Ohio: Pilot Year 1984-1985.* (Technical Report). Columbus: The Ohio State University.

Moore, G (1991) The road to reading recovery. *Child Education,* March, 45-47.

Pinnell, G S (1989) A systemic approach to reducing the risk of reading failure. In J B Allen and J M Mason (Ed.) *Risk Makers, Risk Takers, Risk Breakers.* Heinemann Educational Books: Portsmouth, NH.

Richter, K (1989) Reading Recovery: a point of view. *The VTU Journal,* 8 June, p. 10.

Simmons, K (1987) Withdrawal symptoms. *Times Educational Supplement,* 3 April.

Smith, J (1986) Reading Recovery in Central Victoria: what we have learnt. *Australian Journal of Reading,* 9, 4, 201-208.

Wells, G (1986) *The meaning makers: Children learning language and using language to learn.* Heinemann: Portsmouth, NH.

18 - The Reading Recovery programme in Surrey Education Authority

ANNA WRIGHT and JEAN PRANCE

What is Reading Recovery?

Marie Clay devised the Reading Recovery programme between 1976 and 1979 in New Zealand. It has now been adopted in the whole of New Zealand, much of Australia and forty-one states in the USA. In 1989, Surrey Education Authority, with the help of the Hamlyn Foundation, arranged for one of the authors to be trained as a Reading Recovery Tutor in New Zealand. As a result Surrey are now running their third Reading Recovery training course.

The Reading Recovery programme is an effective programme for reducing the number of children with reading difficulties in New Zealand schools (Clay 1985, Clay and Watson, 1982). It is a second chance, early intervention programme. Its aim is to pick up the children who have not begun to read and write after one year at school and provide them with intensive instruction for 30 minutes daily and individually. As a result of accelerated progress the children typically leave the programme with average levels of performance in 12-15 weeks. The success gained with the poorest performers of the age group at 6 years runs counter to the assumptions, expectations and experience in most Western education systems. It is probably related to the specific nature of the instruction delivered by very well trained teachers.

Results gained in New Zealand show that for every 100 children in the population at age 6, if the 20 lowest achievers participate in the programme, 19 will reach average levels after a maximum of 20 weeks' teaching (average = 12-15 weeks). In New Zealand the figures shown in Figure 18.1 were obtained in 1988.

Less than 1 per cent of the birth cohort required referral for specialist help after Reading Recovery. The rest were reading at average levels for their schools. The surprising factor in Reading Recovery is that it takes the lowest achieving pupils at age 6, irrespective of their IQ, category of special educational need, and level of maturity, and accelerates their learning. This is illustrated graphically in Figure 18.2.

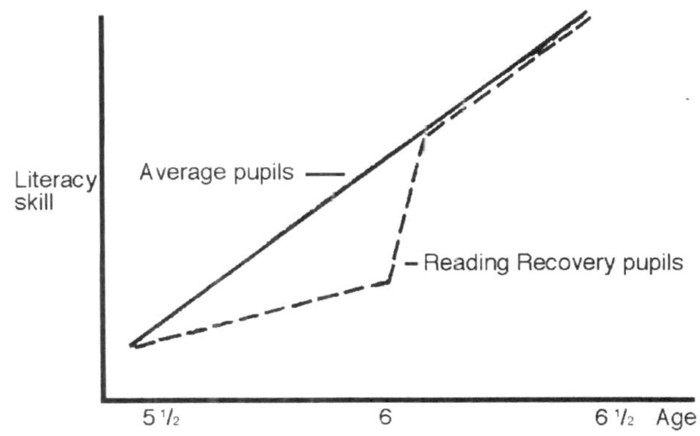

Figure 18.2 - Accelerated learning of Reading Recovery pupils.

The Reading Recovery pupils appear to learn faster than their peers. Follow-up studies carried out three years later, both in Ohio and New Zealand, show that those gains are maintained in that ex-Reading Recovery pupils are still functioning within the average band for their age at age 9 years (Clay 1986, Pinnell, DeFord and Lyons, 1988). Reading Recovery has been found to be superior to alternative educational programmes that deliver one-to-one teaching. A factor in its success appears to be the intensity and effectiveness of the training received by the Reading Recovery teachers (Pinnell *et al*, 1991).

	Birth cohort	*In Reading Recovery*	*Completed programme*	*Started programme*	*Left programme*	*Referred on for specialist help*
Number of pupils	**49,482**	**10,511**	**6,494**	**2,976**	**648**	**390**
Per cent	**100**	**21.24**	**13.12**	**6.01**	**1.31**	**0.8**

Figure 18.1 - New Zealand children in the Reading Recovery programme in 1988.

The Reading Recovery programme

In Reading Recovery, children receive individual daily 30-minute lessons from a specially trained teacher. These lessons do not take the place of good classroom instruction. As they say in New Zealand, Reading Recovery is 'something extra'. Reading Recovery is not intended to be a long-term or permanent programme. Teachers provide daily lessons, during which they involve children in reading many books, and in writing and reading their own stories and messages. During each lesson, teachers ensure that children are actively involved in reading and writing. The teacher carefully observes the child reading and writing texts, and finds opportunities to draw attention to the details of print to work on letter-sound associations and spelling patterns within those activities. The goal is to teach children how to use their knowledge and to see the purpose for it. When the children have made accelerated gains and caught up with their peers, they are then released from the programme as successful readers. This process takes on average 12-15 weeks. During this time 'teachers aim to produce independent readers whose reading improves whenever they read' (Clay, 1985).

A child is released from the programme when he or she 'has a system of strategies which work in such a way that the child learns from his own attempts to read' (Clay, 1985). When the programme for an individual child is discontinued, then another qualified child begins to receive individual teaching.

In Reading Recovery lessons, the teacher and the child sit side by side, reading and writing collaboratively. This setting provides many opportunities to support literacy learning. No one method or approach to teaching reading is used. Reading Recovery teachers try to follow the child and select from the trialed procedures appropriate intervention. By observing closely what the child is doing and systematically recording everything that takes place, the teacher can take advantage of the ways in which the child is making discoveries for him- or herself. From knowledge of the theory of the reading process and experience in observing reading behaviour, the teacher is able to hypothesise about the strategies the child is using, based upon the way the child is operating on the text. The teacher aims to keep the child constantly pushing at the frontiers of his or her knowledge, by making informed decisions about when and how to help.

A Reading Recovery lesson includes the following components:

1. Reading familiar stories: Re-reading familiar books provides the child with opportunities to engage in fast, fluent reading with some opportunities for problem solving.

2. Taking a running record of text reading: The teacher records the child reading a book that he/she has read once before by taking a running record of the child's reading behaviour. This record is subsequently analysed to infer which cue sources and strategies the child is using and this informs future teaching.

3. Working with letters: The teacher works with the child using plastic letters on a board to identify letters, construct words, or analyse words.

4. Writing a message or story: Each day the child composes a brief message in collaboration with the teacher. In this supported situation children learn to analyse words and make the link between sounds and letters.

5. Reading a new book: The teacher and child explore a new book together, and the child reads it for the first time.

The lesson's framework has the flexibility within which teachers can respond to individual children. The procedures were developed and refined with teachers in New Zealand after 'a large number of techniques were piloted, observed, discussed, argued over, related to theory, analysed, written-up, modified and tried out in various ways, and most important, many were discarded' (Clay, 1985). Reading Recovery teachers receive very intensive training which is described below.

The training of Reading Recovery teachers

Reading Recovery training is unlike other in-service courses. It is not the usual one- or two-day session but involves 'on the job' training over one full school year, during which teachers spend over 400 hours in training and practice on Reading Recovery.

Teachers begin their training by attending an initial meeting with the headteacher of their school. This is followed by five half-day assessment training workshop sessions, where they learn to administer and analyse the six-part diagnostic survey test (Clay, 1985). The skills and understandings gained in assessment training enable the teacher to begin assessment testing with 6-year-old children within their school, in order to select the lowest achieving children who will receive individual, intensive teaching.

Throughout the school year, teachers then attend fortnightly two-hour in-service training sessions, held in the afternoon, in which they learn the components of the lesson and the basic procedures.

Simultaneously, the teachers apply and expand their new knowledge as they work with four children in a one-to-one situation. This involves an additional 10 hours a week of teaching time within their own schools.

A special feature of the Reading Recovery training is the 'teaching behind the screen'. Three times during their training year, each teacher brings a child to the training centre and teaches a lesson behind a one-way mirror in a sound-equipped room. The other teachers in training observe and discuss the child's behaviour and the effects of the teacher's instructional decisions. A lively discussion is guided by a tutor who challenges the observers with questions that require analysis.

Two lessons behind the screen take place at each in-service training session. After the lessons, the two demonstrating teachers join the tutor and the remainder of the group in a lesson discussion. Often, the group can increase the teacher's understanding by describing the child's or the teacher's behaviours. The demonstrating teacher is often astonished at what the group has observed. The in-service training sessions also focus on helping teachers to learn the specific Reading Recovery procedures and new concepts.

The role of the tutor is to get the teachers to think about and analyse their own teaching decisions for each of the children they teach. The in-service training course is not designed to train the teachers to use a fixed set of procedures for the Reading Recovery programme. Although the Reading Recovery lesson has a framework, the procedures should be seen as a menu from which the teacher selects those most appropriate for a particular child, at a particular time, and in a particular context.

During the training, the teachers gain insights into the process of analysing, thinking and talking about their own teaching decisions. They look more closely at the pupils they are teaching and find it easier to see their strengths. This leads them to greater understanding of the reading process and to develop a more refined theory of how children learn to read and write. The training is carried out by tutors, who in turn receive very extensive training.

The training of Reading Recovery tutors

The Reading Recovery tutor is the person who trains Reading Recovery teachers. The University of London Institute of Education currently runs a one-year full-time training course for Reading Recovery tutors. Tutor training normally consists of:

1. daily teaching of 6-year-olds using the Reading Recovery procedures;

2. academic and theoretical study relating to current issues in reading and the concepts on which the programme is based;

3. development of techniques for training teachers, which involves participation in on-going training of Reading Recovery teachers;

4. gaining experience in the planning and running of Reading Recovery in-service courses.

Ideally, a local education authority (LEA) wishing to start the programme would send a very experienced and well-qualified teacher to be trained as a tutor, and meanwhile in the LEA one or two administrators, advisers or psychologists would become completely familiar with the conceptual and organisational aspects of the programme. In the next year the tutor can train twelve teachers, and six to ten children in each of their schools will receive individual tuition. The following year each tutor can maintain those twelve teachers and train twenty-four more. So at the end of a three-year period an LEA could have sixty schools with a teacher working a half-day on the programme, a tutor maintaining quality control over the programme, and 450-600 of the lowest achievers in the 6- to 7-year-old age group in reading and writing, receiving individual tuition which raises them to average levels.

Reading Recovery in Surrey Education Authority

Surrey has run two Reading Recovery courses, from March 1990 to March 1991 and from September 1990 to July 1991. The third course started in September 1991 and a fourth is due to start in September 1992. By July 1993 Surrey will have 40 Reading Recovery teachers able to take 400 children a year through the programme. Results from the first two years in operation have been encouraging. All pupils were assessed using Marie Clay's diagnostic survey at the beginning and end of the programme. The diagnostic survey investigates:

1. the level of text the child can read (books are graded from 1 to 20);

2. the number of upper- and lower-case letters, names or sounds the child can identify (0-54);

3. the child's understanding of concepts about print (score 0-24);

4. the child's word-reading ability;

5. the number of words a child can write in 10 minutes;

6. the child's accuracy on a short piece of dictation (maximum score 37).

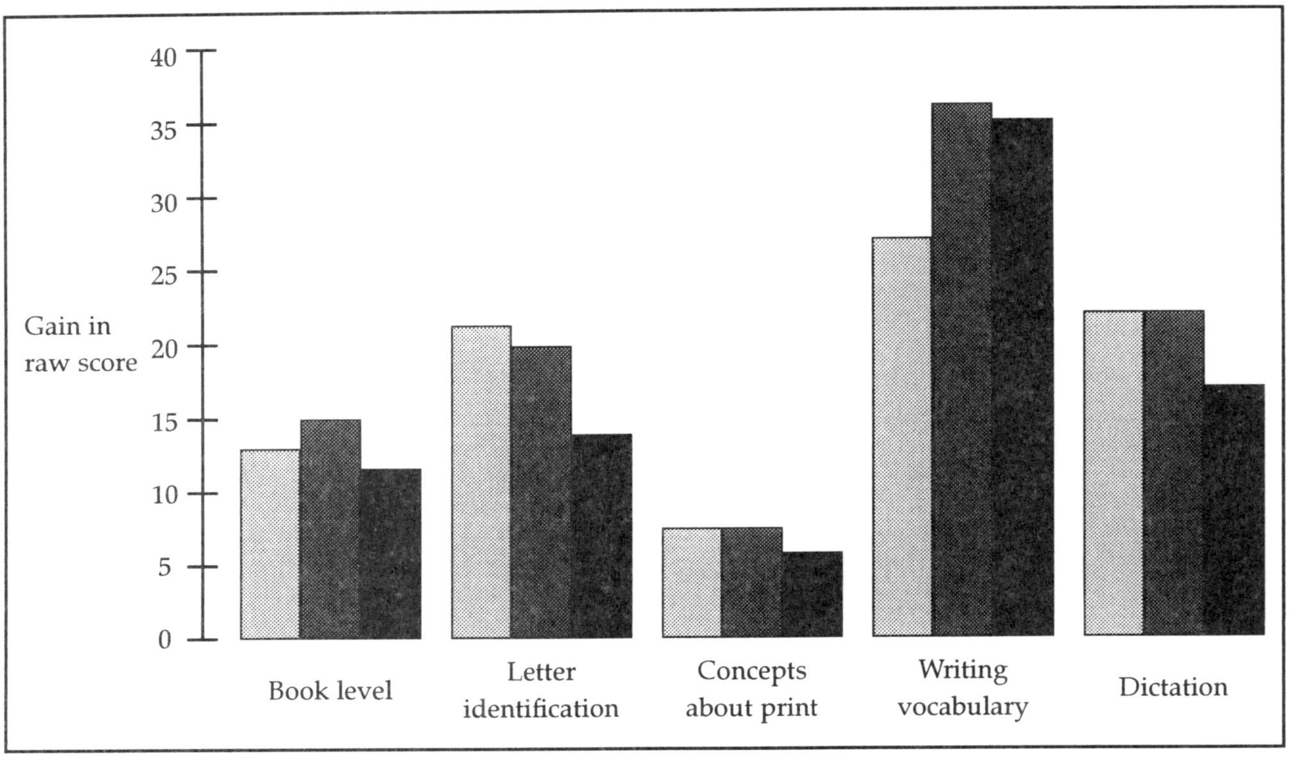

Figure 18.3 - Mean gains of Surrey pupils in Years 1 (▒) and 2 (▓) and of New Zealand pupils (█) on Reading Recovery. (Progress across measures cannot be compared here as each measure uses a different scoring scale.)

The gains of the seventy-seven pupils in total taken into the programme at the beginning of the two training courses were compared with gains pupils made in New Zealand in the first year of the programme there. Figure 18.3 compares gains made by Surrey children directly with gains made by New Zealand children on five of the assessments in Marie Clay's diagnostic survey, reported in Clay (1985). This result clearly indicates that the Reading Recovery programme is as successful in Surrey as it has been in New Zealand.

In Surrey, pupils spent an average of 16.8 weeks in the programme. On starting they were able to read only their name or very simple texts with only one or two words in them. They could identify, on average, 27 of the letters in the alphabet, and write, on average, 5 words unaided. At the end of the programme they were reading text at levels 15 and 16 (equivalent to a 6.7- to 7.0-year readability level), identifying 51 of the letters in the alphabet, and writing 38 words unaided in 10 minutes. Figures 18.4 and 18.5 show the progress of pupils on letter identification and writing vocabulary. Figure 18.4 demonstrates that pupils moved from reading at an average book level of 1-2 to reading at an average book level of 14-16. Figure 18.5 shows that pupils could write, on average, 6 words unaided in 10 minutes at the start of the programme, and that by the end of the programme they could write, on average, 37 words unaided in 10 minutes. This progress occurred after an average 16.8 weeks in the programme.

To provide a clearer picture of the effects of the Reading Recovery programme on these children, we provide here a description of the effect of the programme on one pupil at a Surrey first school.

An individual pupil's response to Reading Recovery

This pupil is Katie, aged 6 years 2 months. She is in a class of twenty-nine pupils. Her teacher stated that Katie's level of reading placed her amongst the lowest group of her class in reading. Katie is the younger of two children, has an older brother, and lives within a traditional family group. She has a history of ear, nose, throat related illness and was fitted with grommets shortly before her sixth birthday. An initial assessment within the school of all the lowest progress readers aged between 6 years and 6 years 3 months was made using the diagnostic survey. This clearly identified Katie as being the lowest progress reader within the group examined. This led to her subsequent selection for the Reading Recovery programme.

Katie at the start of the programme

At initial testing Katie read three one-line caption books - *I Like, I Go Go Go,* and *My Family* - with 97, 92 and 75 per cent accuracy. Using the assessment

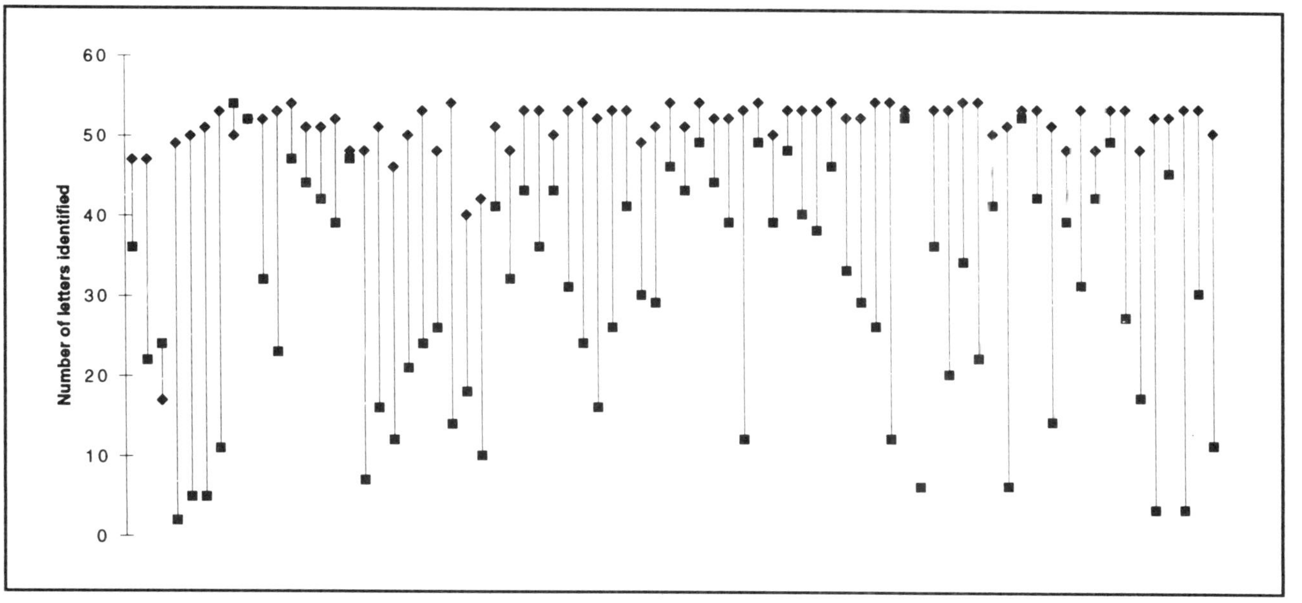

Figure 18.4 - Initial (■) and final (◆) scores of 77 Reading Recovery pupils on letter identification.

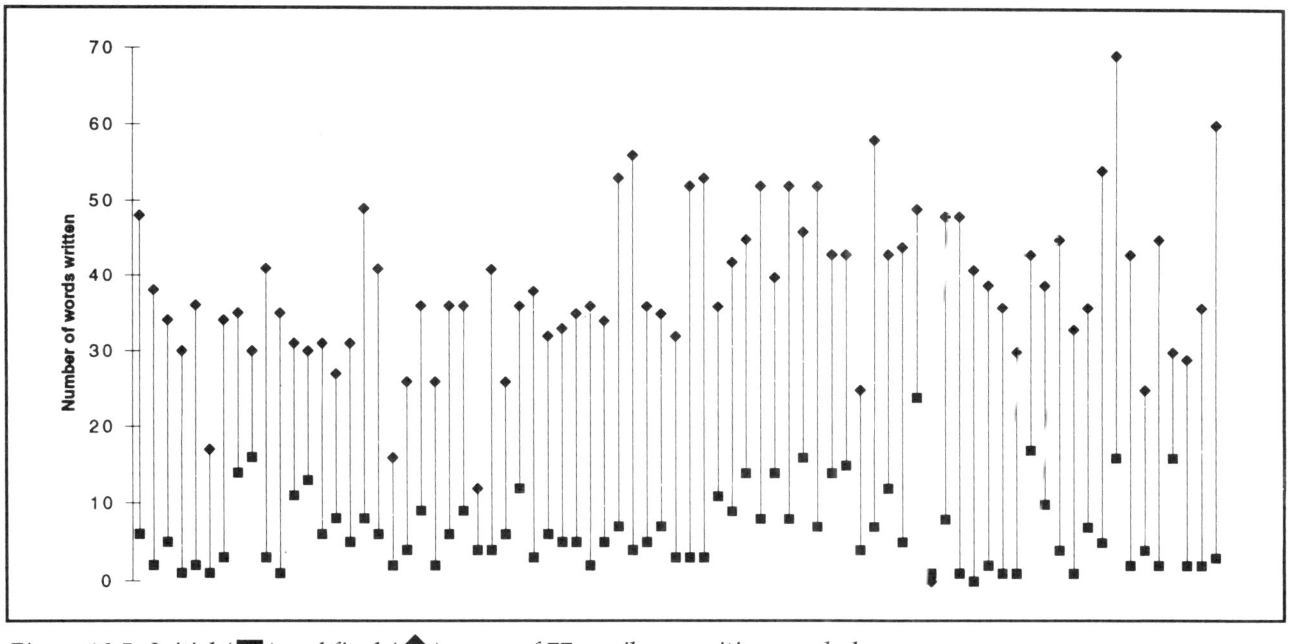

Figure 18.5- Initial (■) and final (◆) scores of 77 pupils on writing vocabulary.

tasks Katie could identify 30 of the 54 letters; she scored 11/24 on concepts about print, 2/15 on the word test, and 13/37 on the dictation and could write 5 words unaided within an allowed 10 minutes.

Katie at the end of the programme

Fifteen school weeks after being taken into the programme Katie was able to meet the demands of the class teacher for the high average children within her class and was subsequently assessed for being discontinued from the programme. Final testing showed Katie reading *The Very Hungry Caterpillar, The Treasure Chest* and *Mr Gumpy's Outing* with 98, 92 and 89 per cent accuracy. Using alternative forms of the assessment tasks Katie could identify 53 out of 54 letters; she scored 23/24 on concepts about print and 14/15 on the word test, wrote 58 words unaided in 10 minutes, and obtained a perfect score of 37/37 on the dictation.

As can be seen from Figures 18.6 and 18.7, Katie had made considerable gains across the battery of tests administered and was subsequently discontinued from the programme.

Figure 18.8 shows clearly Katie's accelerated rate of reading which was plotted on the same day each week from running records of text reading.

	Text title	*Accuracy*	*Self-correction rate*
Initial test, 4 December 1990			
1. Easy	*I Like*	97%	Nil
2. Instructional	*I Go Go Go*	92%	1:2
3. Hard	*My Family*	75%	Nil
Final test, 8 April 1991			
1. Easy	*The Very Hungry Caterpillar*	98%	1:2
2. Instructional	*The Treasure Chest*	92%	1:3
3. Hard	*Mr Gumpy's Outing*	89%	1:5

Figure 18.6 - Summary of initial and final text-reading testing of Katie.

	Letter identification	*Concepts about print*	*Word test*	*Writing vocabulary*	*Dictation*
Initial, 4 December 1990	30	11	2	5	13
Final, 8 May 1991	53	23	14	58	37
Max. possible	54	24	15	Open	37

Figure 18.7 - Summary of Katie's initial and final testing other than reading text.

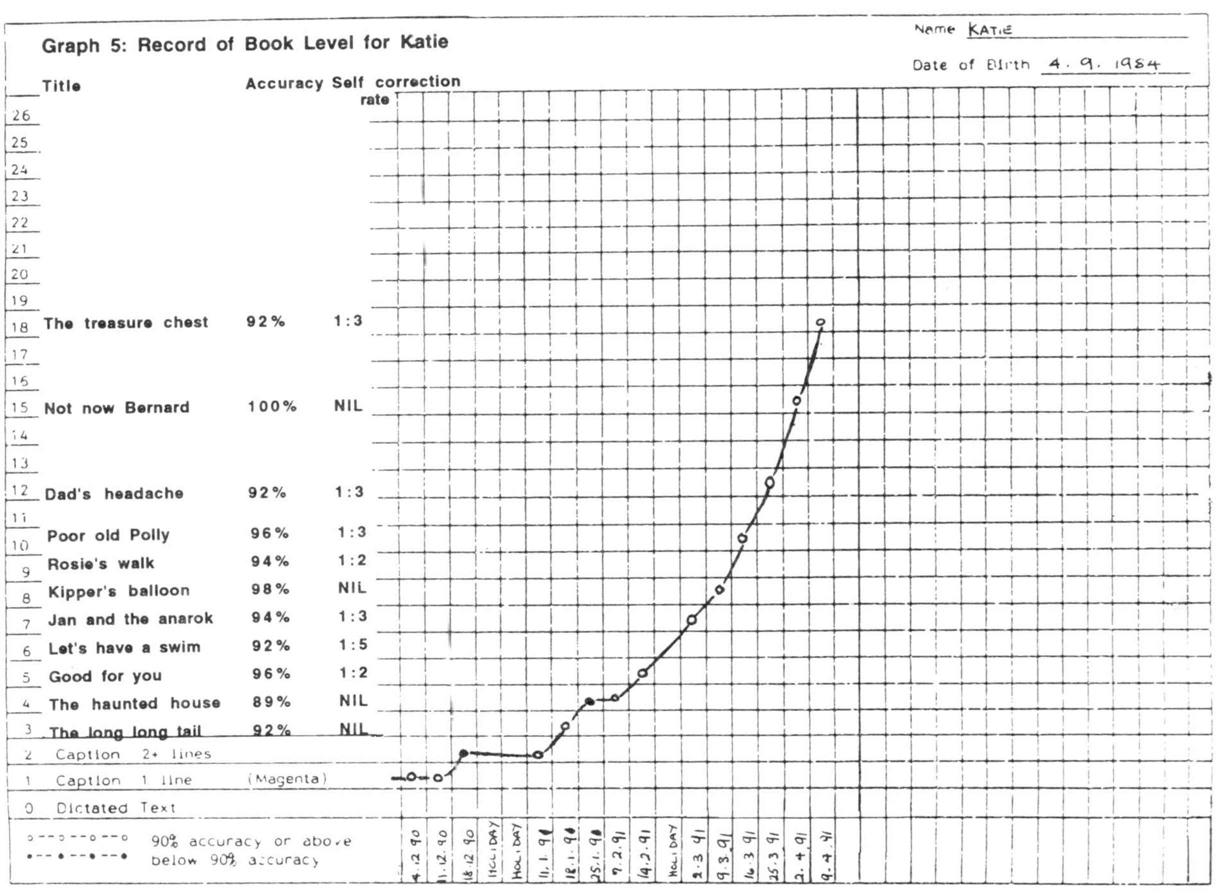

Figure 18.8 - Record of book level for Katie.

How Katie progressed during the programme

During each thirty-minute lesson, Katie worked at a variety of reading and writing tasks carefully selected to meet her particular needs and covering a range of familiar and new materials. Lessons were conducted on a daily basis, except when illness made Katie's attendance impossible. For the first two weeks many opportunities were provided for Katie to move around her own personal corpus of knowledge in many different ways. She was helped to make books for herself (her first reading books) and encouraged to write using the few words she knew in a sentence. Many opportunities were provided for sharing a number of simple story books. Katie began to notice many new things in both reading and writing, and new and useful behaviours began to appear as she began to relate things one to another. For example, during her first week in instruction she talked about the similarity between the words *cat* and *mat* when reading Brian Wildsmith's book *Cat on the Mat.* This was quickly followed with the discovery that *sat* also followed the same pattern. Four weeks into the programme Katie began to dispense with finger pointing, following the words in sequence carefully with her eyes. She was able to monitor her own work and make one or two self-corrections. In writing Katie was able to construct simple messages and hear and identify as letter symbols the most dominant sounds in words. Even at this early stage, Katie's class teacher, her mother and other staff members began to comment on an overwhelming change in Katie's confidence and attitude to school.

Over time Katie increased her reading and writing vocabularies and began to show accelerated rates of progress in reading. New behaviours began to appear. Katie would re-read at difficulties, started to use all the cue sources in an integrated way, and developed a high self-correction rate. More importantly, she came to see herself as a reader and writer. Katie began to write increasingly long and complex sentences and would use her knowledge of known words to help her to reach out to problem-solve unknown words. She needed less teacher support than previously and was well on the way to becoming an active problem-solver in both reading and writing.

By the end of her programme, Katie was able to read books of increasing complexity in a well-phrased and fluent way with less errors. She used repetition less and made use of a new strategy, which indicated that she could be internalising some of her former behaviour. Her eyes would quickly scan the print before commencing to read aloud and errors would be corrected immediately without re-reading as she quickly searched for further information. In writing she would hear the sounds in words in sequence, had developed control of 's', 'ed' and 'ing' endings, and gained a considerable amount of control of some of the spelling patterns of the English language.

The most important factor which influenced the decision to discontinue at this stage was the way she was able to transfer all the good behaviour she had learned to the classroom situation.

Katie in the classroom

Katie's progress in the classroom was carefully monitored by the Reading Recovery teacher at fortnightly intervals for the first two months after discontinuing and on the last of these occasions Katie presented the Reading Recovery teacher with a twenty-page story she had written unaided, inspired by Jay Cowley's book *Ratty Tatty,* one page of which is reproduced here. The complete story was a truly memorable gift that will serve as a constant reminder of the opportunities both Katie and her Reading Recovery teacher had to learn more about the reading and the writing process. Katie was now functioning at a high average level within her class and seemed a different pupil from the one who started the programme.

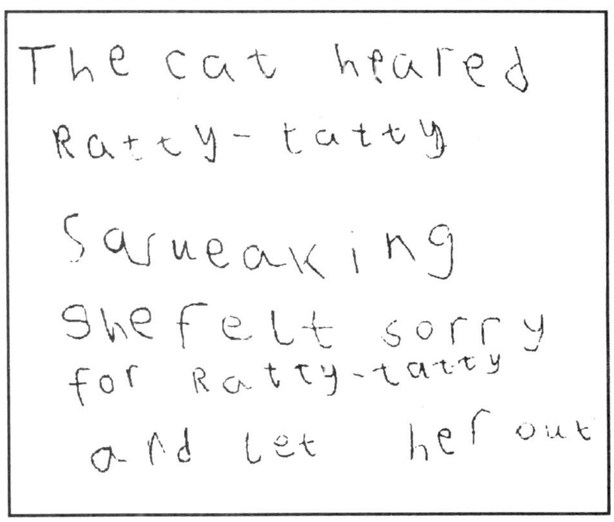
The cat heared
Ratty-tatty
squeaking
she felt sorry
for Ratty-tatty
and let her out

Figure 18.9 - A page from a story written unaided by Katie two months after discontinuing her Reading Recovery programme.

Conclusions

This article provides an informal insight into the effects of Reading Recovery in Surrey. A formal academic evaluation has been submitted for publication. However, we have hoped to provide readers here with a flavour of the effectiveness of the programme in Surrey. It has proved possible to transfer the Reading Recovery programme from New Zealand to Surrey. It was possible to duplicate all aspects of the training and no major problems in implementation were experienced. Pupils in Surrey showed similar accelerated learning to those in

New Zealand; and we have provided an illustration of what that means for an individual pupil in the programme.

References

Clay, M M (1985) *The Early Detection of Reading Difficulties.* Heinemann.

Clay, M M (1986) The Reading Recovery research report: Part 1. *Reading Canada Lecture,* 4, 93-106.

Clay, M M and Watson, B (1982) *The Success of Maori Children in the Reading Recovery Programme.* Report to the Director of Research, Department of Education, Wellington, New Zealand.

Pinnell, G S, DeFord, D and Lyons, C A (1988) Reading Recovery: Early intervention for at risk first graders. ERS Monograph, Educational Research Service: Arlington, Virginia.

Pinnell, G S, Lyons, C A, DeFord, D, Bryk, A S and Seltzer, M (1991) Studying the effectiveness of Early Intervention approaches for first grade children having difficulty in reading. *Educational Report,* No. 16. Martha L King Language and Literacy Centre: Ohio State University, Columbus, Ohio.

(First published in *Support for Learning,* Vol. 7, No. 3, 1992.)

Reading: Issues and Directions

CHARLES W GAINS

In the Introduction to this book David Wray summarises the current situation in the teaching of reading and comes to three general conclusions:

1. Reading is a very complex process and simplistic explanations and approaches, however attractive, are of little use.

2. The teaching of reading should start where the child is most comfortable i.e. looking for meaning, attending to the functional aspects of print and learning through stories.

3. The technicalities of reading *are* important but must be set within a context of real meaning.

The purpose of this summary is to expand on this initial thesis, examine the issues raised by contributors and the directions suggested and finally to incorporate these into some composite models. As many of the readers of this book are dealing with reading failure some attention has been given to this aspect.

Setting the scene: the reading debate

The debate on reading, appearing as it does at regular intervals, generates considerable passion. To the casual observer, there are times when all protagonists, however diverse, appear to be correct. The latest round of charge and counter-charge was led by the revelations of Martin Turner. He claimed to have unearthed evidence of a significant downward trend in reading standards among primary school children. He went further in attributing this to particular teaching methods particularly those of a 'psycholinguistic' or 'whole language' type.

David Wray's carefully argued response questions, in the first instance, the statistics quoted by Turner claiming that the figures collected are far from conclusive. He reserves most of his anger, however, for the assertion that a decline in standards is due to teaching methods. He maintains that the overwhelming majority of teachers do not rely on a single method but deploy a variety of strategies. If there is a decline in standards it may well be due to matters beyond teacher control, in particular the connection between performance and social background.

What can we learn from this ongoing debate? First, there *is* an unease about standards of reading. No one can be really satisfied with current levels of performance, particularly as the demands of training and employment are accelerated. Second, teachers can meet this challenge if freed from some of the bureaucratic demands imposed on them from above. Third, as this book demonstrates, there is a great deal of exciting research, information and advice available to do that very thing.

Providing a reading environment

Figure 1 summarises the five major areas focused on in this publication:

- the beginnings of reading;
- moving reading on;
- extending reading;
- engaging readers;
- supporting readers.

Much of the reading debate focuses largely on the early stages of reading, the acquisition of 'basic skills'. Here Henrietta Dombey has provided a wide ranging and masterly summary of the key areas of knowledge and expertise children require in order to proceed competently and confidently. In strongly supporting such elements as phonic awareness she does much to dispel the myth that reading experts discount this fundamental skill. Usha Goswami reinforces this in introducing us to the concepts of 'onset' (the initial consonants) and 'rime' (corresponding vowels and final consonants). Recent research confirms that such units are easily distinguishable by young children, even before they begin to tackle serious reading. For teachers the implications are that they can have confidence in the multiplicity of approaches they currently use but can add to their repertoire some of the specific skills now being unearthed in the area of phonological awareness.

Moving reading on takes us into the controversial world of 'real books'. Henry Pearson makes a substantial case for the better use of well-written stories in developing reading. Although he makes no claim that children left alone with good and entertaining literature will automatically want to read, he does highlight the powerful effects of engagement with compelling texts. Technical ability is not dismissed but Pearson certainly sees motivation springing from exposure to quality experiences.

Element	*Issues*	*Directions*
The beginnings of reading (Dombey and Goswami)	Young children require a variety of teaching approaches if they are to embark on the reading adventure with confidence. Some 'code cracking' skills are essential.	Reading is a complex task with many interwoven elements. Beginner readers should be provided with situations that: • offer a wide variety of experience • promote positive attitudes • stress pleasure and enjoyment in text • develop specific decoding skills • involve their parents
Moving reading on (Pearson and Coles)	Sustained exposure to quality reading material plays a major part in stimulating a life-long love of reading and must not be sacrificed in the pursuit of simple mechanical proficiency.	Teachers should carefully consider: • whether the material on offer is of sufficient quality to engage and motivate the reader • whether there are aspects of the 'apprenticeship approach' that can be incorporated into existing practice
Extending reading (Wray and Lewis et al)	As readers grow mechanically more proficient we cannot assume that comprehension and research skills automatically follow.	A variety of interesting and enjoyable techniques has been developed to promote such skills including: • comprehension monitoring • reciprocal teaching • discussion and dialogue • systematic patterns of research
Engaging readers (Poulson and Sawyer et al)	A fundamental aim of reading is to introduce pupils to the pleasure that can be derived from literature and poetry.	There are a wide range of approaches that encourage reading for pleasure including: • choice of text • re-reading • discussion • sharing experiences
Supporting reading (Topping and Medwell)	Reading can be supported in many ways. Parental involvement is now an established and well-documented practice. School policies can ensure that all participants in the process are brought together in a cohesive way.	Successful reading strategies require: • planning • development • monitoring • renewal • parental and other inputs

Figure 1 - Providing a reading environment.

Martin Coles pursues this theme examining, in a fairly exacting fashion, the concept of 'apprenticeship' i.e. learning through observation, coaching and practice. He acknowledges weaknesses in the approach but suggests the technique can be incorporated successfully in current classroom practice. What both writers remind us of is that unless reading is seen as enjoyable and the material used is of good quality we cannot simply hope that children will acquire a life-long interest and love of books.

The University of Exeter is playing an important role in researching methods of extending reading. David Wray, for example, examines an area known as 'comprehension monitoring' i.e. how individuals can monitor their own comprehension and take remedial action when the process is in danger of breaking down. He recommends 'reciprocal teaching' in which pupils enter into dialogue about their reading experiences and difficulties. Maureen Lewis and her colleagues are pursuing the processes that will enable pupils to become more skilful researchers. She gives examples of how children have been lured from passive copying into undertaking interesting personal research. The Exeter team give substantial indications of how reading skills can be extended and enhanced in powerful ways.

Michael Lockwood and Angela Redfern remind us of the pleasure and enjoyment that is derived from exposure to the written word. Lockwood recounts some experiences in the teaching of poetry coming to some simple guidelines for its promotion in classrooms. His stress on rhythm interestingly echoes the work of Usha Goswami elsewhere. Like Lockwood, Redfern wants to emphasise the joy of literature and is clearly uneasy about the more instrumental demands of the National Curriculum. She neatly describes the collaborative partnership of parent, teacher, child and book as the 'quintessential quartet'. These writers reinforce arguments used elsewhere that for reading to really matter it must touch and uplift the soul.

This section on providing a reading environment concludes with two contrasting contributions on how the reader might be supported. Keith Topping takes to task those who continually complain about falling standards and cast doubt on the role parents can play. He rejects the pessimism of some and reiterates his strong views, whilst shrewdly pointing out their cost effectiveness. Jane Medwell's school policy for reading attempts to pull together all the elements and actors in the equation. This provides an important base from which planning, development, monitoring and renewal can take place. The writers here remind us of the support needed in terms of parental involvement and the need for an agreed whole school statement of policy.

Dealing with reading failure

Figure 2 summarises the three areas that deal with reading failure in this book:

- assessment and readability;
- dyslexia;
- reading recovery.

Both the contributors on assessment and readability raise serious questions about the National Curriculum. Louise Poulson is clearly unhappy about the 'obsessive concern' in British education with assessment. Her research leads her to the conclusion that teachers are already very sophisticated in the assessment and monitoring of children's work and this ranges far beyond the somewhat simplistic demands of official requirements. Indeed, she would argue that assessing literacy in such narrow terms demeans the nature of what constitutes a literate human being. Chris Sawyer and his colleagues address a rather different sort of assessment, that of reading material itself. Examining materials in use in schools using readability formulae, they come to some staggering conclusions. In certain circumstances the readability levels are so high as to preclude the

Element	*Issues*	*Directions*
Assessment and readability (Poulson and Sawyer et al)	Assessment criteria frequently used in English are not representative of the wide range of measures informally deployed by teachers. Materials presented to pupils may require investigation as they often have extremely high readability demands.	Teachers should: • continue to develop their own informal methods of assessment as these may be of more relevance to the task. • review and assess the material placed in front of pupils as this may, unwittingly, contribute to reading difficulties
Dyslexia (Hellier and Connor)	The concept of specific learning difficulty (dyslexia) arouses considerable emotion. Continual debate is unhelpful. Pupils are best helped by concentrating on its presenting features and seeking the most appropriate combination of methods for the amelioration of the condition.	As yet there is no single agreed approach to dealing with dyslexia. Evidence, however, supports a balanced programme of: • phonological awareness • graded texts • multisensory strategies • collaborative teaching • information technology inputs • reading recovery techniques • appropriate counselling
Reading recovery (Simmons and Wright and Prance)	Reading Recovery offers a highly structured approach to attacking reading failure. Research evidence is convincing and suggests it will spread and be adopted in a wide variety of situations.	The programme is particularly effective in: • identifying weaknesses in reading • encouraging reading fluency • developing a range of 'coping' strategies

Figure 2- Dealing with reading failure.

vast majority of pupils from getting any coherent meaning from the text. They would argue that any purported fall in reading standards may well be connected with the difficulty children are experiencing in wrestling with incomprehensible material.

Dyslexia, or specific learning difficulty (SpLD), generates highly charged confrontations between those who see it as a discrete medical condition and those who support the concept of a continuum of learning disability. The authors of the two complementary contributions in this section, Cyril Hellier and Michael Connor, wisely choose not to pursue this somewhat sterile argument. Instead they concentrate on the manifestations of the problem and discuss the wide range of strategies available for dealing with SpLD. As supported by others elsewhere in this volume they favour balanced and sensitive programmes rather than any short term 'quick fix' solutions.

The Reading Recovery programme, as pioneered by Marie Clay in New Zealand, has attracted considerable attention as a structured means of helping pupils with reading difficulty. It is a detailed and systematic approach with five basic components:

- reading and re-reading familiar stories;
- recording and analysing records of reading behaviour;
- working with letters and constructing words;
- writing messages and stories;
- exploring new books with the teacher.

Katy Simmons outlines the programme, giving some indication of its strengths and weaknesses, and suggesting there is still a lack of hard evidence for its effectiveness. Anna Wright and Jean Prance have no such reservations, bolstering their argument with statistics derived from the impressive Surrey project. The concept of reading recovery is very attractive and undoubtedly offers hope to many pupils. Significantly, its key elements are familiar to teachers and its absorption into the range of existing remedial strategies poses no great problem. It is likely to appeal to the profession and to become a standard way of handling reading failure.

Towards a synthesis of reading development

Having extracted key elements from this selection of articles it is possible to begin to discern patterns of strategies and techniques that enable one to move towards some synthesis of reading development. *Figure 3* illustrates a number of phases which:

- ***state*** those aspects that contribute to an over-arching school policy;
- ***collect*** carefully the information and ***audit*** those resources necessary for the implementation of a school policy;
- ***implement*** the process of reading by detailing and elaborating on the logistics of delivery and the monitoring of progress;
- both ***promote*** and ***support*** reading development with emphasis on the act of reading development and, where appropriate, the support that can be given by sympathetic adults and peers;
- ***expand*** on this process by stimulating the understanding interpretation of text and the use of reading as an investigative tool.

Clearly the above no way represents a strict hierarchy of events. However, this tentative model can be used to:

- identify sources of weakness in policy and programmes;
- focus on particular phases that need further development and strengthening;
- anticipate staff development programmes;
- give clearer indication as to the direction in which school policy might proceed;
- provide a basis for predicting resource requirements.

Overcoming reading difficulties

Reading failure can rarely be attributed to a single cause and is even more unlikely to respond to one particular technique. Among the factors that may contribute to reading difficulty are:

- identifiable genetic or physiological handicaps;
- emotional/psychological disorder;
- discouraging environmental circumstances;
- poor self-image and lack of motivation;
- unfortunate prior learning experience.

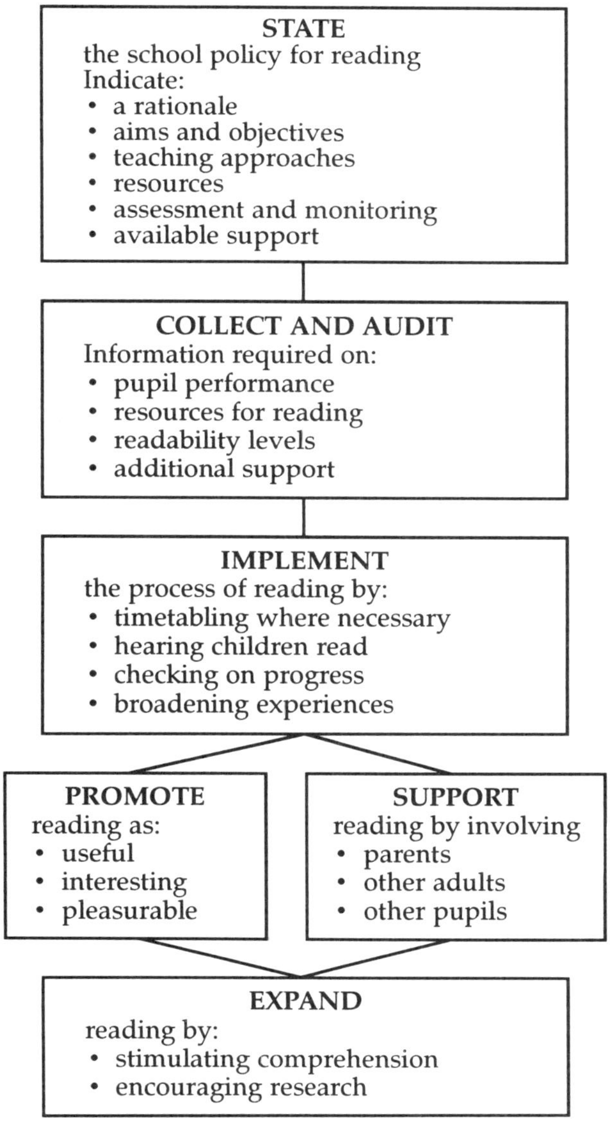

Figure 3 - Towards a synthesis of reading.

The permutations of these factors are so numerous that it is understandable that simple diagnoses and treatments are so seductive. However, most teachers remain aware of the complexity of the task and deploy a variety of techniques, often with considerable skill and subtlety.

Drawing on the general strategies advocated for dealing with reading difficulty it is possible to identify a four-pronged means of attack. This is illustrated in *Figure 4* and comprises:

- ***Teaching methods*** - Children in trouble respond to all manner of approaches but undoubtedly need substantial 'code cracking' skills. However, exclusive concentration on word building skills can be extremely counter-productive and lead to sterile responses to text. The technique needs careful balancing with other approaches that illuminate the process of decoding, ensure meaning is simultaneously garnered from text and, above all, guarantee some real pleasure is derived from the task.

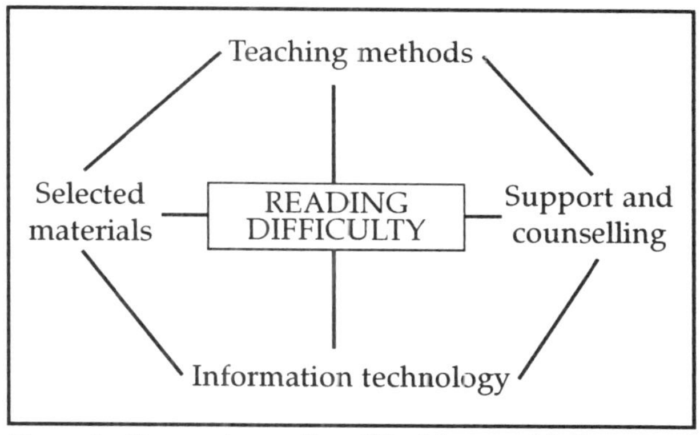

Figure 4 - Overcoming reading difficulties: a multi-dimensional approach.

- ***Materials*** - The above obviously indicates teachers need to carefully select books and other materials that provide graded readability experiences in combination with those which are of high interest and likely to motivate.

- ***Support and counselling*** - Because reading provokes so much emotion, failure in any aspect can cause considerable damage to the individual's self-image. A whole variety of techniques has emerged that can promote confidence and motivate reluctant learners.

- ***Information technology*** - We remain very much at the early stages of deploying information technology and interactive learning. Initial experimentation is highly encouraging and suggests that IT represents the most potentially powerful means ever devised for preventing reading failure or correcting specific difficulties.

These four broad features would seem to be essential in the provision of a structured and supportive learning environment for pupils with reading problems.

Conclusion

The purpose of this publication is to pull together a range of contemporary opinion and recommended practice and to extract from this collage some key issues and directions. This process has encouraged the belief that in many respects views are beginning to converge, that some kind of synthesis is possible. It is an optimistic scenario which it is hoped the reader will share.